Shakespeare and I

Shakespeare

Shakespeare Now!

Series edited by Ewan Fernie and Simon Palfrey
Web editors: Theodora Papadopoulou and William McKenzie

First Wave:
At the Bottom of Shakespeare's Ocean Steve Mentz
Godless Shakespeare Eric S. Mallin
Shakespeare's Double Helix Henry S. Turner
Shakespeare Inside Amy Scott-Douglass
Shakespearean Metaphysics Michael Witmore
Shakespeare's Modern Collaborators Lukas Erne
Shakespeare Thinking Philip Davis
To Be Or Not To Be Douglas Bruster

Second Wave:
The King and I Philippa Kelly
The Life in the Sonnets David Fuller
Hamlet's Dreams David Schalkwyk
Nine Lives of William Shakespeare Graham Holderness
Shakespeare and I edited by Theodora Papadopoulou and
   William McKenzie

Visit the *Shakespeare Now!* Blog at http://shakespearenowseries
.blogspot.com/ for further news and updates on the series.

Shakespeare and I

**Edited by William McKenzie
and Theodora Papadopoulou**

continuum

Continuum International Publishing Group

The Tower Building   80 Maiden Lane
11 York Road   Suite 704
London SE1 7NX   New York NY 10038

www.continuumbooks.com

British Library Cataloguing-in-Publication Data
A catalogue record for this book is available from the British Library.

ISBN: HB: 978-1-4411-4371-6
      PB: 978-1-4411-3718-0

Library of Congress Cataloging-in-Publication Data
Shakespeare and I / edited by William McKenzie and Theodora Papadopoulou
      p. cm. – (Shakespeare Now!)
Includes bibliographical references and index.
ISBN 978-1-4411-3718-0 (pbk.) – ISBN 978-1-4411-4371-6 (hardcover)
1. Shakespeare, William, 1564-1616 – Influence. 2. Shakespeare, William,
1564-1616 – Appreciation – English-speaking countries. I. McKenzie, William,
1976- II. Papadopoulou, Theodora, 1981-

PR2965S365 2012
822.3'3–dc23   2011035035

Typeset by Newgen Imaging Systems Pvt Ltd, Chennai, India
Printed and bound in India

Contents

Notes on Contributors   vii

General Editors' Preface to the Second-Wave of the Series   xiii

Acknowledgements   xv

Notes on Editions   xvi

Introduction: The 'I' Has It   1
Theodora Papadopoulou and William McKenzie

1. Mea Culpa   19
Ewan Fernie

2. Othello, Marriage, Middle Age   40
Eric S. Mallin

3. Discovering Transgression: Reading from the Passions   61
David Fuller

4. Ghosts and Heartbeats   78
Philippa Kelly

5. Going to Shakespeare: Memory and Anamnesis   87
Peter Holland

6. Stand Up for Bastards   107
Richard Wilson

7. My Language!   126
Thomas Docherty

8. Mrs Polonius and I   144
Julia Reinhard Lupton

9. 'Who Is It That Can Tell Me Who I Am?'   161
   Graham Holderness

10. Hierophantic Shakespeare   178
   Philippa Berry

11. No 'I' in Shakespeare   201
   Philip Davis

12. Real Men Don't Cry   221
   Sarah Klenbort

13. Ghostly Selections   233
   Simon Palfrey

   Afterword: 'Speak what we feel, not what
   we ought to say'   258
   Paul Edmondson

   Bibliography   269

   Index   283

Notes on Contributors

Philippa Berry is the author of books and articles on Shakespeare and Renaissance culture, including *Shakespeare's Feminine Endings: Disfiguring Death in the Tragedies* (Routledge, 1999), and is co-editor of *Textures of Renaissance Knowledge* (Manchester University Press, 2003).

Philip Davis is a Professor of English Literature, University of Liverpool. His books include *Sudden Shakespeare* (Athlone/Continuum, 1996), *The Victorians* (OUP, 2002) and *Shakespeare Thinking*, as part of the *Shakespeare Now!* series (Continuum, 2007).

Thomas Docherty is a Professor in the Department of English and Comparative Literary Studies at the University of Warwick. He has published on most areas of English and comparative literature from the Renaissance to the present day. His works include *After Theory* (Routledge, 1990; revised and expanded 2nd edn, Edinburgh UP, 1996), *The English Question, or Academic Freedoms* (Sussex Academic Press, 2007), *For the University* (Bloomsbury, 2011) and *Confessions: The Philosophy of Transparency* (Bloomsbury, 2011).

Paul Edmondson is Head of Knowledge and Research and Director of the Stratford-upon-Avon Poetry Festival for The Shakespeare Birthplace Trust. He is co-series editor for Palgrave Macmillan's *Shakespeare Handbooks*, Manchester University Press's *Revels Plays Companions* and co-supervisory editor of the *Penguin Shakespeare* (for which he has contributed to several introductions). His other publications include *Twelfth Night: A Guide to the Text and Its Theatrical Life* (Palgrave Macmillan, 2005), and (co-authored with Stanley Wells) *Shakespeare's Sonnets* (Oxford Shakespeare Topics series; OUP, 2004) and *Coffee with Shakespeare* (Duncan Baird, 2008). He is a priest in The Church of England.

Ewan Fernie is Professor of Shakespeare Studies and Fellow at The Shakespeare Institute, University of Birmingham. He is the author of *Shame in Shakespeare*, editor of *Spiritual Shakespeares* and co-ordinating editor of *Reconceiving the Renaissance*. He has recently completed a *Macbeth* novel with Simon Palfrey, with whom he is General Editor of the *Shakespeare Now!* series. Fernie is Principal Investigator of the AHRC / ESRC funded project, 'The Faerie Queene Now: Remaking Religious Poetry for Today's World', for which he wrote *Redcrosse: A New Celebration of England and St George* with the poets Andrew Motion, Michael Symmons Roberts and Jo Shapcott and the theologian Andrew Shanks. *Redcrosse* was premiered at St George's Chapel, Windsor and Manchester Cathedral in 2011 and is due to be taken by the RSC to Coventry Cathedral in its jubilee year of 2012. Fernie is completing a critical book for Routledge called *The Demonic: Literature and Experience*.

David Fuller is Emeritus Professor of English in the University of Durham, UK. He is the author of *Blake's Heroic Argument* (1988), *James Joyce's 'Ulysses'* (1992), *Signs of Grace* (with David Brown, 1995), and essays on a range of poetry, drama, and novels from Medieval to Modern. He is the editor of *Tamburlaine the Great* (1998) for the Clarendon Press complete works of Marlowe, of *William Blake: Selected Poetry and Prose* in the series Longman Annotated Texts (2000), and co-editor (with Patricia Waugh) of *The Arts and Sciences of Criticism* (1999). He trained as a Musicologist, and has written on opera and ballet. His *The Life in The Sonnets* was published in 2011 in the series *Shakespeare Now!*

Graham Holderness is a writer, Professor of English at the University of Hertfordshire, and author of *Nine Lives of William Shakespeare*, as part of the *Shakespeare Now!* series (Continuum, 2011).

Peter Holland is McMeel Family Professor in Shakespeare Studies in the Department of Film, Television and Theatre and Associate Dean for the Arts at the University of Notre Dame, USA. He was formerly Director of the Shakespeare Institute, Stratford-upon-Avon. He is editor of *Shakespeare Survey* and co-general editor (with Stanley Wells) of the *Oxford Shakespeare Topics* series. He is currently co-editing with Adrian Poole the series *Great Shakespeareans* for Continuum.

Philippa Kelly is a Shakespeare scholar serving as a resident dramaturge for the California Shakespeare Theatre, USA. She teaches regularly in Australia, North America and the Middle East. She is the author of *The King and I* for the *Shakespeare Now!* series (Continuum, 2011). She has also written on the subject of the mirror and, more generally, autobiographical identity in early modern England.

Sarah Klenbort teaches literature at the University of Western Sydney. Her fiction and non-fiction have been published in literary journals and magazines in Australia, Britain, and the United States. She won the 2010 *Mslexia* Short Story Competition and was one of four winners of the 2011 Josephine Ulrich Short Story Prize in Australia. She is currently working on a novel.

Julia Reinhard Lupton is Professor of English and Comparative Literature at the University of California, Irvine. Her most recent scholarly books are *Thinking with Shakespeare: Essays on Politics and Life* (Chicago, 2011) and *Citizen-Saints: Shakespeare and Political Theology* (Chicago Press, 2005). She is the co-author with Ellen Lupton of two books on the everyday life of design. Her newest project is on Shakespeare and hospitality.

Eric S. Mallin is Associate Professor of English at the University of Texas at Austin. He is author of *Inscribing the Time: Shakespeare and the End of Elizabethan England* (University of California Press, 1995), and *Godless Shakespeare* for the *Shakespeare Now!* series (Continuum,

2007), as well as numerous articles on Shakespeare and film. He is currently studying the perverse in literature and politics.

William McKenzie completed his Ph.D. on in English and French at Royal Holloway, University of London in 2009. His thesis argued that Shakespeare and Montaigne rework themes first crystallised in Ovid's Echo-Narcissus story; and the way they do this at once challenges and enriches our modern conception of narcissism. He has since taught in the French Departments of King's College London (where he won a prize for Teaching Excellence), University College London, and St. Hilda's College, Oxford. He has published book-chapters on *Shakespeare's Sonnets* and on the circulation of Ovidian texts in Renaissance France. He is currently working on a book based on his Ph.D. thesis.

Simon Palfrey is Professor of English Literature and Fellow of Brasenose College, University of Oxford. With Ewan Fernie he is the founding editor of *Shakespeare Now!* and co-author of the novel *Bloodhill*. His other books include *Late Shakespeare: A New World of Words* (OUP, 1997), *Doing Shakespeare* (Arden, revised 2nd edn, 2011), *Romeo and Juliet* (Short Books, 2012), and *Shakespeare in Parts*, co-authored with Tiffany Stern (OUP, 2007), which won the 2009 Medieval and Renaissance Drama Society's David Bevington Prize for best new book. He is currently working on a monograph about possibility in early modern drama and philosophy, and a play inspired by Spenser's *Faerie Queene*.

Theodora Papadopoulou completed her Ph.D. at Royal Holloway, University of London. Her thesis focuses on the subjectivity of Stephen Greenblatt's critical work, out of which she develops an argument for the value of subjectivity as such, in criticism and beyond. Her essay '"Circulating through languages and tales": Stephen Greenblatt's *Cardenio*' will appear in *Reinventing the Renaissance: Shakespeare and his Contemporaries in Adaptation and Performance* (ed. Sarah Annes Brown, Robert I. Lublin, and Lynsey McCulloch;

Palgrave Macmillan, 2013). Theodora is currently teaching at the Department of English Studies at the University of Cyprus.

Richard Wilson is Professor of English Literature at Cardiff University and the author or editor of numerous books on Shakespeare and theory, including *Will Power: Studies in Shakespearean authority* (1993), *Secret Shakespeare: Essays on theatre, religion, and resistance* (2004), and *Shakespeare and French Theory: King of Shadows* (2007). Previously Director of the Shakespeare programme at Lancaster University, he is well known for research on Shakespeare's response to Catholic terrorism. He has been a Visiting Fellow of the Shakespeare Institute, University of Birmingham, and Visiting Professor at the Sorbonne Nouvelle (Paris III). He was the 2006 Fellow at Shakespeare's Globe, and he is the 2011 Distinguished Visiting Professor at the Sorbonne (Paris IV).

General Editors' Preface to the Second-Wave of the Series

We begin with the passions of the critic as they are forged and explored in Shakespeare. These books speak directly from that fundamental experience of losing and remaking yourself in art. This does not imply, necessarily, a lonely existentialism; the story of a self is always bound up in other stories, shared tales of nations or faiths or of families large and small. But such stories are also always singular, irreducible to the generalities by which they are typically explained. Here, then, is where literary experience stops pretending to institutionalized objectivity, and starts to tell its own story.

Shakespeare Now! is a rallying cry, above all for aesthetic immediacy. It favours a model of aesthetic knowledge as *encounter*, where the encounter brings its own, often surprising contextualizing imperatives. Implicit in this is the premise that art is as much a subject as an object, less like aggregated facts and more like a fascinating person or persons. And encountering the plays as such is unavoidably personal.

Much recent scholarship has been devoted to Shakespeare *then* – to producing more information about the presumed moment of their inception. But this moment of inception is in truth happening over and over, again and again, anywhere that Shakespeare is being experienced anew or freshly. For the fact is that he remains, by a country mile, the most important *contemporary* writer – the most performed and read, the most written about, but also the most remembered. But it is not a question merely of Shakespeare in the present, as though his vitality is best measured by his passing relevance to great events. It is about his works' abiding presence.

In some ways criticism needs to get younger – to recover the freshness of aesthetic experience, and so in part better to remember why any of us should care. We need a new directness, written responses to the plays which attest to the life we find in them and the life they find in us.

Ewan Fernie and Simon Palfrey

Acknowledgements

We are grateful to the following for permission to use material originally published elsewhere. Michael Hinchliffe from E-rea ('Revue électronique d'études sur le monde Anglophone') agreed the reproduction of material from Graham Holderness, ' "A Word-Web Woven": Autobiography in Old English Poetry' (E-rea, 5.1 2007, stable URL: http://erea.revues.org/178). John Lucas confirmed permission to reproduce material from Graham Holderness's *Craeft: poems from the Anglo-Saxon* (Shoestring Press, 2002). A version of Sarah Klenbort's essay first appeared in the magazine *Ninth Letter*.

Every effort has been made to secure permissions or ensure that the use of material falls within fair dealing guidelines but the editors would be happy to address errors and omissions in subsequent editions.

The staff at Continuum (David Avital, Colleen Coalter, Rachel Eisenhauer, Anna Fleming, Laura Murray, Nick Church) were continually patient, warm and a joy to work with, as were Srikanth and the production team at Newgen Imaging. Ewan Fernie and Simon Palfrey gave us invaluable help, support and advice every step of the way. The contributors to this volume were all indefatigable in their energy and passionate commitment to this project. Warm thanks to them all.

Notes on Editions

Unless otherwise stated, the edition of Shakespeare cited and referenced in this book is the 1997 edition of *The Norton Shakespeare: Based on the Oxford Text* (edited by Stephen Greenblatt, Walter Cohen, Jean E. Howard and Katharine Eisaman Maus). All act, scene and line numbers refer to this edition.

Introduction
The 'I' Has It

Theodora Papadopoulou and
William McKenzie

The book you're reading speaks up for the value and importance of self-investment in any consideration of literary art, especially its most celebrated practitioner: Shakespeare. It offers writings which challenge the familiar stylistic decorum and professionalized idiom of literary criticism, and which ask if the purpose of criticism is instead to articulate existentially meaningful effects of reading, writing and thinking. The same questions echo through the book time and again: how do the historicized complexities of Shakespearean language and performance affect those who encounter them? How does Shakespeare shape, construct, or even aggress, the reader's or playgoer's ongoing and changing sense of him- or herself? And how might any such free, frank, even confessional depiction of such experience be represented? In this sense we have asked our contributors to try and practise a genuinely 'literary' criticism, which not only takes literature as its field of enquiry but also strives to share and partake in its spirit of linguistic experimentation.

As this book stresses so intently the necessity of articulating personal investment in literature, perhaps we might start by briefly setting out our own positions and impulses. As recently graduated PhD students in Shakespeare and Renaissance literature and literary criticism, and as 'Early Career Researchers' (to use current terminology) much contemporary scholarly writing about literature and poetry strikes us as dispiritingly unpoetic. In an increasingly market-led academy, scholars are obliged to generate lists of publications at speed, and in convincing sequence. A scholarly factory or rather factories have grown up, all driven by fierce competition. As a result, a distinctive mode of critical writing has emerged which is, more often than not, formulaic, easily reproducible, mechanically objective, and coldly impersonal. What has come to be definable as literary 'expertise' now seems to us to have little or nothing to do with 'literature': the distinctively, emotionally and libidinally engaging form of language worthy of the name.

Not only in its forms of writing but also in its modes of thought and inquiry, Shakespearean literary criticism seems to have lost some sense of the need to witness and convey the aesthetic energy and delight that is, presumably, what drives people to the study of Shakespeare in the first place. Recent years have seen scholars bemoan an 'intellectual stagnation' in the field (Grady, 2005, p. 112). Historical, materialist and other such contextualizing and 'post-theoretical' approaches to the text have become mainstream – perhaps because they slot more readily into the kinds of modes of production advocated by the scholarly industry. Granted, the best of such work has been indispensably valuable for the development of our knowledge and understanding of Shakespeare's life and world. But any effort to construct such a context risks by definition neglecting the literary text's linguistic and formal singularity and the role of the living respondent in constructing his or her invested and involved aesthetic response. As this happens, we worry that current critical practice insufficiently engages with the artistic qualities and emotional pleasure afforded by the experiences of reading and watching Shakespeare. After all, these are the very qualities and pleasures that make the playwright's work compelling also to those who do not share the professional scholar's drive and instincts.

Perhaps more so than ever before academic literary criticism seems out of touch with the world beyond the university wall.[1] Increasingly specialized academics write for progressively smaller readerships; the culture of exclusion and exclusiveness that the academy fosters is reinforced by the general reader's suspicion and intolerance of abstract, impersonal jargon. But the chasm that seems to have opened up between the academy and the world outside it is more than a problem of accessibility. With the proliferation of cultural forms of literary criticism, 'culture' has become an abstract theoretical concept, rather than the space we live within and share; discussions of artistic experience are correspondingly isolated from discussions of life experience. Making an impassioned plea for the pertinence of expressly personal experience to literary criticism in *Blake's Heroic Argument*, David Fuller states:

> The discussion of values, in art or in life, cannot be carried on with a proper honesty without including some account of the experience which has led to those values. Literary criticism which gives rise, as it should, to cultural criticism needs, like any other discussion involving values, to include the personal. (Fuller, 1988, p. 226)

For Fuller, and for us, what seems to have got lost in contemporary critical thought and practice is a sense of the importance and irresistibility of self-expression, even while in the 'outside' world of blogs and Facebook people seem to be doing little else. Ever disappearing in scholarly discourse, subjectivity is more often than not seen as an intellectual embarrassment. Even arguments for a more accessible, less insular form of critical writing warn against 'the kind of self-revelation that can be used to mock or trivialize' the critic's work (see Reisz, 2010). Yet it seems to us that literary critical discourse that militates against subjectivity also precludes an honest, genuine engagement with literature and with the world. And such writing, we feel, can have little to do with the art in which its writer professes to be expert. Literature affects the person reading or experiencing it. What is the value or relevance of a work in which nothing – or no one – really seems to be at stake? If you can't write about literature in a way that offers the opportunity – and challenge – of self-expression, then where *can* you write in such a way?

We began by introducing ourselves as 'young Shakespeareans', new to the academic fray. But we don't want to imply a false generational divide between ourselves and the academic community we are joining by editing this book. The frustrations we express are shared by many, not least by the writers contributing to this volume. In the opening chapter, for example, Ewan Fernie argues that the writing 'the academy typically asks for and rewards . . . may, of all things, betray passionate and vital reading experience, may betray art as what traffics with and in such experience'. And Philip Davis similarly bemoans the loss, 'not just within the theatre', of the 'dramatic life' that flows throughout the Shakespearean text. If the writers in *Shakespeare and I* imply and attack a kind of *rigor mortis* in contemporary criticism, we do so only to stress all the more urgently the potential for creative life that criticism could represent and which is passing us by. We believe in a criticism that is committed to human creativity in literature and culture, and one which expresses and explores this commitment. The possession of a creative imagination should be more of a help than a hindrance for professional readers. And if 'all fine imaginative work is self-conscious and deliberate', as Oscar Wilde's spokesman in 'The Critic as Artist' has it, we further agree with Gilbert that 'self-consciousness and the critical spirit are one': 'criticism is itself an art', it is 'a creation within a creation' and, as such, it is 'the purest form of personal impression' (Wilde, in Abrams, 1993, p. 1623).

* * *

It might go without saying that situated in any experience of a Shakespeare play or poem there is a thinking, responding energy or agency: this energy or agency is (for example) computing the myriad and multiple senses of a Shakespearean word or sentence; following the rhythmical modulations of the verse; considering the meanings (or thrilling to the visuals) of the costumes, lighting, bodies and movement of the stage spectacle.

But the central traditions of literary interpretation that have dominated Shakespeare studies over the last thirty or so years have not readily used the vocabulary of the 'self' to describe these energies or agencies. For these early 'cultural materialists' and 'new historicists' (as they came to be known), the issue of subjectivity was a central preoccupation, while a heightened historical and interpretive self-consciousness was also a defining characteristic of their critical practices.[2] Both new historicists and cultural materialists would acknowledge the critic's particular 'situatedness' in the present as that which prompts and determines their interrogations of literature and history. Thus the 'self' was for many of them a bourgeois chimera, complicit with the newly entrepreneurial and 'individualist' politics and economics of Thatcherite and Reaganite governments and those that followed them. Catherine Belsey's 1985 comments on Prince Hamlet – surely the most introspective, individualized Shakespearean character – give a good idea of the critical mood of the time: '[Hamlet's soliloquies are] traversed by the voices of a succession of morality fragments, wrath and reason, patience and resolution. In *none of them is it possible to locate the true, the essential Hamlet*' (Belsey, 1985, p. 42, our emphasis). Belsey agrees with the late Francis Barker's bleak, Orwellian conclusion dating from 1984: 'At the centre of Hamlet, in the interior of his mystery there is, in short, *nothing*.' (ibid., p. 41; quoting Barker, 1984, p. 33; our emphasis)

These dismissals of the self or subjectivity were extended and substantiated by work by theorists of post-1968 Paris, especially Louis Althusser and Michel Foucault. Althusser and Foucault (especially in his early work) both argued, albeit in different ways, that people's conscious senses of themselves are merely the superficial 'effects' of deeper and more powerful unconscious forces of social conditioning. Althusser's favoured term for such forces is 'ideology'; Foucault's is 'power'.[3] Correspondingly, Foucault attacked the notion of the 'human', and its implied sense that individuals are fully in control of their own consciousnesses and destinies, as a comforting illusion that keeps existing circumstances and conditions of 'power' in place. These arguments extended within Shakespeare studies into the subject of 'Literature' itself. Questions of aesthetic judgement and personal taste became political. Art, literature, and the responses they elicit, tended not to be analysed via the relatively interiorized and personal vocabulary of (say) affect, emotion, physiology or psychology; they were increasingly conceived and articulated as the mere resurfacing of fully internalized sociological and class-based pressures. The 'aesthetic' itself thus came under scrutiny, deemed to be false and reactionary. The implication was that hierarchies of artistic value were inseparable from the hierarchies of power and society the theorists of 1968 and their acolytes in English Literature Departments were seeking to subvert. Thus, the literary canon of Dead White European Males was exposed as such; 'literary' and 'non-literary' texts were read in conjunction and in the same manner.

In this way 'new historicism' (in the United States) and 'cultural materialism' (in the United Kingdom) became the dominant critical approaches in late twentieth-century Shakespeare studies. But 'post-theoretical' criticism sought to challenge their established hegemony. There subsequently emerged a reinforced interest in the material – not only the material form and existence of Shakespeare's text but also the material conditions in which the playwright was working. This new materialism primarily sought to rescue historicism from the charges of 'narcissism' that were frequently levelled against it. As David Scott Kastan puts it, new historicist and cultural materialist readings of literature seemed 'too overtly self-interested to be compelling as historical accounts, significant more as records of our present needs and anxieties than as reconstructions of Shakespeare's past' (Kastan, 1999, p. 17). With the proliferation of new materialist criticism, then, critical thought decidedly turned its back on the problem of subjectivity which defined the previous critical models at their earliest stages; yet it also seemed dangerously to veer back to older modes of a more positivist historicism that would seek 'objectively' to reproduce history.

The same 'point of divergence' between the work of new materialism and that of new historicism is also the point of departure
and 'enabling foundation' for 'presentism'– an umbrella-term with
which Hugh Grady and others describe 'an array of critical practices
that consciously situate themselves in the "now" or present of our
own day' (Grady, 2005, p. 113). Indeed, this most recent critical
trend has sought to complement rather than compete with the previously established practices of new historicism and cultural materialism. It prescribes a profound critical self-awareness that goes all the
way back to Stephen Greenblatt's oft-cited assertion in the introduction to *Renaissance Self-Fashioning*: 'It is everywhere evident in this
book that the questions I ask of my material and indeed the very
nature of this material are shaped by the questions I ask of myself'
(Greenblatt, 1980, p. 5).

Presentist critics, therefore, similarly begin with the assumption
that 'our' understanding of the past is produced in, conditioned by,
and contingent to 'our' situation in the present: 'Facts and texts, that
is to say, don't simply speak, don't merely mean. *We* speak, *we* mean,
by them. And we do so in the present' (Grady/Hawkes, 2007, p. 3).
So by taking issue with the 'deepening apoliticism' in contemporary
Shakespeare studies that it understands as the effect of the prevalence
of an increasingly positivist historicism, presentist criticism expressly
seeks to reinvigorate the commitment of literary studies to the present,
'a present in which Shakespeare is an icon politically contested and
fought over' (Grady, 2005, p. 113). And by dispelling 'the myth of
objectivity' and dismissing the possibility of a single, rigid and undi-
versified 'history' of human creativity, presentist critics insist upon
'the existence of "histories" produced by subjects variously positioned
within the present social formation and motivated by quite different
senses of *present* needs and *present* problems which it is hoped will be
clarified through the study of the past' (Howard, 2003, p. 463).

It is this challenge that presentist criticism offers to current critical thought that *Shakespeare and I* seeks to extend further, but it
does so by challenging some of this critical movement's defining

characteristics. Presentist criticism, as Grady and Terence Hawkes explain it, interrogates the 'paradoxical presentness' of historical works of art, how 'they evidently continue to speak to us with urgency and insight' (Grady/Hawkes, 2007, p. 4); yet the implied 'we' alluded to remains largely unspecified. In its efforts to reinvigorate the commitment of literary studies to 'the probing and questioning of our cultural and political norms and values' (Grady, 2005, p. 111), presentist criticism seems to lose sight of the distinctive 'presence' of a living self – a self unstably and unpredictably engaged in the aesthetic experiences of reading and writing about literature.[4] Any real sense of personhood and life seems, instead, to become co-opted by presentism's faithfulness and duty to a collective present. In this sense, it appears that Friedrich Nietzsche's complaint still stands true: 'Present experience has, I am afraid, always found us "absent-minded": we cannot give our hearts to it' (Nietzsche, trans. Kauffmann, 1967, p. 1).

So where presentist discourse typically represents a collective 'we' that is responsible for the political and cultural present, *Shakespeare and I* perceives 'our present' as it is crucially reflected and refracted through each writer's own particular lived (and living) experience and partial perspective. By bringing the writer's sense of being expressly and meaningfully to bear on his or her criticism, it insists on the rich privacy and particularity of aesthetic experience, which cannot be determined in advance.

Germs – but only germs – of what the authors in this book are trying to achieve might be said to exist in the 'latent presentism' evinced by Stephen Greenblatt's mode of new historicism.[5] This is a writer who frequently resorts to using the personal pronoun 'I' in his critical writing. Not only in *Renaissance Self-Fashioning*– as noted above – but throughout his critical oeuvre, Greenblatt seems to implicate himself in the discursive processes of reading and writing about history and literature.[6] What emerges is a nascent sense of critical subjectivity, but one that is subtly and carefully 'performed', that is immanent to the specific context of his critical investigations and that needs to be construed and interpreted through nuanced readings of his work. *Shakespeare and I* ventures further than that: the authors in this volume genuinely assay themselves; that is, they put their own selves at risk in the effort to convey something truly real about Shakespeare as experienced. To this extent, they no longer 'remain unknown to [them]selves', as Nietzsche bemoans is the case for those who seek knowledge. They want to know: '"What really was that which we have just experienced?" and moreover: "who *are* we really?"' (Nietzsche, trans. Kauffman, 1967, p. 1).

So while we do acknowledge our indebtedness to contemporary critical practices, we also mean for *Shakespeare and I* to stand on its own as genuinely and proudly different from anything that has come before it in contemporary literary studies. We appreciate presentism's insistence that literary criticism should involve 'the radical act of putting one's cards on the table' (Grady/Hawkes, 2007, p. 4); and we respect the value that Greenblatt's style of new historicist writing places, however covertly and ambiguously, on 'the single voice' (Greenblatt/Gallagher, 2000, p. 16). Thus, finally, we conclude that 'the I has it':

> Because your voice is important. Literary criticism is on the whole almost unbearable to read because it lacks much in the way of personal stakes and commitment. The only way to get those qualities is to actually put yourself on the line as somebody. (Greenblatt, quoted in Blume, 2001)

Shakespeare and I takes Greenblatt's advice seriously, perhaps even more seriously than Greenblatt himself does. This call for literary critics to hold on to and take responsibility for their individual 'voices' is only dimly and imperfectly heard in current criticism. The writers in *this* book by contrast celebrate the risk involved in having, using and exploring one's own 'voice'. They reveal and insist upon the existence of multiple, diverse and varied 'presents' in the same way as presentist criticism acknowledges a plurality of coexisting 'histories'. And they do so by producing a form of writing about Shakespeare that is grounded in the singular aesthetic experience from which that writing originates, a form of writing in which 'the self is something that is observed and experienced, something that acts and performs, and something that feels and judges' (Grady, 2000, p. 131).

* * *

One writer kept on cropping up in our many discussions about this project in the coffee bars of London (as he does on occasion in this volume): Michel de Montaigne. Perhaps this is apt: *Shakespeare and I* takes off from the underlying principles and values of the *Shakespeare Now!* series, and Montaigne is the main proponent of the vigorous, performative 'assaying' mode of writing that makes the 'minigraph' so unique and distinctive. Montaigne is now becoming interesting to Shakespeareans who feel something like an 'anxiety of influence', challenging cultural historicism and new historicism's sceptical attitude towards the self, while still acknowledging the theoretical sophistication and politicized values of their arguments. Scholars like John Lee, Hugh Grady and Peter Holbrook all look to the sixteenth-century essayist to restore, and work with, the hypothesis that human beings – in Shakespeare's and Montaigne's time as in ours – do indeed intuit and act upon their senses of themselves as distinctive and unique, however provisional, contingent and changeable such senses may be.[7]

Montaigne suggests at several points the 'vain, various and wavering' nature of human beings in general, and of himself in particular (Montaigne, trans. Screech, 2003, p. 5). At one point he calls his massive book 'a register of varied and changing occurrences, of ideas that are unresolved and, when needs be, contradictory, either because I myself have become different or because I grasp hold of different attributes or aspects of my subjects' (ibid., p. 908). Nevertheless, despite such protestations of instability and inconstancy, certain recurrent patterns of self-consistency also emerge. Montaigne maintains throughout for example a distaste for lying and dissimulation (see ibid., pp. 32–7, pp. 753–8); his affection for his lost friend Étienne de la Boétie and for his father (see ibid., pp. 205–19, p. 444); even his inability to have sex standing up (ibid.,

p. 1230)! Montaignean writing thus emerges as a kind of continual self-vigilance, testing the consistency with which Montaigne 'grasps' his 'subjects', establishing which are relatively characteristic and which are relatively contingent. This is the only kind of test according to which Montaigne may justly say whether a particular pattern of response is distinctly *his*, distinctly *him*.

Readers of Montaigne, from Pascal's time to the present, have accused him of egotism, arrogance and solipsism. But, if the potential criticisms of Montaigne's self-writing project could just as legitimately be levelled at ours, we have taken from Montaigne a similarly determined stance in response. Yes, it is conceivable that the kind of criticism we are advocating and striving to practice could be seen as the mere Shakespearean extension or corollary of a much wider and more pervasive contemporary culture of the self, a 'me' culture that encompasses the aggressively competitive individualism of modern business, as well as the vapid narcissism of reality TV. For Montaigne, however, to 'talk about yourself' and 'to think about yourself' is not the sign of such vanity; it is its 'sovereign remedy' (Montaigne, trans. Screech, 2003, p. 426). People must talk and think about themselves, Montaigne implies; otherwise they risk 'fall[ing]' passively into 'an injudicious self-love' (ibid.). Considered thus, narcissism is not an active arrogance; it can just as easily be an unthinkingly automatic acceptance – you sleepwalk into it. Perhaps our 'culture of narcissism' (as Christopher Lasch calls it), (see Lasch, 1978), should therefore be reconsidered: in this culture, most people don't have the time, space or energy to think about themselves honestly and responsibly; they cannot construct their own life-narratives independently from the extremely expensive and powerful messages created by a technocratic mass-media. Perhaps modern narcissists, like Narcissus himself, are melancholy and frustrated because they are dominated by unexamined images of the self, compelled to 'be' a self constructed from advertising and consumerism, a self that feels unsatisfactorily unsustainable and even unattainable.

We therefore hypothesize that self-writing may challenge and resist self-love and narcissism, rather than succumb to or encourage it, following Montaigne's description of his own brand of self-writing, which explicitly sets out to reflect self-consciousness adequately and accurately, in all its complexity, its quivering changeability. Such writing is difficult, a 'thorny enterprise' (Montaigne, trans. Screech, 2003, p. 424). And, because it is difficult, it becomes much more worthwhile than it might seem. It necessarily entails on one hand the risk of exposing, perhaps even discovering, unconsciously held or long-forgotten memories, associations, sensations, values or beliefs. It also entails the difficulty of formulating these often contradictory and simultaneous perceptions as time-bound and grammatically coherent linguistic structures: sentences, paragraphs, chapters, books. But these difficulties also make the written self more complex to the reading self; and the person doing (and being) both feels more interested, more interesting. Perhaps this is why Montaigne found the process so inexhaustibly addictive.

What may emerge from such experimentation is a new, supple, formally expressive and experimental form of writing; one that reflects, witnesses and perhaps even elicits life-changes in its writer. This is the kind of 'self-writing' – writing as unique, irreplaceable and irreducibly personal as the self writing it – with which we are striving to challenge contemporary academic discourse about literature. Not only might it potentially make the self more interesting to itself and others, thereby offering meaningful communication and affective pleasure to writer and reader alike; it might also offer useful ways of considering the distinctions between 'professional' and 'non-professional' modes of writing. Part of the challenge, Montaigne suggests, in any genuine self-writing is the groping search for a distinctive vocabulary, idiom, rhythm, style. Montaigne's answer to such questions was to invent his own *genre* – the essay. But, whatever the answer, this approach to writing literary criticism implies and practises a real engagement in questions of literary creativity, the implicit questions posed and answered by the writers we profess to study. And unlike academic writing on literature which tends to sideline questions of critical voice or personality by means of a coldly restrictive 'professional' idiom, we believe that such *personable* writing could potentially reach readers and writers outside as well as inside the university, enabling productive dialogue between them.

* * *

So, by positioning our project in relation to contemporary intellectual and cultural realities as we see them, and in relation to the history of the idea of the 'self' in recent Shakespeare studies, and by explaining the particular relationship of our project to Montaigne's writing, we hope we have gone some way to explain and justify our decision in this book to focus on the writing self. But we also hope here to show how we seek to breathe new life into the forms and goals, as well as the themes, of contemporary literary criticism. The questions of self-articulation we outline necessitate to some degree distinctive forms of language, of verbal expression; the kind of self-expression we wish to exemplify depends not simply on a revelation of the writer's selfhood but also on the aesthetic individuality of his or her text. The essays in *Shakespeare and I*, therefore, do not seek only to describe or interpret the text (conventional, traditional goals of literary criticism); free as they are to adopt personal, authentic, creatively and distinctively personal styles, the authors also seek to *relay* their particular aesthetic experience elicited by Shakespeare's work and, in doing so, to elicit or evoke similar or comparable affective responses to their own texts from their readers.

David Fuller urges writers to acknowledge and work with the idea that truly personal discussions of artworks may share and communicate their aesthetic 'life': 'In the discussion of art the personal is vital: finally it is the only truly vital thing, the one essential without which everything else is vacuous mechanical motion without spirit' (Fuller, 1988, p. 225). The authors here have taken on the task of writing an experimental, innovative kind of criticism which shares the hard struggles of self-expression, self-articulation, and self-exploration posed in and by literary art itself. We feel that such a writing is truer to the 'creativity and agency that blaze in the Shakespearean text as the promise of human possibility' (Fernie, 2005, p. 183). By insisting on the intense pertinence of reading, watching, thinking and writing about Shakespeare to personal life, we hope to address the questions that the *Shakespeare Now!* series most crucially raises: 'Why read? Why go to plays? Why are they important?' And how, as Fernie puts it in his piece, might we 'do justice to the sheer life and life-potential' of Shakespeare's writing, in and through our own?

It is precisely to this vital, pleasure-giving impact that reading and watching Shakespeare has on life that this book seeks to bear witness. By offering fully personal accounts of their complexly experienced and long sustained encounters with Shakespeare's work, our essayists hazard a genuinely performative, even improvisatory criticism, in which the self emerges freshly, provocatively – and often, as some of our writers informed us as they worked on their pieces, unexpectedly. Past and present selves fuse, in complex but vivifying ways, within the furiously complicated present moment of thinking and writing. We think a new Shakespeare emerges in this book: a cubist mirror, in which different and constantly changing selves find new angles to view and think of themselves. And the ability of the texts, as witnessed in these pieces, to continuously generate complex sensations from readers, auditors, playgoers, explains the Bard's enduring life-giving force for *everybody* – academics and non-specialists alike.

The accent of *Shakespeare and I* is very much on the future. But the personal encounters with Shakespeare collected here are not intended as a rigid prescription for future scholarly practice. We hope instead to encourage passionate readers of Shakespeare to write texts that in their own style and subject matter shimmer creatively at the edge of literature, criticism and philosophy, much like (or not much like?) those of Montaigne, Proust, Sartre, Barthes, or Hazlitt. In the end, all we want is an 'inter-esting' response to literature. 'Inter-est' in its Latin etymology implies to be *within*. We think, and in working on this book we are convinced, that the only texts that will interest the reader will be those that have interested its writer.

* * *

How, then, have our contributors responded to the difficult, unique challenge we have set them? What might their explorations of their

own changing personal relationships with Shakespeare involve or
entail? The vocation, duty and responsibility of a Shakespearean
career? The person-making force of religious belief, political conviction or sexual desire? The changing memory of a life-changing film
or play? Such experiences and sensations, we contest, are as vital to
'literature' as the analytical processes taught and analysed by the
university, possibly more so.

The opening chapters in the volume are powerfully confessional,
in more than one sense of that word. Ewan Fernie's childhood dream,
where he destroys an ideal world by his mere presence, resonates
with his guilty, intense investment in *Measure for Measure* and its
discovery of the lustiness of even, perhaps especially, the most sacred
affections. Eric S. Mallin fragments critical writing's conventionally singular, unassailably omniscient voice and creates something
more recognizably human; his brave and tender chapter on *Othello*,
marriage and middle age is punctured and disturbed throughout
by other voices of guilt, recrimination and vulnerability. David's
Fuller's intensely personal memoir recounts the myriad sensations
and experience of his youth – the '[p]ost-War dreariness'and 'post-
War opportunities' of 60s London – in relation to his complicated
identifications with the dramatic characters and verse-melodies of
Wagnerian opera, *Antony and Cleopatra, Romeo and Juliet* and *Phèdre*.
While Fernie, Mallin and Fuller provocatively explore sexuality
and sexual relations, in her own searingly honest account, Philippa
Kelly turns to Shakespeare as a form of mourning. Hamlet's Ghost,
Constance's speech on grief in *King John* and Othello's meditation
on death's irreversibility become for her shockingly and fiercely real
in the wake of the recent, shockingly sudden loss of her brother.

Several writers in this volume sensitively and intricately probe
their changing memories of Shakespearean experience. Starting from
stories of his own childhood trips to the theatre, Peter Holland uses
his own reflections on Shakespeare and his career as a theatre historian, to put forward the intriguing suggestion that theatre was also
for playgoers of the seventeenth, eighteenth and twentieth centuries
an act of anamnesis. The history of Shakespearean performance

becomes a kind of history of remembering; a memory of memory, where the sharing of the play matters as much as, if not more than, the play itself. Richard Wilson offers a vividly observed memoir, hilarious and moving by turns, of his Shakespearean schooling as actor, director and student. Along the journey from Crawley, to Lewes, to York University, Wilson includes deeply felt, fully inhabited readings of *The Winter's Tale,* shrewd critical portrayals of F. R. Leavis, George Wilson Knight and a sweetly sad portrait of his long term, deeply missed mentor and friend John Davies. Similarly taking as a starting point his own early educational experiences, Thomas Docherty's 'My Language!' dissects his complicated, memory-charged response to the notes and handwritten marginalia in his torn 'Junior School' copy of *A Midsummer Night's Dream.* As a result, Shakespeare comes back to life in 60s Glasgow, the Glasgow of Celtic's European Cup win, on one hand reaffirming class barriers and class consciousness, on the other hinting at solidarity and song.

Other writers have chosen to stress moments in Shakespeare that witness or elicit profound transformations. Inventing an *alter ego* as brilliant as Clark Kent's Superman, Julia Reinhard Lupton in 'Mrs Polonius and I' creates a fully individualized historical 'persona', who guides her emotionally and imaginatively through the challenges of grasping Shakespeare's world and managing her own. Graham Holderness, a convert from Marxism to Christianity fifteen years after the loss of his father, offers a movingly thoughtful meditation on internalized plurality and self-difference, juxtaposing with his own experience Lear's conversion from pride to humility, from bleak to redemptive attitudes to death. Philippa Berry also considers – albeit in very different ways – the deeply (trans-)formative impact of Shakespeare at school. Her entrance examination to Cambridge – an analysis of *The Merchant of Venice*– emerges in hindsight as a kind of 'myesis' ('preliminary initiation') into the 'quasi-mystical' power of Shakespeare's metamorphic metaphorical language, the enriching 'soul-music' of his poetic rhythms, which '[animate] what we think of as ordinary reality'.

Philip Davis, Sarah Klenbort and Simon Palfrey each offer different responses to these kinds of Shakespearean energies and the way a reading and writing self is caught up in them. Davis's response to the challenging question of what makes Shakespearean language so uniquely and distinctively compelling puts forward the idea of a 'secret text'. Thus, the dramatic power of *Coriolanus* is described and analysed not in terms of individualized characters but of 'preconceptual excitement', an 'electrical Shakespearean effect' elicited by the protagonists' interactions, the dense metaphorical richness of the language, and the myriad of implicit meanings secretly sparked off in a listener's mind. In 'Real Men Don't Cry', Klenbort writes out of a similar process of Shakespearean stimulation: she uses *Titus Andronicus* and *Coriolanus* to spark off an extremely rich and wide-ranging meditation on masculinity, maternity and violence. Palfrey's 'Ghostly Selections'– the closing piece of the collection before Paul Edmondson's perceptive and generous Afterword – may be read as a stream of literary-critical consciousness. Palfrey's piece unfolds a relatively simple question: 'how was it that at age twenty-three I came to spend years thinking about the late plays of Shakespeare?' Comments of startling acuity on these plays oscillate with rich, detailed accounts of the fugitive situations, sensations and thoughts that gave mysterious rise to them, like his raw, bewildered response to his mother's long-term, terminal illness.

As rich, vibrant and resonant as the people writing them, and rewarding with every rereading, we hope these life-writings will encourage other readers and playgoers to trust and explore their own living experience with Shakespeare's texts. We also hope writers of all backgrounds and persuasions will undertake similar experiments, performing and witnessing those moments when Shakespeare generates the genuinely 'human affections' for which Ariel in *The Tempest* so jealousy yearns:

ARIEL:	Your charm so strongly works 'em
	That if you now beheld them your affections
	Would become tender.
PROSPERO:	Does thou think so, spirit?
ARIEL:	Mine would, sir, were I human. (*The Tempest*, 5.1.18–20)

Notes

1. It should be noted that recent years have seen several Shakespeare scholars attempting to cross over this divide by writing studies of Shakespeare's life and work intended for popular consumption. See Duncan-Jones, 2001; Wells, 2003; Greenblatt, 2004; Shapiro, 2005.

2. Some of most influential productions of these critical approaches in the early 1980s were studies of Renaissance subjectivity and its formation. See two notable examples: Greenblatt, 1980 and Belsey, 1985.

3. For a general discussion of Foucault, Althusser, and the use of their ideas in cultural materialism and new historicism, see Lee, 2000, pp. 5–69.

4. See Fernie, 2005, for a challenging countervoice and a positive attempt to reinscribe 'presence' into 'presentism'.

5. See Grady, 2005, p. 115: 'There is no historicism that does not imply a latent presentism. All reconstructions of the past are interested and motivated by our current history and situation.'

6. At least a majority of Greenblatt's studies singularly involve evocations, explorations or 'dramatizations' of the critic's own subjectivity, thoughtfully and craftily woven into the relevant historical scrutinies. In *Marvellous Possessions* (1991), for example, the critic appropriates the discourses of travel, exploration and 'wonder', which he is studying in relation to the early modern Europeans' colonial encounters in the New World, and interjects his own modern-day traveller's tales into the critical narrative. And in *Hamlet in Purgatory* (2001), Greenblatt introduces his investigations into the Catholic institution of Purgatory by relating his own experience of undertaking to recite the Jewish prayer for the dead (or 'kaddish') to honour the memory of his father.

7. At the time of writing this Introduction, Stephen Greenblatt's *Shakespeare's Montaigne* is forthcoming (2011). See Lee, 2000, Grady, 2000 and 2002 and the essays collected in Bradshaw, 2006.

Chapter 1
Mea Culpa

Ewan Fernie

I want to start with a notion of literature as a 'biographeme'. It might seem a silly word but I use it to signal not just concentrated life but also *embryonic* life – that sort of vitality which can generate new life in the reader, for better or worse. For the art-work might say for itself with Falstaff, 'I am not only witty in myself, but the cause that wit is in other men' (*2 Henry IV*, 1.2.8–9). I also want to distinguish the life of art-experience from the dissipation of life in biography in its windy contemporary mode.[1] Intense art-experience is often experienced as a revelation of life itself – or as a revelation of a possibility of life. It is, for the reader, viewer or listener, something like what Thomas Mann's young hero experiences on the Magic Mountain:

> As he lay there above the glittering valley, lapped in the bodily warmth preserved to him by fur and wool, in the frosty night illumined by the brilliance from a lifeless star, the image of life displayed itself to young Hans Castorp. It hovered before him, somewhere in space, remote from his grasp, yet near his sense; this body, this opaquely whitish form, giving out exhalations, moist, clammy; the skin with all its blemishes and native impurities, with its spots, pimples, discolorations, irregularities, its horny, scalelike regions, covered over by soft streams and whorls of rudimentary lanugo. It leaned there, set off against the cold lifelessness of the inanimate world, in its own vaporous sphere, relaxed,

the head crowned with something cool, horny, pigmented, which was an outgrowth of its skin; the hands clasped at the back of the neck. It looked down at him beneath drooping lids. (Mann, 1985, p. 276)

Such visions are thrilling and menacing. Or they are, as Stevenson notes in his letter to J. A. Symonds on reading Dostoevsky, *for one kind of reader.*

Raskolnikoff is easily the greatest book I have read in ten years; I am glad you took to it. Many find it dull: Henry James could not finish it: all I can say is, it nearly finished me. It was like having an illness. James did not care for it because the character of Raskolnikoff was not objective; and at that I divined a great gulf between us, and on further reflection, the existence of a certain impotence in many minds of to-day, which prevents them from living in a book or a character, and keeps them standing afar off, spectators of a puppet show. To such I suppose the book may seem empty in the centre; to the others it is a room, a house of life, into which they themselves enter, and are tortured and purified. (Stevenson, 1999, pp. 127–8, appendix 3)

This sort of profoundly vital experience is clearly foreign to objectivity. It may derive from just *part* of a work. In Stevenson's letter, he says he is moved by Dostoevsky's Sonia and her drunken father and by other characters, but it is evidently 'Raskolnikoff' and his fate which shakes his soul, which nearly finishes him off, which both 'tortures and purifies'. That's why 'Raskolnikoff' displaces *Crime and Punishment* as the title of Dostoevesky's novel in Stevenson's recollection. It might even be just a line or phrase, which triggers such powerful, revelatory experience. '*When violent sorrow seems/A modern ecstasy*' . . . '*To sin in loving virtue*' (*Macbeth*, 4.3.170–1; *Measure for Measure*, 2.3.187). From such seeds a comprehensive vision of things may grow, as when the smallest, most intangible feature of a work of art – or (alternatively) its broadest outline – inspires another or others. I think here, given what will be my demonic theme, of the way Dostoevsky grew his most demonic character, Nikolai Stavrogin, from the germ of his perception of 'a sudden demon of irony' in Hamlet (Dostoevsky, 2006, p. 189).

Part of the problem is the place of literature in the academy. What the academy typically asks for and rewards is a correct or balanced appreciation: objectivity. But an informed or balanced response may, of all things, betray passionate and vital reading experience, may betray art as what traffics with and in such experience. Information is so often an evasion, an attempt to master as fact an agency which addresses us with the authority of a personhood that belongs to the work rather than the author. There are other criteria for judging criticism than balance or expertise. How interesting is any given reading? How far does it do justice to the work's *varying* charisma and possibilities of meaning? Some things in even a great work may be less good than others. How fertile is it? What is its generative potential, in terms of art or life? – I'm thinking now partly of Rilke looking at the Apollo Belvedere and writing, 'You must change your life!' (Rilke, 1992, p. 143). Can it be owned by a living human being, at his or her most intimate and exposed, in the sudden depths of a surprising conversation, in the prone moment of consciousness before falling asleep, when engaged in the rawest and most agonizing self-reflection?[2]

Of course scholars know all this, and it conditions our response to the critical work and art we most like and respond to, but, I feel, too secretly and too much in the background, to the effect that scholarship is now a professional business largely sealed off from enthusiastic reading. It is hard for contemporary academic readers to do justice to the sheer life and life-potential of a book. Professional identity and standing in an epoch of unprecedented professionalization stand in the way. And if a critical orientation towards history typically proffers facts in place of the subjectivity of aesthetic encounter, theory involves abstraction from experience. I've recently felt that a good question of any theory or philosophy is: what kind of model or 'image of life' – realized, say, in novel form – would it express? If we can't imagine this as anything other than hopelessly thin or facile, then it's simply not suitable to the dense complexities of art. And political criticism also steps away from experience, being ethics at a higher level of abstraction. One reason for its righteous tendency is that politics enables a comfortable distance from the ambivalence of one's own moral life. That of course is properly the domain of ethics. But ethical criticism has, in recent times, tended to be too pious, too liable to neglect not just the temptation to privilege oneself over 'the Other', but the real reasons for and desirability of doing so. It often degrades into ethical kitsch.

It is interesting that Stevenson is writing about a Russian masterpiece, as expressly opposed to an Anglo-American tradition. Intensity is a well-known predicate of Russian and German literature. And it may be that for English or American readers such dislocated traditions communicate all the more suddenly and powerfully with raw life, because they are from elsewhere, beyond familiarity, beyond mastery. Scottish authors are a bit of a special case and the author of *Dr Jekyll and Mr Hyde* seems closer than his typical English counterparts to these alternative traditions. I believe that Shakespeare should be read much more often in such contexts, and that to read him there would be to discover or rediscover a more powerful and existentially compelling Shakespeare.

I also believe, strange though it is to say, that another way of renewing an intense and serious intellectual engagement with art is via a new engagement with theology. Jonathan Dollimore once said to me that theology at least engages with 'the Big Stuff' – life, death, meaning, value. And Martin Luther wrote in the same vein, in a letter of 17 March 1509, to his friend, the Eisenach priest Johannes Braun, 'From the outset I would rather have exchanged philosophy for theology. I mean for a theology that gets at the meat of the nut, at the kernel of the corn, or the marrow of the bones' (quoted in Lohse, 1999, p. 36). But if theology might help repair criticism's connection with life, we need the right kind, the sort of theology that really connects up with the Big Stuff, nothing too pious, pompous or metaphysical. Luther, remember, had to lay his life (and much else) on the line in his effort to keep it honest.

And as he knew, one thing which keeps theology honest is the demonic – because the Devil is a tempter, because he is a possessor of souls, because he gets right in, making it plain that moral objectivity and pride are unsustainable, that life's a struggle in which we are always messily and ambivalently involved. Here's Kierkegaard on the subject:

> Commonly, one hears little about the demoniacal, notwithstanding that this field, particularly in our time, has a valid claim to be explored, and notwithstanding that the observer, in case he knows how to get a little *rapport* with the demon, can, at least occasionally, make use of almost every man for this purpose. As such an explorer Shakespeare is and constantly remains a hero. That horrible demon the most demoniacal figure Shakespeare has depicted and depicted incomparably, the Duke of Gloucester (afterwards to become Richard III) – what made him a demon? Evidently the fact that he could not bear the pity he had been subjected to since childhood. His monologue in the first act of Richard III is worth more than all the moral systems which have no inkling of the terrors of existence or of the explanation of them. (Kierkegaard, 1955, p. 114)

It's instructive that both Kierkegaard's and Stevenson's testimonies to literature's vitality are inspired by demonic masterpieces: the *Macbeth*-like story of an unnecessary murder that is *Crime and Punishment*, and Shakespeare's portrayal of Richard III which Kierkegaard expressly nominates as 'demoniacal'. Kierkegaard asserts the pertinence of the demoniacal for nearly all of us, provided we can bear to recognize it in ourselves. But he also asserts the particular pertinence of the demoniacal *in our times*. This might be because of secularization, because the demonic is now the back door into spirituality where the front door appears to be shut, because the demonic is the prevalent form of modern religious experience – and it is in this context that the demonic theme in Shakespeare can be said to anticipate and foretell modernity. But Kierkegaard's emphasis falls on the true-to-life challenge of such demoniacal art to theoretical abstraction: 'moral systems which have no inkling of the terrors of existence or the explanation of them'.

Kierkegaard relates to Richard as a demonic hero. Disadvantaged in the social sphere, Shakespeare's Crookback becomes an avatar and exponent of the egotistical sublime. His unlikely existential victory attracts me too, but I feel even more compelled, moved and accused by another demonic Shakespearean character, one who is less defiantly demoniacal, one who from the first is humbled and humiliated by a lucid recognition of demonic tendencies within himself even while he energetically pursues them.

I mean, of course, Angelo from *Measure for Measure*.

* * *

Angelo's career, like Richard III's, reveals, judges and hungers to transcend the anguished embodiment of human being, but also points specifically to a perverse and wrecking covetousness hidden in desire – even desire that could or should be sacred. His fate is to be more like the carrion than the violet in the sun. *He corrupts with virtuous season.*

And yet, Shakespeare makes Angelo curiously engaging and attractive. His name and dramatic fall associate him with the demonic, and quite specifically with a fallen angel. His absolutist legalism of the beginning of the play has a religious flavour, which contrasts with merely worldly accommodations. From the point-of-view of the world, Angelo is radically deformed and dehumanized – an 'ungenitured agent', who urinates 'congealed ice', and wasn't begotten by the 'downright way of creation' (3.1.406, 355, 350–1). But, in a play which also affords the view through the grille of the convent on a dispiritingly corrupted society, such palpably imagined weirdness has its own mysterious charisma and allure. Who *is* this Angelo, this straitened stranger among men? His seeming transcendence of mortal conditions might just be the mark of sainthood. By the end of the play he is an angel with horns. Guilty (as he thinks) of the hurried rape of a nun in the dark, he laments that though you can write 'good angel' on the devil's horns, they remain the devil's crest (2.4.15–17). And yet, Angelo isn't left in completely demonic ruins; a better nature burns in his self-condemnation – and the Devil himself after all remains a fallen *angel*, so there is scope within an angelic name and nature for a fall. Nor is it the case that Angelo just falls into the non-being and privation of Good which characterizes the orthodox Christian conception of Evil. Throughout his reversals in *Measure for Measure* Angelo's ambivalent intensity remains his distinguishing feature, and this endues him with life.

And, for me at least, a corresponding magnetism.

Angelo and the nun he supposedly rapes, Isabella, are together the most spiritually ambitious characters in the play. Their uncompromising opposition to sex doesn't much impress liberal criticism but the play reveals their shared tendency to violent chastity as itself a form of libido, and one characterized by superior energy. So these two, puritanical judge and nun, are also the most flammable, the *sexiest* characters in *Measure for Measure*. Moreover, it is Angelo, of all the characters in the play, who falls farthest and hardest, he who is convinced he is damned and begs only for death. What really gives us his measure is comparison with the play's putative victor, that self-saving pragmatist Vincentio – who deliberately sets Angelo up for a fall in order that he might return to the polity he originally failed as its saviour. Compared with him Angelo goes out in a blaze of demonic glory. Indeed, as he coldly engineers Angelo's exposure, the disguised Vincentio says with a shrug, 'Let the devil/Be sometime honoured for his burning throne' (5.1.287–8). It's a form of pious sarcasm but, given Angelo's superior dramatic intensity, it also demands to be taken straight. The line even betrays a shimmer of erotic possibility by resonating with the greatest sexual epiphany in

Shakespeare. 'The barge she sat in, like a burnish'd throne/Burned on the water' (*Antony and Cleopatra*, 2.2.196 ff.).

It is possible to construe the love of *Measure*'s most mainstream romantic couple as a wholesomely organic foil to the brothel-haunting sexuality of the play.

> Your brother and his lover have embraced;
> As those that feed grow full, as blossoming time
> That from the seedness the bare fallow brings
> To teeming foison, even so her plenteous womb
> Expresseth his full tilth and husbandry. (1.4.39–43)

And these are indeed beautiful lines, but the truth is that *Measure* is not otherwise much interested in Claudio and Juliet. And, for all their organic wholesomeness, the passage strangely lacks energy and intensity. It's all about *afterwards* – the satisfaction of passion or life; as Dollimore remarked in response to an earlier draft of this essay, it seems to be gesturing towards that sort of ordinary life where, say, Romeo and Juliet marry, have kids and get fat! And while there is a kind of knockabout warmth and kindness expressed by the Viennese sex workers, all the sexual heat is generated in an abstract argument between a self-castrating lawman and a novice nun: 'She speaks, and 'tis such sense/ That my sense breeds with it' (2.2.144–5). That a brother's life depends on this contributes extra force. The explanation to us worldly moderns must seem obvious: sublimation. What's interesting about sublimation in *Measure* is that it makes for better sex. But we think we can deal with sublimation. And in fact something much more disturbing is going on, as Angelo reveals in this magnificent soliloquy:

> ISABELLA: At what hour tomorrow
>   Shall I attend your lordship?
> ANGELO: At any time fore noon.
> ISABELLA: God save your honour.
>   [*Exeunt* ISABELLA, LUCIO *and* PROVOST]

ANGELO: From thee: even from thy virtue.
            What's this? What's this? Is this her fault, or mine?
            The tempter or the tempted, who sins most, ha?
            Not she: nor does she tempt: but it is I
            That, lying by the violet in the sun,
            Do as the carrion does, not as the flower,
            Corrupt with virtuous season. Can it be
            That modesty may more betray our sense
            Than woman's lightness? Having waste ground enough
            Shall we desire to raze the sanctuary
            And pitch our evils there? Oh fie, fie, fie,
            What dost thou or what art thou, Angelo?
            Dost thou desire her foully for those things
            That make her good? Oh, let her brother live!
            Thieves for their robbery have authority,
            When judges steal themselves. What, do I love her,
            That I desire to hear her speak again,
            And feast upon her eyes? What is't I dream on?
            Oh cunning enemy, that, to catch a saint,
            With saints dost bait thy hook! Most dangerous
            Is that temptation that doth goad us on
            To sin in loving virtue. Never could the strumpet
            With all her double vigour – art and nature –
            Once stir my temper; but this virtuous maid
            Subdues me quite. Ever till now
            When men were fond, I smiled, and wondered how.
            (2.2.164–91)

There is some desublimation in this. And there can scarcely be a
more frightening and humiliating testimony to the imperative and
shattering force of repressed desire than the image of this punctili-
ous man talking his would-be rape victim through their anticipated
assignation *twice*.

ISABELLA: He hath a garden circummured with brick,
        Whose western side is with a vineyard backed;
        And to that vineyard is a planchèd gate,
        That makes his opening with this bigger key.
        This other doth command a little door
        Which from the vineyard to the garden leads.
        There have I made my promise
        Upon the heavy middle of the night
        To call upon him.
DUKE: But shall you on your knowledge find this way?
ISABELLA: I have ta'en a due and wary note upon't.
        With whispering and most guilty diligence
        In action all of precept, he did show me
        The way twice o'er. (4.1.25–38)

It all evokes Angelo very vividly – this fastidious man with the sweat and gum of pure lust on his brow. And let's not forget the victim he has so carefully instructed in her coming rape is a novice nun, one who would expressly forswear carnality.

And yet, the most terrifying thing about Angelo's soliloquy is not, I'd submit, the return of the repressed, nor even its terrible intensification, but rather the revelation of the demonic corruptibility of desire as such *even in its most virtuous forms*. Angelo doesn't want Isabella because he can see the curve of a beautiful body under her cassock. Nor is it even that he can see through her cassock to the desire it masks and disavows and therefore perhaps radically inflames. There's nothing so vulgar or predictable in the desire he expresses. Angelo really is interested in Isabella's virtue – in the soliloquy quoted, he alludes to it three times, comparing it, in Spenserian vein, with sunshine; he's interested in her modesty, her saintliness. His desire for her channels and expresses even as it soils a metaphysical hunger for the Good. 'To sin in loving virtue.' Ay, there's the point! And it takes us beyond familiar psychoanalytic categories.

There's great paradoxical pathos in Angelo's prayer to be saved from Isabella's goodness. He's tortured by the fact that, having waste ground enough, he desires to raze that sanctuary and pitch his evils there, even as that torture further inflames his desire. We might think he wants her out of spiritual *ressentiment* and hatred of the Good. He might very well resent any rival claim to goodness since he knows, after breaking off his engagement with Mariana, he can't really measure up. But his foulness truly *honours* Isabella's virtue – or the virtue he sees in her: it doesn't much matter here whether he's right; what matters is his sincerity. He desires 'her foully *for those things which make her good*'. He is the victim of a desire which simultaneously discloses him at his best (venerating virtue) and his worst (venturing in that very veneration to defile it). A leering Satan is seen here baiting his hook with a saint in order to catch a saint. It raises the question as to whether our purest and most sacred feelings can ever be free of demonic elements. For love itself – perhaps the last touchstone of humanist criticism – is a temptation here, even love of what is highest and most rightly lovable.

But *what* sins in loving virtue? Partly it's sex. For what conditions these thoughts uttered in soliloquy is Angelo-the-future-rapist's exposed consideration of the sex-act: his vivid tasting of what it would be – *what it will be* – to fuck Isabella. I apologize for the obscenity but no euphemism will do. Angelo wants to, even as he recognizes that sex is horribly at variance with what he wants of or from her: her spiritual virtue. Of course, he's still partly being a puritan, and yet his agony poses a real and hard and maybe even tragic question about what sex might be beyond idealization. Even if we object that there is no sex beyond idealization, that sex is the means by which lovers summon each other into bodily personhood and presence, a wrecking consciousness of the brutality of sex is never far away. In Angelo's soliloquy, sex grossly obtrudes into religious desire and ruins it, pitching our evils in the razed sanctuary. But perhaps there is always a religious, in the sense of metaphysical, ambition in sex, to which it is tragically unsuited as vehicle, to the effect that sex always promises but cannot get what it wants; and so we want more and more sex. Sex is as a bull in a china shop in Angelo's speech, pathetically, inevitably ruining what it wants. Yet all of this, perhaps, only makes sex more sexy as an approach to the truth of our tragically disintegral condition.

And there's more, for Angelo comes to grief not so much on the rocks of sex, as on something which is active in but irreducible to sex, something much more basic than sex: this is where we come up against the possessive element in all desire. For isn't even desire of the most rarefied sort in some sense possessive? Can we conceive of the Holy of Holies without desiring to enter it, or otherwise hug it to ourselves, at least in imagination? And must not such an entrance, or seizure, corrupt its sacred otherness? That's why Dostoevsky's paradisal 'dream of a ridiculous man' is infected and ultimately ruined by the mere presence of the dreamer (Dostoevsky 2004).

I recall a haunting dream from my own childhood, where I was running, in a panic, down a white corridor, trying false doors which opened hopelessly onto solid white walls. Finally, I was able to pass through a door, finding myself in a strange but beautiful land, a pastoral world full of tall and twisting tree-like forms, washed in extraordinary colour. It was populated by slender, tall and soulful rabbit-like beings who went upright on two legs. Well, they did till I arrived. Because when I had, they all instantly started to crumple with pain and die. And there was no way back into the corridor. . . .

'Shall we desire to raze the sanctuary and pitch our evils there?' Such is the temptation to profane. What makes profanation demonic is that it depends on knowledge of the Good, to which it constitutes negative testimony. The fact that profanation knows the Good brings it in range of spiritual sympathy but at the same time rules such sympathy out of court – for how, given that it knows the Good, could it so raze and defile that sanctuary – *how could it*? Angelo is more sympathetic because he experiences this violating impulse as an irresistible and self-estranging mystery. 'What dost thou or what art thou, Angelo?' He is possessed by desire; he doesn't *coldly* choose to raze the sanctuary like, say, Dostoevsky's Raskolnikov. But the real horror in *Measure for Measure* is the sneaking suspicion that *we* can't *not* raze the sanctuary. We can't simply keep Angelo at arm's length. To sin in loving virtue: there's a flaw in desire as such which responds sensuously and sharply to the vivid, resplendent otherness of what it beholds but simultaneously moves against it, to compromise it and possess it for its own.

Of course, though Isabella seems pure to Angelo, this quality in desire which hurts or soils both the other and the soul or self infects her too. She much less consciously reflects Angelo's experience of inevitable profanation in these infamous lines:

> The impression of keen whips I'd wear as rubies,
> And strip myself to death, as to a bed
> That longing have been sick for, ere I'd yield
> My body up to shame. (2.4.101–4)

The glistening wounds and pining for death suggest martyrology, hinting, like the ungenitured agent urinating congealed ice, at a desire and subjectivity not of this world. They might be the badge or stigmata of sainthood but for the cruel fact that they evoke exactly such a physically relished yielding to shame as they are defined against. The thrill inhering in such deliciously anticipated impressions of whips, and the sensuous self-satisfaction of rubious ornamentation, amply demonstrates the world and the flesh returning in their disavowal. But the irony here is tragic, and Isabella, like Angelo, not simply its victim, much as we might like to enjoy the humiliation of their pride. For what would a non-possessive desire be like? What would it mean to desire something *without* identifying one's self and pleasure with it? How could such a thing even be desirable? Eastern doctrines of non-attachment may come in here, but perhaps one advantage of the Christian tradition with its doctrine of incarnation is the justice it does to the erotically and ethically complicated fact that we always desire in and as a self and body, to the effect that as *Measure* instructs us the very otherness we honour in desire we want immediately to compromise by enjoying it as ours. Angelo's and Isabella's spiritual predicament is that they are each inspired by a lovely vision of that which exceeds mere selfish life and condemned, brutally or subtly, one way or another, to kill it in the cradle.

The rape of a nun Angelo does not quite commit is the most concentrated and terrible image of the perverse paradox of desire that is the burden of the play's tragic knowledge. But before Angelo falls, and leaving his history with Mariana aside, his attitude to the Good is already a guiltily possessive one: 'My gravity,/Wherein – let no man hear me – *I take pride*' (2.4.9–11; my emphasis). We have seen that Isabella too enjoys virtue by identifying with it – as her own – in emotionally complicated fantasies of godly debasement. In cooler mode she says, 'I have spirit to do any thing that appears not foul in the truth of my spirit', and the folding of 'spirit' into 'my spirit' here as well as the note of purse-lipped pedantry bespeak a horribly proud self-arrogation of the Good (3.1.203–4). But the play's cheapest and most conspicuous rape of goodness is surely the Duke's. At the curtain, remember, Vincentio was full of melancholy feelings of guilt and failure as regards the anarchy in Vienna. His trick, and admittedly it's impossible to say that he consciously knows what he's doing, is to install Angelo as his deputy precisely because he doubts him. Then when Angelo fails, this enables Vincentio's moral and political triumph, and thorough evasion of his own guilt. Angelo is Vincentio's fall guy, and Vincentio's forgiveness of Angelo is callow and thoroughly incidental to his process of exculpating himself. Worse than that, he has the gall to clothe himself in the mantle of a saviour. And then to take the body of the nun which his Deputy has failed to obtain. The difference between Vincentio and the other characters I have considered is that whereas Angelo and Isabella are powerfully possessed by that which they want to possess, and completely abandon themselves to their obsessions, Vincentio is just a cynic.

Lucio has his number. He is a habitual user of prostitutes and though it's theoretically possible to use prostitutes passionately, ecstatically, even in fear and trembling, here such behaviour is precisely revealing of one who refuses to be possessed by what he possesses. Lucio recognizes Vincentio as just the same sort of bloke, testifying, for instance, that the Duke would 'mouth with a beggar though she smelt brown bread and garlic' (3.1.413–5). But Vincentio scapegoats Lucio at the end of the play. When he decrees that Lucio must marry Kate Keepdown, a prostitute by whom he has a child, this ensures that Lucio henceforward will be possessed by that which he took so cheaply. It's astonishingly hypocritical. Not least because Lucio conspicuously and surprisingly did honour the separateness of Vincentio's own intended, Isabella, which Vincentio now spectacularly fails to honour when seeking her hand in marriage. At the gate of the convent, Lucio referred to Isabella as 'a thing enskied and sainted/By your renouncement an immortal spirit' (1.4.33–4). Nuns are by definition 'separates', and later Angelo's anguished desire for Isabella agonizingly worshipped that very separateness which he would prevail upon and defile. There is an anguished ethical dignity in this compared with the casual arrogance of Vincentio's throwaway proposal. In his ethical grandstanding at the end of the play, Vincentio just assumes goodness for himself, and thereby completely squanders it; and then, in an absurdly premature equivalent gesture, just takes, or at least wants to take, the nun as well. Talk about a would-be rapist. It's as if he doesn't really become a subject of desire at all, because he does not sufficiently recognize the space desire posits between itself and what it desires. This is partly true of Isabella in her priggishness, but her extraordinary spiritual ambition does at the same time measure out that space. In the end, the dissipated image of Angelo raping a nun in the dark returns to haunt *Measure for Measure* as its deepest truth, but it is Vincentio who is doing the raping in the guise not of a tormented angel with horns but of a complacent husband. Angelo may entertain sensationally extraordinary desires, but Shakespeare doesn't let more ordinary ones off the hook.

And this is where the play's moral diagnosis threatens almost literally to come home.

* * *

I am not a rapist (not a sentence normally called for in a critical essay). But *Measure for Measure* troubles this admittedly minimal and unimpressive moral assertion. My life is ordinary and law-abiding but Shakespeare seems to link it to Angelo's extreme experience, discovering under also my cloak of relative decency and decorum a gross and criminal guilt. We are less equipped than was Shakespeare's day to recognize the general resonance of Angelo's weirdness. It would have given Luther no trouble at all. The following, from his *Commentary on Galatians*, could practically be a gloss on or amplification of *Measure for Measure*:

> So it happeneth at length to all justiciaries, who being drunken with the opinion of their own righteousness, do think, when they are out of temptation, that they are beloved of God, and that God regardeth their fastings, their prayers, and their will-works, and that for the same he must give unto them a singular crown in heaven. But when that thundering, lightning, fire, and that hammer which breaketh in pieces the rocks, that is to say, the law of God, cometh suddenly upon them, revealing unto them their sin, the wrath and judgement of God, then the selfsame thing happened unto them which happened to the Jews standing at the foot of Mount Sinai. (Luther, ed. Dillenberger, 1961, p. 143)

What happened on Sinai was that, in Luther's words:

> [T]he children of Israel did behold the horrible sight of the mount smoking and burning, the black clouds, and the lightnings flashing up and down in this thick darkness, and heard the sound of the trumpet blowing long and waxing louder and louder; and moreover when they heard the thunderings and lightnings, they

were afraid, and standing afar off they said unto Moses: 'We will do all things willingly, so that the Lord speak not unto us, lest that we die, and this great fire consume us. Teach thou us, and we will hearken unto thee' [Exodus, 20.19; Deuteronomy. 5.24 ff.].

Luther comments:

I pray you, what did their purifying, their white garments, their refraining from their wives, and their holiness profit them? Nothing at all. There was not one of them that could abide this presence of the Lord in his majesty and glory: but all being amazed and shaken with terror, fled back as if they had been driven by the devil. For God is a consuming fire, in whose sight no flesh is able to stand. (Luther, ed. Dillenberger, 1961, p. 142)

We don't live in such searing proximity to truth; I don't anyway. Luther evokes a massive panorama and a proto-universal experience of existential guilt. But it's Shakespeare's intimate portrayal of Angelo's tragedy of desire which has the power to get under my skin and disturb my moral self-conceit.

It's Angelo whom I *recognize.*

It's true he starts out from somewhere beyond sympathy (but isn't that somewhere we all have stood?). As Eric S. Mallin wrote in response to an earlier draft of this, Angelo is like a visiting spirit which has taken flesh, which has in turn taken him. Angelo is *dead* in the beginning of the play, or at least not fully alive.

Ever till now
When men were fond, I smiled, and wondered how

But that 'now' changes everything. As the rhyme indicates, it undoes Angelo's weird distinction. He is brought to recognize he is just like others. But the resonance, equally, flows the other way, which is much less acknowledged. All others are, equally, just like him – *and never more so than at the inception of rape.* 'Now' stands for the tender, vulnerable and ambivalent induction into desire which everyone experiences, and not just once, but again and again. As we have seen, Angelo's experience lays bare desire as the most intense experience of the inviolable autonomy of another person and the simultaneous impulse to destroy that autonomy by means of violent possession. 'To sin in loving virtue'. His fate involves not just an assault on a nun, but also a terribly condensed experience of spiritual life and death. Angelo's is the agony of a still-born soul, born in the inception of a virtuous love but born dead because of the attempted rape this synonymously inspires. Of course we don't all fall for nuns, but any love is virtuous in its cherishing of another's inimitable separateness, which desire indissociably acts against. And if the grim ambivalence of love forms the basis of Angelo's solidarity with other men, we have seen that Isabella shows that it is not just a male problem, for she cannot love her God without loving Him as her own. Luther was on to it. He developed a new definition of sin as Curvitas, writing 'Our nature has been so deeply curved in upon itself because of the viciousness of original sin . . . it not only turns the finest gifts of God Himself to achieve these aims, but it also seems to be ignorant of this very fact, that in acting so iniquitously, so perversely, and in such a depraved way, it is even seeking God for its own sake' (quoted in Lohse, 1999, pp. 70–1). *Measure for Measure* describes the soul's experience of spoiling sanctity, including its own, the soul's unavoidable experience of *spoiling itself.* It is this which the play emblematizes as a would-be-good man raping a nun, an X-Ray image it reveals at the heart of political, legal and religious life and, in the end, also in the more sinisterly everyday, domestic shape of a complacent husband making a move on his bride.

Angelo is a scapegoat, and not just for Vincentio and Isabella. He is also a revealing mirror and, again, not just for Vincentio and Isabella. This is easy enough to take in general terms *but I am not a rapist*! And yet, *Measure* seems to compel confession, not so much in the gut-spilling as the spiritually serious sense. And the confession it compels is of a horrible failure to love, a deeply ingrained and systematic practice of rape in moral and spiritual life. I am *not* a rapist, not in the ordinary sense of the word, but nor for that matter is Angelo, and is he not absolutely one? The play seems to turn on me here. For, as we have seen, Angelo is a rapist not just in relation to Isabella, but also in his usage of the Good for his own purposes, his arrogation of a meticulous probity in the interest of his own self-security, precedence and pride. And am I not guilty likewise? Isn't it the case that everything I admire and desire to honour for itself I also energetically covet for myself? Even, weirdly, as myself. Is it literature (or Shakespeare) I profess? Or is it – when all is said and done – me? Oh fie, fie, fie! Isn't everything a Trojan horse for self-assertion? So, then – demonic sneer – shall we desire to raze *the sanctuary* and pitch our evils there? Yes, yes, that too, even the holiest of affections! *My* mother. *My* wife. *My* child. *My* God. There's no twisting off the coil. For these very ideas unmasking self-assertion are themselves me and mine, to the effect that this supposed attack on my own integrity in fact slyly reinforces it. Angelo seems clearer and more honest than I am able to be, and it moves me to a kind of love – though even this is no doubt partly an opportunistic appropriation of Angelo's virtue of moral honesty in an attempt to save my self-esteem. But then part of what Angelo sees and shows is that there is nothing other than such ambivalence. I find myself wanting to address him personally.

Yes Angelo, me too, me especially, mea culpa.

And yet, as soon as I do there bubbles up in me a fugitive and half embarrassed hope, and one which seems to me not to be wholly self-serving. For Angelo's metanoia involves a kind of theology of desire, one which sees that sex and ethics and religion are all part of the life of desire, one which could be spelt out something like this:

1. In desire we know the beloved/Good/God.
2. But in desire we also know that we cannot but desire the beloved/Good/God for our own.

What Angelo does not himself articulate but perhaps nevertheless embodies is:

3. Our chastened knowledge of desire is the closest we get to the beloved/Good/God.

In other words, in falling so painfully short Angelo recognizes what transcends him. And I too have experienced something thing like this, a precious intimation of enlightenment which can only be accessed but is also betrayed by and remains beyond desire. But I am hardly so identified with this as Angelo is. It is through him that I acquire a better sense of it and begin to intuit what a life might be that was lived in accordance with such knowledge. In respect of Shakespeare criticism, it would mean recognizing that Shakespeare is unavailable except via a limited and partial experience which, as it were, negatively reveals what truly transcends it.

But that's just Shakespeare criticism. *Measure for Measure* is about more serious things.

Notes

1. I thought I'd come up with the term 'biographeme' but Roland Barthes uses the word in *Sade, Fourier, Loyola*:

   Were I a writer, and dead, how I would love it if my life, through the pains of some friendly and detached biographer, were to reduce itself to a few details, a few preferences [tastes], a few inflections, let us say: to 'biographemes' whose distinction and mobility might go beyond any fate and come to touch, like Epicurean atoms, some future body, destined to the same dispersion; a marked life, in sum, as Proust succeeded in writing his in his work. (Barthes, 1977b, pp. 8–9)

   Barthes emphasizes concentration here, and the capacity to touch other lives, as well as intuiting the link with literature. He offers a life of

Fourier in twelve anecdotes spanning less than two pages. Here is one of them:

11. His concierge found him dead in his dressing gown, kneeling among the flowerpots. (ibid., pp. 182–4)

Earlier he envisions Saint Ignatius's 'beautiful eyes, always a little filled with tears' (p. 8). In his second preface to *Philosophy in the Tragic Age of the Greeks*, Nietzsche said, 'It is possible to shape the picture of a man out of three anecdotes. I shall try to emphasize three anecdotes in each system and abandon the rest.' (Nietzsche, 1998, p. 25). Even where great art is capacious and expansive (Barthes's example of Proust comes to mind) it remains, at least at its best, concentrated, intensely interesting. Shakespeare of course is both rich and concentrated, as well as supremely affecting in his impact on other imaginations, works and lives.

2. For powerful and considered arguments in favour of the involvement of personal experience in literary criticism, see especially the last chapter of Fuller, 1988 and Fuller, 2010.

Chapter 2
Othello, Marriage, Middle Age

Eric S. Mallin

> *Our preferences (what we long for and crave) and our standards (the
> kinds of creatures we would rather be) usually have a sadomasochis-
> tic relationship of taunting and teasing and punishing (think how
> difficult it often is to justify our sexual desires to ourselves). What
> we want and what we should want has become an endless drama of
> mutual humiliation.*
>
> (Phillips, 2005, p. 102)[1]

* * *

The first infidelities in the play are his. He steals the precious
jewel Desdemona from her father, violating guest–host relations
and social order. Then he hides the marriage from everyone. Even
Cassio, who supposedly 'came a-wooing' many a time with his
General (and how did Brabantio miss this embassy?), oddly seems
not to know about the match: in response to Iago's information
that 'He's married', the puzzled lieutenant asks 'To who?' (*Othello*,
1.2.52). He is unfaithful to Iago, swiping the lieutenancy from him
and handing it to Cassio, right out from under the noses of 'three
great ones of the city' (1.1.8). His spiritual infidelity is great, too:
as a literal convert, he has already abandoned his religious belief
(or unbelief) once, this time for the new promise of Christianity.
But his deceptions hide under the guise of that impressively
noble diction and heroic demeanour, so his renegade thefts and

trickery can pass unnoticed. He can even play the victim of his own transgressions.

Othello never admits it, but he has a larcenous, untrue heart. So much for 'my . . . perfect soul' that will 'manifest me rightly' (1.2.31–2). He fits surprisingly well into the sneaky culture of Venice, with its multiple 'beguilings' and misdirections ('[I] did beguile her of her tears'–1.3.155). One of his more artful betrayals involves the prop with which he feigns betrayal: the handkerchief.

That overdetermined scrap of cloth helps convince Othello of his cuckoldry, but it ought to be unconvincing from the start, non-dispositive in the trial of Desdemona's faith. The first time Iago attempts to deploy it as ocular proof against Cassio, the effort falls a bit short, thus hinting at the token's provisional meanings:

IAGO: Did you perceive how he laughed at his vice?
OTHELLO: O Iago!
IAGO: And did you see the handkerchief?
OTHELLO: Was that mine? (4.1.164–7)

Strange indeed, given the fetishizing of this object, that '*any* handkerchief would have served as evidence' (Booth, 1995, pp. 23–4). Othello has an unpredictable attitude towards the token. It's the most important thing in the world, its loss would cause 'such perdition/As nothing else could match', and yet he abandons it, pushing Desdemona's hand away and letting the rag fall, while seeming to instruct her to 'Let it alone' (3.4.66–7, 3.3.292). Once it is lost, he fabricates a threatening, symbolically weighty history for the object, first ascribing its source to an Egyptian charmer who gave the token to his mother, who gave it to him. Later, however, he strays from that vital tale, saying the hanky was 'an antique token/My father gave my mother' (5.2.223–4). Perhaps most surprisingly, Othello claims the Egyptian allegedly told his mother that while she kept it

'Twould make her amiable [i.e., desirable] and subdue my father
Entirely to her love; but if she lost it

Or made a gift of it, my father's eye
Should hold her loathèd, and his spirits should hunt
After new fancies. (3.4.56–61)

This punitive lie performs wicked double business. It makes Desdemona insecure about her own desirability (based solely on her possession of some magic silk). And, more cravenly, the lost handkerchief explicitly gives the husband leave to cheat on and abandon the wife, as he is no longer subdued 'entirely to her love'. The story furnishes an occult alibi for the man to pry himself from marital subjugation: a free pass for infidelity and abandonment on the grounds of the wife's failure to remain sufficiently appealing. It's all her fault.

* * *

Othello is Shakespeare's only marital tragedy; it underscores the wretched difficulty of the wedded condition.[2] This vexation has little to do with jealousy per se, or even the misogyny that figures so pervasively in Venice and elsewhere; it is instead about marriage's revelatory constrictions, its demand on men for self-exposure. Marriage causes men to fall into nets of their own secrets, inwardness, rationalizations, lies, because of their unaccustomed vulnerability. Positing such ethical descent as the consequence of marriage seems a lame and impotent sort of excuse, but the married men in the play – both of them – depend on the idea. Sometimes, so do I. The play has always, at least since I've been married, frightened and embarrassed me intensely.

But why? Surely I needn't worry: *Othello* describes something hyperbolic, not inevitable. Furthermore, I don't much resemble the hero or his situation; I am not of direct African descent, and I lack military experience. My wife and I are about the same age and skin colour; I have never had the complicated luxury of suspecting her of infidelity. Still, Shakespeare can make familiar what ought to be strange, and he is able to turn Othello's peculiar circumstance into an allegory for all married men.[3]

The play's unpredictable oscillation between distance and identification, the way it comforts an audience with its hero's extremity
and then disturbs us – me – with his psychological familiarity, gives
the drama much of its fearful power. What seems eerily recognizable is not so much Othello's rage or susceptibility to suspicion as
what these signify: a faithlessness that provides a safety-valve for his
considerable insecurities. The play stages erotic paranoia as a cower-
ing estrangement from the convictions of self-worth, potency, and
lovability – and as an excuse for every male marital transgression.
As the clown Lavatch says in *All's Well that Ends Well*: 'If men could
be contented to be what they are, there were no fear in marriage'
(1.3.44–5). Ontological discontent occupies the fear in and around
marriage; it certainly bothers Iago. From the moment of his conspicuous self-negation 'I am not what I am' (1.1.65), Iago stands as an
archetype of sorry self-alienation and, not incidentally, marital misery. Emilia confirms as much, exposing her husband without knowing it: 'some such squire he was/That turned your wit the seamy side
without,/And made you to suspect me with the Moor' (4.2.149–51).
('Squire' slaps hard at Iago's resentful servitude, a gratifying if accidental insult.) Iago's self-spawning, fragmenting jealousy, however,
does not stop him from pronouncing self-help platitudes: 'since I
could distinguish betwixt a benefit and an injury, I never found man
that knew how to love himself' (1.3.310–11). But a purely negated
consciousness ('I. . .not. . .I') would be categorically and logically
incapable of that elusive self-love.[4] And of course, Iago is peculiarly
awful at distinguishing 'betwixt a benefit and an injury'. His entire
marriage-demolishing scheme slaughters the benefits he seeks and
turns the entire world into an injury. Loving oneself proves perversely complicated; like Iago, most people cannot tell what helps,
what harms, until many aches and dangers have passed.

Which may be why Othello's tragic paranoia attempts to rescue
benefit from injury: the real shock of Desdemona's presumed infidelity is that it seems to be a *projection*. Othello's conviction of his
cuckoldry functions like the handkerchief, a prop that relieves him

of the immense vulnerability he feels in marriage. As Kenneth Gross writes, 'It is as if he suddenly perceived the world to be full of secrets, but in a way that robbed him of his privacy' (Gross, 1989, p. 825; see also Cavell, 1987). Othello realizes that these secrets are desires, and they are shamefully his own.

Let me consider some of Othello's secrets, but not as if I were isolated from them. His deferral of blame, his defensive, wandering faith, and the vague erotic insufficiency to which the drama points: the play is weirdly continuous with my uncertain experience of self in marriage. The 'endless drama of mutual humiliation', as Adam Phillips calls it – the psychomachia of embarrassing wants and stupid self-idealizations – connects me to, and affects my ideas about this play more intensely than any other. So my reading will be unreliable in the most basic sense: over-identified, nervous, grandiose. Othello frequently sponsors dismaying interpretive self-disclosures; it seems to compel readers' confessions. But the play also thematizes 'confession' as wickedly unreliable and manipulative, reminding us that tortured revelations can also camouflage deeper secrets. In this respect, my confessional reading of *Othello* may be a protective lie I tell myself. However, I can at least claim this advantage over the General: I have had the chance to acclimate to matrimonial rhythms and grapple with my deficiencies. Othello, who weds for the first time in middle age, cannot cope with the sudden clash between his desires and ideals; he keeps his secrets pursed up, and they ruin him.

* * *

Pieces of the past: I do not wish to remember most of it. But start here: Attractive young woman in the office, watching as I speak to my wife on the phone. The conversation was unremarkable, but after we hang up the woman says: 'she's your best girl, isn't she?' A long, sweet look. Then she asks me to kiss her. Happy that she sees who I love, feeling safe in this recognition, I consider the request. Not for too long.

When called to account for his marriage before the Senate, Othello speaks hidingly: his description of the stories that won

Desdemona's heart shows someone in the act of public conceal-ment. His account lacks explanations or aetiologies: what battles did he fight? How old was he when he was freed from slavery? Why did he convert? More important for the occasion: at what point did Desdemona's curiosity about him become passion? The speech, designed to explain the genesis of love, or at least of Desdemona's desire ('She gave me for my pains a world of sighs' [1.3.158]), is airy nothing.[5] Certainly, discourse, whether love talk, poem, political utterance, or personal essay, typically negotiates between concealment and disclosure. So it is all the more remark-able that after confessing his obliviousness to Desdemona's desires in the courtship – 'Upon this hint I spake' (1.3.165) is his comic line after describing her unsubtle pursuit – Othello should then baldly reveal an ill omen for the romance. Seconding Desdemona's request to follow him to the wars, the General tries to persuade the Senate thus:

> Let her have your voice.
> Vouch with me, heaven, I therefore beg it not,
> To please the palate of my appetite,
> Nor to comply with heat – the young affects
> In me defunct – and proper satisfaction,
> But to be free and bounteous to her mind;
> And heaven defend your good souls that you think
> I will your serious and great business scant
> When she is with me. No, when light-winged toys
> Of feathered Cupid seel with wanton dullness
> My speculative and officed instruments,
> That my disports corrupt and taint my business,
> Let housewives make a skillet of my helm,
> And all indign and base adversities
> Make head against my estimation! (1.3.259–73)

Can we believe him? After all, Brabantio, the father of the bride, has just told the white politicians all about Othello's witchcraft, animality, and unnaturalness; the black man on informal trial may thus want to expunge any hint of sexuality in his reply. But. . . this! Here he swears not to possess any desire for sex or even for the 'proper satisfaction' that would permit the consummation of the marriage. He swears that he is effectively impotent – what else could 'those young affects in me defunct' signify? His desire to gratify his new wife's request combines an admirable idealism about companionate marriage ('to be free and bounteous to her mind') with a chaste, misogynist hostility to the eroticism that actually helps sustain such marriages ('disports corrupt and taint my business').[6] Othello remarkably claims not to 'comply with heat', which amounts (in a marriage to a new young bride) to a publicly confessed debility, framed as a virtue.

By his own admission, then, he may be radically under-sexed. Perhaps he could get some help: enter Iago. Readers have noticed that the villain's function in the play is to arouse the General; as a personal pornographer, Iago will later incite Othello to an erotic pitch undreamt of (and utterly foreclosed) in the testimony before the Senate. Rather than prove a marital aid, however, Iago shows what a potent neurotoxin sexuality can be in a marriage.[7] Still and all, Othello's public account is not entirely false. It is, instead, inauspicious, untimely, perhaps aspirational. For at this point in the play he has yet to discover how vulnerable he is to the notion of an exuberantly sexual wife.

Iago's later insinuations about Desdemona may be *too* arousing – they send Othello into a cataleptic frenzy[8] – but he merely exaggerates, if grossly, a fact that Othello cannot successfully ignore: Desdemona's positive passion and his own discomfort with his wife's erotic energy. To be sure, her vigour should not surprise him. In recounting the history of his courtship he recalls that Desdemona would 'come again, and with a greedy ear/Devour up my discourse' (1.3.148–9). He receives her sighs for his pains – a proleptically sexy transaction – and he hears her say 'That I did love the Moor to live with him,/My downright violence and storm of fortunes/May trumpet to the world' (1.3.247–9). (Iago will lewdly pun this passion into his own ugly idiom: 'The Moor – I know his trumpet' [2.1.177].) And she unashamedly asks to accompany her husband so as not to miss out on 'the rites for why I love him' (1.3.256). Although his response to her request hardly seconds that emotion, no one can know, early in the play, how profoundly the erotic differential between husband and wife will affect them. We get a better idea when they reunite in Cyprus.

* * *

– So. That was fast. Is it over already?
The light plays off her back, smooth and curved like the outrounding of a ship's hull.
– (She continued:) I don't want to say it, but. . .
– You're not going to say that we need to talk, are you? I know you're unhappy.
– Hey, don't put this on me. Obviously something's wrong. . . You just back and fill, turn away. What aren't you telling me?
I have nothing for her. I can't bring myself to speak my embarrassment. The rumours, the looks – an outcast already – I can't spy happiness from here. I don't know, maybe we can go back. She says:
– This was a mistake, wasn't it? But it doesn't have to end badly.
– No, it doesn't.
– Except it isn't fair. You think you're the one at risk, but I'm doing the heart on the sleeve thing. You've got shelter.
– True enough. I'm sorry. (Pause, indicating my sincerity.) What do you want? Do you want everyone to know?
(And wouldn't you just leave me anyway?)

Othello sees Desdemona again on the shores after a storm has swallowed the Turks. He exclaims: 'If after every tempest come such calms,/May the winds blow till they have wakened death./. . . If it were now to die,/'Twere now to be most happy' (2.1.182–7). The lines expose a dismal mismatch: Othello is so happy to see

Desdemona he wants to die; she is so happy, she wants to live and flourish. He receives a proper rebuke from his excellent wife, who instructs him with her first, best contradiction: 'The heavens forbid/ But that our loves and comforts should increase/Even as our days do grow' (2.1.190–2). Her corrective (increase, grow) sounds like a biblical injunction. But the damage is done: Othello is caught out, having already failed to imagine a future with her.

He fails in other, related ways. Despite Desdemona's best intentions, and even without Iago, their married life would have always been troubled, particularly in the erotic realm.[9] We know as much because of the delicate, taunting stagecraft around their consummation. Their coupling is repeatedly postponed, even after we are (repeatedly) led to think – confessions of impotence notwithstanding – it certainly must have occurred.[10] The play invites us to wonder what the many delays signify. Boito's libretto for Verdi's *Otello* puts the blame wholly on the villain Iago, who instructs Roderigo: 'Then shalt thou cry a mutiny and disturb/The Moor in the arms of his love!'[11] In the operatic reading, Othello and Desdemona fail to consummate their marriage only because of strategic, cunning interruption. Certainly, this is part of Iago's plan too; but he receives aid from other sources, such as the abortive war.

Implied parallels between sex and warfare in the play cast light on both (Calderwood, 1989, pp. 75–8). Othello is called to the Mediterranean battle, interrupting his wedding night. Answering the call, Othello expresses eagerness for the fight, and no shred of reluctance at leaving his new, young wife on their nuptial eve. Indeed, his reassurance to the Senate makes war sound like a recumbent pleasure, even if framed as subjection: 'The tyrant Custom. . ./ Hath made the flinty and steel couch of war/My thrice-driven bed of down' (1.3.227–9). While waiting for Othello's return from the Turkish battle, Cassio oozes out a prayer, asking Jove to let Othello's sails swell, his 'tall ship' enter the bay, and, abandoning such subtle metaphor, to 'Make love's quick pants in Desdemona's arms,/ Give fire to our extincted spirits' (2.1.81–2). This vicarious refresher for the troops aligns with the crucial impression that the Turkish campaign has been in some measure unsatisfying. The war needs a capstone, something to consummate it. Literally, it needs (or the Venetians need) sex between the General and Desdemona.[12] And the impression of incompleteness, of the somehow failed success of the war, sharpens when Othello announces with uncharacteristic brevity on his return: 'News, friends: Our wars are done, the Turks are drowned' (2.1.199). An audience might think: my, that was fast! Quite the anti-climax.

The war never does come to satisfying fruition, and it ends just after it starts. However, its proper analogue is not, as Calderwood suggests, *coitus interruptus* (Calderwood, 1989, p. 81). The General takes up arms, he enters the fray, he wins. Yet he does not engage in the back-and-forth of battle, and he claims no combat triumph or enemy surrender. Indeed, the vanquished Turks simply disappear, a vast, deflating disappointment. The closest physical analogy for what occurs in the war must be premature ejaculation: an incomplete, frustrated, ambiguous consummation that represents a mid-point between 'no sex' (which would equate to pacifism or treaty) and successful, masterful intercourse, complete with explosive orgasm (decisive military victory). The Turkish wars end not with a bang, nor with a sense of achievement, and so resemble Othello's and Desdemona's wedding night. *Coitus interruptus* is an unconvincing dramatic metaphor because the mere adventitious prevention of sex, as in Verdi, would be little obstacle to determined lovers; instead, the notion that something inherent in Othello curtails the possibility of sex with his wife offers more compelling, suggestive, if uncertain, theatre. Where mere interruption provides some possibly comic annoyance, Othello's premature ejaculation (or his unclear, partly functional impotence) would vex, embarrass, and confuse the pair; and it would reveal the psychic limitations of the match.

The problem makes a half-truth of Othello's supposedly defunct 'young affects'; it suggests those feelings are surely present (as indeed his mad jealousy confirms), but self-undoing, or perpetually voided and debilitating. The statistically common problem of premature orgasm in some way stands opposite to that of erectile dysfunction, or Othello's confessed dead affects; premature release signifies one who is young, perhaps overeager, guilt-ridden, or sexually inexperienced: '[Premature ejaculation] is most common in younger men (aged 18–30 y), but it also may occur in conjunction with secondary impotence in men aged 45–65 years.'[13] In the evocative terms of a well-known medical dictionary, Othello may be suffering a dendritic problem: premature ejaculation is

> ejaculation consistently occurring either prior to, upon, or immediately after penetration and before it is desired, taking into account factors such as age, novelty of the specific situation, and recent frequency of the sexual act. Used officially [DSM-IV], it denotes also significant resulting distress or interpersonal difficulty. (*Dorland's,* 2003: 593, s.v. 'ejaculation')

Othello's 'interpersonal difficulty', if the play allows us this much speculation – and why wouldn't it? – arises from the stressors of performance anxiety, novelty, and (in)frequency. If his woes signify a young man's more than an older man's problem, perhaps Desdemona *has* rejuvenated him, his young affects tormentingly and very much alive. But these affects, in an aging body, in gentle or passionate collision with a youthful form, discompose him. Early ejaculation ('the Turks are drowned') signals Othello's intense implication in, but lack of control over, his own erotic responses. His technical difficulties could deepen the tragedy: his assumption that he and his wife live at incompatible levels of desire may then be slightly off-centre and exculpatory for his failure.

Othello's erotic dysfunction, as I posit it, can be extrapolated from the General's other complexes: for instance, his tendency to idealize Desdemona and to inflate her significance beyond mortal bounds before absolutely abandoning her ('Perdition catch my soul/But I do love thee. And *when* I love thee not/Chaos is come again' [3.3.92–3]).

In regarding her as transcendent or untouchable, nothing good can happen when he tries to touch her. Othello struggles with an unusually edgy conflict between parthenology, his fetishizing of Desdemona's virgin purity, and his husbandly imperative to sexualize his wife. Combined with this underplot, and contributing to it, is the strong suggestion that the defeated Turks are never in fact destroyed, but rather merge with Othello's own 'Propontic and the Hellespont' (3.3.459), his raging psychic sea: they become the subliminal enemy inseparable from the self. The war itself has erotic implications for a premature ejaculator, one who suffers an inconclusive victory, a conflict with no rival other than his own ideas, his body, and spirit.[14]

Premature ejaculation (more than simple impotence or erectile dysfunction) discloses an attribute of mind, not merely of flesh or circumstance. Othello always arrives too soon at 'preposterous conclusions' (the temptation scene is blindingly fast), his surprising impatience Iago's best tool; Othello is easily brought to the summit of arousal, the peak of anguished pleasure – he jumps the gun. Iago repeatedly finds it necessary, throughout his mental arousal of Othello, to pull back, to stop stimulating him so that both may achieve the proper 'satisfaction'[15]: 'No more of that', and 'Nay, but this was but his dream', 'Nay, yet be wise', and 'Yet be content'. Like a skilled lover, he knows that every brake on the process only heightens desire (and with it, agony). But lest I over-eroticize this engagement, I should simply note that Othello is often too eager, too ready to spring to the ultimate consequence: if it were now to die, and so forth. That quality baffles an audience: why such lack of deliberation? Such a quick dismissal of Cassio? Why so much belief in Iago, so quickly? And why such myopia about his wife? Because cognitively, Othello just cannot help himself. When he reaches a certain pitch of passion, he cannot maintain control, no matter how he tries: the armoured fury that once made him a good warrior now makes him a failed lover. We may even see the figure for premature and pleasureless orgasm beneath the courtship itself: having told Desdemona his stories, having 'ran it through, even from my boyish days' (1.3.131), Othello may be spent, emptied out, a vessel of no self at all.

* * *

– No, don't say that. I don't appreciate these lies and evasions and shit, honey. Why can't you tell me the truth? All this secrecy feels like shame; I'm thinking I've wasted all this time.
– All this time. Really? You want me to blow up my life after a few weeks. Then what kind of life would we have?
– I thought I was your life.
Then me, with my best look, quietest tone.
– 'Voi sapere ch'io v'amo.'[16]
– What bombastic garbage is that? What did you say?
– I just told you that you know I love you. It's Italian.
– Yeah, you <u>would</u> have to say that in another language. And no, I don't know it.

Early on, he spoke ambivalently about his wedded state: 'For know, Iago,/But that I love the gentle Desdemona,/I would not my unhousèd free condition/Put into circumscription and confine/For the seas' worth' (1.2.24–8). It sounds like he has made a loving, rational choice, but the former slave thinks of marriage as imprisonment, in opposition to the sea: openness, boundlessness, liberation. Such a man could not possibly discover the freedom in marriage: unpressured conversation, a shared pleasure in domesticity, a more-secure future, and the relaxation of sexual pressure, which I mean as ambiguously as it sounds. Once loosed from his bonds, granted divorce through Iago's pestering enfranchisement, Othello instantly submits to confinement again – by marrying Iago at the end of Act 3 scene 3, a spectacular moment not merely of adultery but damned bigamy that actually confirms the General's pessimistic sense of what marriage means.[17] Paranoia about infidelity seemingly enables that second marriage. But given his own lies and concealments, his fear is instrumental. It helps him keep his humiliating secrets.

Othello's marriage to Desdemona sinks because he and his wife want radically different things from love; because conflicting ideas about their bodies, risk, a life together perplex their chances of happiness; and most of all because, like Iago, Othello cannot distinguish between a benefit and an injury. Some of these things may be true of my marriage, my self, as well. But for all my flaws and failings, I separate myself from such characters not by wisdom or temperament or even desire, but by luck: my wife's indulgence, and my occasional fortunate choice, have allowed marriage to guide me from youth into middle age. (I speak of chronology, not maturity.) When a marriage is new, it is unquestionably more susceptible to the internal voice that plays on the sexual secret, the *ancient*, debasing reminder: 'you are insufficient, animalistic, undeserving, and yet, deprived of what you deserve'. A substantial problem for Othello in this regard is that his marriage is new, but he is not, and yet he has no experience that prepares him to understand a husband's place. And it surely does not help that he carries a false and dispiritingly common attitude towards married sex, one that has made its way nearly unchanged to the modern era, one that I share: the notion that the erotic being of one's wife is not the same as the erotic being of other people. Whether she seems sacred, marmoreal, untouchable in her way; or sweet and companionable, the bedrock of hearth and centre of affective life, one's wife can all too easily become de-eroticized, so that bodily desires will not debase (the husband's ideas about) her: 'mature love combines the contradictory elements of sensuality and a tenderness that may well be described as desexualized'.[18]

Othello lacks the time to resolve these contradictions: he wishes to desexualize his wife, and cannot; he claims impotence, disavows his bodily desires, but fails in that, too. The play famously accelerates time, collapses into mere hours the lifespan of an unhappy couple: flirtation, love, passion, indulgence, uncertainty, impatience, unfaithfulness, alienation, abuse, divorce, remorse, death. Could they have rescued happiness in a longer life together? The impressionistic tragedy weighs against the possibility, precisely because of

Othello's complexes: a slow tumble 'into the vale of years' (3.3.270) was never in their future. For the husband can see, over the horizon, the plummet of power and regard heralded by middle age, ironically brought into focus by his young bride, who exposes intolerable physical and characterological limitations that do not sort with his heroic self-image. Othello's implacable nervousness about his energetic and erotic wife drives him with Iago's help to a needed peace: 'my relief/must be to loathe her' (3.3.271–2). This 'relief', his belief in Iago's improbable lies, allows him to abdicate his marital responsibility, lets him disown the fear in marriage. In this respect the cuckoldry fantasy does him the strangest favour; it helps hasten the transition to retirement, makes him give up the soldier's glory now. Better to have done with all at once than suffer the contraction and detumescence of old age.

But the specific fear lingers, and exposes him: 'Behold, I have a weapon', he says as he threatens suicide. 'A better never did itself sustain/Upon a soldier's thigh' (5.2.266–8). Even as he grows more phallically potent in proximity to his own death, he imagines an ideal weapon that would be *self*-sustaining; and yet it points down, thighward (or maybe it rests on another soldier). This notionally inevitable failure resurfaces presently in his suicide, which becomes at last a disturbing violence directed below the waist: his final words in the play conflate his imminent death with a self-punishing penectomy: 'I took by th' throat the circumcised dog,/And smote him thus' (5.2.364–5). ('Throat': 'The narrowest part of the shaft of a column, immediately below the capital' [*OED*, def. 6.]). Othello marshals his ultimate rage and sorrow against an image of his own betraying body.

The hero's grisly impatience divulges a fundamental, characteristic misunderstanding: he seems not to know that marriage, in order to prosper, is an *abiding* effort at pleasure. The play, on balance, may not know that either. The most lamentable part of the marital tragedy (excepting the horrific violence, of course) is the simple sorrow of brevity: Desdemona, partly because of her youth, intuitively understands her wedded status in terms of patient anticipation for a new now, the imminent chance for a life of steadily increasing happiness. Othello, partly because of his age, just cannot see that. He so misapprehends love ('she loved me for the dangers I had passed' [1.3.166]) that it never has the chance to recover, to grow into knowledge – of self, of wife, of circumstance. The play's two husbands are alike in this respect: when Iago says Cassio has 'a daily beauty in his life' (5.1.19), he seems at first to mean a quality of soul or spirit. But I think he refers longingly to the bachelor's freedom. For Iago and Othello, as so often for Shakespeare, the unmarried state figures longed-for autarchy. Yet the married men undervalue and misconstrue their circumstances. They forget that daily beauty lies not in being unconfined, but (even I can see it) in the day-to-day future that people promise one another. Matrimony, for all its disappointments and turbulence, for every stretch of erotic ennui or estrangement, has a beauty of its own – given enough time.

The wounded, discontented husband impulsively pushes the spouse to the margins, regards only himself, thinks he and only he suffers, because of the institution. From such narcissistic solitude perhaps only the institution can save him.

This was the last of it:

– What did I want? I wanted you to change your life for me. Then I'd know it was worth it. What did you *want? Why would you do this in the first place?*

– Why wouldn't I? I didn't think much about it. You're lovely, intense, ridiculously smart.

– You didn't mention my age.

– Yes, young. That was exciting at first. But it wasn't just physical. For you either, right?

– No, not at all.

(Hmmm, that didn't help.) She went on:

– Maybe I pushed things. I'm impatient. I want to know you, to travel with you. I want to see what you've seen.

— No, you really don't.

— What are you saying? Oh, OK. You're dug in, aren't you? You're staying, aren't you?

— Come on, you can see the problems. And it's not just this situation. It's you. You scare the hell out of me, all your force, all your. . . desire. I've got nothing for you; and you don't need what I have, anyway. (Not a complete lie.)

— So what now? You think you'll be better off? You think her *life will improve?*

— I do.

Notes

1. The proliferation of parentheses in the quotation may suggest that even our honest avowals attempt to hide themselves. On such subjects, see also Lamb, 2010.

2. *Macbeth* is also a marital tragedy, more hopeful about matrimony in its way than *Othello*, but the dissolution of the relationship between Macbeth and his wife is more the consequence than the cause of the other disasters in the play.

3. I owe to Amad, 2009, the idea that Othello, the 'General', is indeed general, a caricatured Everyman. He observes that Othello traffics in vague, windy magniloquence, plurals, fuzzy rubrics, categoricals, and clichés; Othello's tendency to generalize, Amad notes, makes him a grotesque walking pun. His absurdity tends at once to diminish and confirm his representationality as Every(married)man.

4. Many modern critics understand Iago's misogyny as Othello's psycho-sexual baseline, suggesting a common, soldierly bond in woman hating. I think that emphasis is not quite right; rather, I believe the villain's animus is primarily self-directed, which is to say, aimed at Othello whenever possible. To the extent he and Iago are both 'slaves', 'fools', failed husbands, mutually constituting mirrors and shadows, Iago is a formal embodiment of Othello's limits. Iago figures Othello's self-loathing, or at least his rogue discontent, come to insinuating life.

5. 'A world of kisses' (the F1 reading) makes no sense, unless you also accept that after giving such a world, Desdemona still finds it necessary to 'hint' that Othello's friend could win her simply by telling the stories again. In any case, we see in that hint the imaginary presence of a third person in the dyad from the very beginning, a sure sign that Othello's and Desdemona's relationship in some ways always revolved around (imaginary) adultery.

6. Calderwood (1989, p. 76) notes the 'tone of Puritanical disapproval' and its appearance 'at the point where sexuality comes into potential conflict with the hero's military "business"'.

7. He has his reasons. Iago's plot, which centrally includes the staging of a man's cuckolding in front of him, is something the villain has already experienced. When Cassio smooches a surprised Emilia in his presence (2.1.96–103), Iago suffers the nausea of his own impotence: 'this bold show of courtesy', as Cassio calls it, amounts to social death and the irreparable emasculation of the not-lieutenant. 'Let it not gall your patience, good Iago', the slick operator says, enlisting the husband's consent in his own humiliation. The operational misogyny of the play is thus a gauge of erotic helplessness. Iago takes a small measure of revenge out on *his wife* right away by immediately launching into slander about women's deceptions, how they are 'Players in . . . housewifery' (2.1.115). Cassio, who is inculpable even as Iago is incapable, of course agrees.

   On the problematics of voyeurism and erotic arousal, see Daileader, 1998, pp. 35–40. Genster (1994, p. 230) offers this comment about *Othello* that neatly explains its pornographic edge: 'If the cuckold's shame is that he is rearing another man's children, in *Othello* . . . the cuckold's shame, and Othello's tragedy, is that his imagination is no longer his own: he is bringing up the children of another man's fancy.' Neill (1994, p. 200) also discusses the fantasies spun by Iago and the way the play transfers those to the audience.

8. Hagstrum (1992, p. 472, n.10) quotes Luther, seemingly anticipating Othello's fit, on 'the epileptic and apoplectic lust of present-day marriage'; for Luther, then, perhaps all eroticism inside marriage has *Othello*-like pathological resonance. Yet Othello's fit seems to arise from not fully achieving such lust.

9. The idea that Iago is in some sense superfluous to the inevitable failure of their relationship can be found, among other places, in Bloom, 2005 and Fiedler, 1972.

10. Even though the newlyweds' bed-time is repeatedly disturbed, there are still more than enough chances for consummation. No one ever explains, for instance, why they did *not* make that two-backed beast on their wedding night. Yet whenever we think sex has happened, or could have, we either find out definitively that it has not, or are led to believe it could not. Their sole chance at lovemaking comes before the brawl in 2.3; but by the *end* of the play we cannot really think that consummation occurred there, either. Because (first) if it had, Othello probably would have noticed that his wife had been a virgin, which would render Iago's subsequent, morning-after implications about her ridiculous, even for a dimbulb such as the General; and (second) Desdemona would probably not want love-bloodied sheets to make an appearance on stage in Act 5, when she explicitly asks Emilia to bring the wedding bedding. On these issues, see Bradshaw, 1993, pp. 148–201.

11. 'Pensa che puoi cosi del lieto Otello/ Turbar la prima vigilia d'amore!' (Boito, n.d, p. 7).

12. The couple's coupling concerns Daileader, who discusses Iago's obsession with the offstage sex, but doesn't see that he may be misleading or wishful-thinking (Daileader, 1998, p. 36). Typically, we do not prosper interpretively by believing Iago; he repeatedly publicizes Othello's active sexuality, and repeatedly proves wrong. Neill (1994), gives the most judicious if ambivalent consideration of the theme of off and onstage sex.

13. From http://www.dapoxetine-online.biz/notorganic.php (accessed 28 September 2010). The site also contains this important information: 'An estimated thirty percent of men suffer from premature ejaculation on a consistent basis.' Such a large percentage of particularly male sufferers of this ailment (there is no female equivalent in the literature) implies – unless such things have changed markedly from the Renaissance – that Shakespeare may be addressing, however glancingly, a knowledgeable audience.

Lopate (2008, pp. 89–90) has sharp things to say about performative 'duration'. Many thanks to Hannah Chapelle-Wojciehowski for the reference.

14. All of this suggestion is, on Shakespeare's part, *aggressively subliminal*: no one on stage will voice it but it still calls insistent attention to itself.

    Indeed, as far as the touchy subject of Othello's erotic dysfunction goes, even Iago maintains uncharacteristic reticence, but not for reasons of either tact or craft. Iago seems oddly imperceptive about this one glaring feature, the much-postponed consummation. His blindness must come from a simultaneous racist regard of Othello as inevitably oversexed and his soldierly idealization of Othello as perfectly potent. (Even the caveat to Roderigo that Desdemona's 'appetite shall play the god/ With his weak function' (2.3.321–2) seems to refer more to the husband's mental, not penile power.) We should keep in mind the considerable stake Iago has in neutering presumptively potent men, which is how he can 'plume up' his own 'will' (1.3.375). The General's functional impotence would take the wind out of Iago's sails.

    The staging of Desdemona and Othello's sole consummation in the play, the on-bed murder, likewise reflects the notion of the General's failure. Othello cannot manage to kill his wife the first time, and as she springs back up to forgive him she claims that *she* has 'done this deed' herself (5.2.132). Even Othello's certainty about her death is premature.

15. The word (along with satisfy, satisfied) occurs more often in *Othello* than in any other Shakespeare play. It is important to remember that 'satisfaction' is a theological term as well. See Hassel, s.v. 'satisfaction' (2005, p. 307). Since only Christ can provide satisfaction to God, perhaps we are meant to think that all true 'satisfaction' is humanly impossible.

16. Jago to Otello, from Boito's libretto, *Otello*, 2.3.35.

17. I agree with Neill that this scene is 'the one real adultery of the play, the seduction of Othello in which Iago is at this very moment engaged' (Neill, 1994, p. 198). 'Engaged', in keeping with Othello's profound

if paradoxical commitment to infidelity, is the point: 'I am your own forever', Iago says, not insincerely.

18. See Hallstead, 1968, p. 109, n.3, discussing Herbert Marcuse's insight that love 'to the wife . . . is sensual as well as tender, aim-inhibited as well as aim-attaining'. Othello misses or represses most of the sensual elements, until Iago magnifies them beyond love.

Chapter 3

Discovering Transgression: Reading from the Passions

David Fuller

The transgression was sexual, the Shakespeare *Antony and Cleopatra*, the context post-War London.

When my eyes were opening to sexual feeling my desires were criminal. Lord Wolfenden's report of 1957 did not pass into law, and so decriminalize my desires, until 1967, when I was twenty – and only when I became twenty-one ('adult') could I benefit from the new law's provisions. Growing up queer in a rough district of north London ('queer' was the word, its pre-recuperation tone mocking and violent) focussed one's vulnerabilities. What was expected of boys was that they should pursue girls; if they did not play football, they should at least support a football team; if they were intellectually able they should study science, but not show intellectual interests except when compelled to do so; and they should enjoy pop music and whatever else fitted one for participating in the group. Aesthetic interests were girly, and should not be shown, even under compulsion. Boys who recognized all this – healthy, open, friendly, at ease with themselves, not held back by deviance driving them to introspection – I variously liked, adored, and desired. I saw them as my own antitypes; and, though I was intellectually defiant in private (to myself) about the legitimacy of my passions, at times at least I also regarded myself with horror and loathing. Even now it is not difficult to recapture the constant and sometimes intense terror of having recognized by others the queerness that was so constantly present to me, and that conditioned (as it seemed) every aspect of private self-awareness and social behaviour.

Other aspects of the social context of 1950s north London were more helpful. I was enjoying a good education at a grammar school that became one of the first comprehensive schools in England while I was at it. The education system had already thrown in my way an energetic primary teacher who, having introduced me to the delights of acting and singing, decided she should teach me to play the piano, and taught me well because her sole aim was musical pleasure. A peripatetic music teaching scheme, staffed partly by middle-European Jewish pre-War émigrés-refugees who were very good musicians, meant access to free string instrument lessons of a high standard. A high-spending (Labour) local authority, with patrician views, not led by popular taste, provided a well-stocked public library that included a comprehensive collection of scores and recordings from the Baroque to living composers. This context produced other teenagers who could play – so, as well as being alone with a piano and recordings, I was able to participate in chamber music groups that played Mozart and Beethoven, Schubert and Brahms. Post-War dreariness (bomb-sites, prefabs, general greyness and dirt) was combined with post-War opportunities.

The illicit desires that could not find direct outlet among my school friends were diverted into music. Finding I could relieve pent-up feelings by hammering out at the piano a Chopin Polonaise or Brahms Rhapsody, or by listening to Romantic period composers whose relief to the passions also fed and intensified them, I became obsessed with music. Preferring Tchaikovsky to Bach, I remember wondering whether all music was deflected desire. At about fourteen I discovered Wagner, and in *Tristan* and *Die Walküre* particularly I recognized (perhaps largely unconsciously) dramas in which illicit sexual passions (adultery, incest), which I must have felt had some congruence with my own, were viewed as exalted, even salvific. While aesthetic pleasures were not nearly so forbidden as queerness, they were on the same spectrum, as not for proper boys. And since I recognized that some of my pleasure in music was derived from deflected desire, that pleasure had about it a savour of the illicit – the delicious-cum-horrifying secret taken a little towards the daylight.

Still none of this craving for aesthetic experiences encountered any serious literary focus until at sixteen I read *Antony and Cleopatra* and Racine's *Phèdre*. These two plays, read alongside one another – again works of (queer-congruent) irregular passions – were a revelation: dramatic poetry too could provide the intensity of pleasure that until then I had found only in music.

In all these works I identified with the transgressive women – Wagner's Sieglinde (brother-incest) and Isolde (adultery), Racine's Phèdre (stepson-incest), and Cleopatra, whose relish of her abilities as Isis and Venus was antithetical to Phèdre's sex-horror. Whether traumatized or liberated by their passions, these characters acted as surrogates for what I felt, or what I wished to feel, about my own more secretive transgressions. My healthy school friends were supposed analogous not (of course) to the enraptured lovers in Shakespeare and Wagner but to the horrified stepson in Racine. Reading *Antony* in these circumstances gave rise to an account in which excited participation in all that the protagonists say about how love validates their choices had to be endorsed, and all that might count against endorsement had to be confuted. My aims were far from purely literary: I was fighting about who I wanted to be, and what I wanted to establish for myself as modes of feeling in life generally. My fellow school students who wanted to enforce a Roman view of Shakespeare's lovers seemed to me doing the Devil's work. While some critics have read *Antony and Cleopatra* as a Hegelian tragedy of equally valued irreconcilable opposites, on the stage it has regularly been presented as showing a contra-mundane road of excess which, though it has foul bypaths, leads finally to a palace of wisdom. That was my reading then. It is broadly my reading now. I would also still defend the general way of integrating lived and aesthetic experience with which circumstances entangled me as a teenager: I see it as fundamental to giving any work the only worthwhile reality it can have – a reality to the actual experience of a particular reader, with which it interacts, and which, by that interaction, it extends.

To endorse Shakespeare's lovers meant partly engaging with character and situation. Fundamentally I saw the play as accepting Antony's verdict that 'the nobleness of life/Is to do thus' – put love before all other values – and that in so doing the lovers 'stand up peerless' (1.1.38–42). Despite all that can be said against this from a Roman perspective, and in disillusionment by Antony himself, it is finally valid: the lovers find through each other their highest selves, selves that can only be achieved through the extremes to which they are pushed by love. Cleopatra as 'low', whether violating proprieties of gender and hierarchy by passionate violence (2.5), or playing a stereotype of woman to the hilt by inviting and enjoying flattery (3.3), was no bar to this view. 'Royal Egypt' and 'no more but e'en a woman', paradox is part of her power (4.16.74–5). 'Vilest things/Become themselves in her': she makes 'defect perfection' (2.2.243–4, 237). I enjoyed the gamut: erotic energy and comedy, grandeur and pettiness, role-playing and sincere feeling. That we cannot always be sure how to interpret Cleopatra's behaviour – with Thidias, with Seleucus, with Octavius – I saw as giving the audience Antony's experience of inscrutable fascinations. The exhilarating role-playing, with lightning variations of feeling, planned and spontaneous, is part of what evinces Cleopatra's abundance of mental and emotional energy. Since I felt my life depended on successful role-playing I was more than willing to admire consummate performance skills. And a positive reading of the doubts prompted by Cleopatra's staging of the self is always possible: with Seleucus, a show to convince Octavius that she is thinking of a life in Rome; with Octavius, the need to estimate as clearly as possible his likely way of proceeding with her; with Thidias, combining astute political handling with a wittily insinuated reminder of political experience and erotic power (3.13.82–5). Enobarbus fearing betrayal (3.13.62–5) I saw as epitomizing the obtuseness of seeing Cleopatra from only one perspective.

And while I could see that these scenes were open to other presentations, from that I learned that what the reader found was partly what the reader chose to find – though I remember that I was not willing to admit this: it seemed dangerously permissive. Why, then, should my classmates not endorse Roman rectitude? Worse still, why was I so keen to confute it?

But I was willing to admit that unromantic aspects of the lovers' relationship were fully acknowledged. This I thought of as just clear-sighted: you cannot have real passion in which violence and repulsion are not potential. But for me the low aspects were finally subsumed in apotheoses that are unequivocally exalted: 'I dreamed there was an Emperor Antony'; 'I have/Immortal longings in me . . . I am fire and air' (5.2.75, 272–80). Everything about Egypt contributed ultimately to exaltation, everything about Rome to rectitude that was ultimately mean-minded. I resisted the idea that there was anything to be said for the Roman critique of Egypt, which I saw as fundamentally Puritan antagonism to pleasure. I was too keen to escape the Puritanism on which I had been brought up to allow it to inhibit the contrary potential revealed by love in the play.

The Roman view of the lovers, most fully expressed by Octavius (1.4.1–33), was placed for me by its context – admiration for so limited a spectrum of Antony's virtues, those that are conventionally 'manly' (fortitude, endurance); whereas it is part of the lovers' comprehensiveness that they flagrantly violate gender proprieties. The pleasure ('O times!') of Antony dressed in Cleopatra's 'tires and mantles', Cleopatra wearing the sword with which he conquered at Philippi (2.5.18–23): this was (broadly) queer. The lovers' passions were (in conventional terms) feminine, flexile, moist – all that is meant by Egypt in its opposition to Rome. The play presents not only a clash of individuals but also of the contrasts of ethos epitomized by two locations. I was eager to find that it saw Rome as Cleopatra sees Octavius: "Tis paltry to be Caesar', not only (as she says) because he is a mere agent of larger powers ('Fortune's knave'), but also because his Roman spirit has no ability to understand the

feelings that give life value for the lovers (5.2.2–3). I had no difficulty demonstrating to myself that the play was of my mind in this.
Octavius's 'wisdom' about women (3.12.29–31) showed him risibly
shallow beside the emotional strength and political subtlety actually shown by Cleopatra. His sacrifice of Octavia in a political marriage that is to his advantage whether it succeeds or fails indicated
the Roman view of human relationships: whatever lip-service was
paid to another ethic, they were secondary to the drive for power.
Enobarbus's despair when he chooses the world before love (4.9),
and Eros's nobility when he chooses love before life (4.14), were both
equally comments on this. That Cleopatra is so entirely able to fasci-
nate one last Roman that he betrays his master seemed to me a fine
reflection on the paltry spirit of Octavius, who cannot tell 'which is
the Queen of Egypt' (5.2.109).

But I had come to poetry through music, and what most deeply
established for me the play's perspective on the lovers – though this
worked on me less consciously: I knew less how to articulate it –
was derived not from character and situation but from the music of
poetry. I hope I was responding to the sounds of tropes and figures
for which I knew no names, to the richness of diction, to the imaginative suggestion of imagery, to the mythic resonance that gave
characters the dimensions of those gods and heroes I was learning
to adore in Wagner. But mainly I was discovering what I found
later formulated by Wallace Stevens: 'in poetry you must love the
words . . . with all your capacity to love anything at all' (Stevens,
1957, p. 161).

> Where souls do couch on flowers, we'll hand in hand,
> And with our sprightly port make the ghosts gaze.
> Dido and her Aeneas shall want troops.
> And all the haunt be ours. (4.14.51–4)

I loved this, as beautiful in itself, and as talismanic of a view in
which passion is validated by an imagined transcendence. But there

was too a form of engagement that had little to do with what the words meant. As when learning piano music, the pleasure of the sounds was so great that as soon as I got to the end of a favourite passage I read it again. Gradually most of the play became lodged in my memory, so that, while I was reading any part, my mind was resonant with echoes of its place in the whole. With poetry as with music, I was discovering that memory is vital to that concentrated participation that means music is

> heard so deeply
> That it is not heard at all, but you are the music
> While the music lasts. (Eliot, 1963a, 'The Dry Salvages', V, p. 213)

With all these works – *Antony*, *Tristan*, *Die Walküre*, and *Phèdre* – I was very much helped by recordings, which gave me a sense of them that I could never have acquired from books and scores alone. With *Tristan*, Kirsten Flagstad as Isolde (HMV, 1953) was the epitome of a heroine of myth and legend, pouring out sound of all but superhuman beauty and grandeur, as from a horn of plenty. With *Die Walküre*, Lotte Lehmann as Sieglinde (HMV, 1935/1962) was the obverse, 'no more but e'en a woman': as she gasped for breath between phrases, all the bodily effort through which she identified with the character was thrillingly audible. But perhaps most instructive for the music of poetry was Marie Bell in a Comédie-Française recording of *Phèdre* (n.d., 1950s). Marie Bell's speaking of verse, in the classic style of French acting, was as near to singing as voice that remains speech can be. Accustomed as I was to the actual singing of verse, and partially screened from recognizing Marie Bell's extreme declamatory range by my less than completely idiomatic feeling for the intonation of spoken French, I loved her style of performance as a perfect union of poetry and music. And it was about the music of poetry that I learned from a recording of *Antony* (Caedmon, 1963) – how to speak the verse without losing the sense of rhythmic recurrence and rhetorical shape that conveys or supports passion of utterance; and, while phrasing to bring out sense, using a range of intonation that finds in the real character of the voice sounds that fully match meaning. Like any art this can be learned by conscious application of method, but a better school is that of practice – hearing it well done by those for whom method has become intuition. All of these recordings offered models of a particular type of performer, one who was not afraid to present fully the heightening and excess of art. Nothing could have suggested more vividly the values of a world other than the post-War Puritan dreariness of everyday life around me.

I also found that recorded performances help with imagined participation. While there is not the intensity generated by living actors performing in the moment, there are obverse compensations. Being alone with a performance, and confident that it is wholly adequate to the emotions it raises and requires for fulfilment, makes possible complete concentration and passional absorption. And knowing the precise aural form phrases will take I found allowed full identification with their articulation, almost as though the performance were my own. Lehmann as Sieglinde recognizing in a moment of erotic release that the liberating beloved is her brother; Flagstad as Isolde, ecstatically identified with her lover, reckless of the dangers of illicit passion; Marie Bell as Phèdre, in horrified contralto contemplating 'des crimes peut-être inconnus aux enfers' (4.6; crimes perhaps unknown to Hell); Pamela Brown as Cleopatra, relishing and caressing words as the epitome of Desire: 'Ram thou thy fruitful tidings in mine ears,/That long time have been barren' (2.5.24–5); or as the incarnate sound of Desolation, wailing at the finality of death, 'O, withered is the garland of the war' (4.16.66); or even just in the grand simplicity of 'My desolation does begin to make/A better life' (5.2.1–2): for me these became moments of complete absorption in which being able to anticipate the performer's entire adequacy released the fullest possible pleasure.

Finally, I remember being gropingly aware of what I now think of as the overall structural music of poetic drama, feeling in the tones of moment-by-moment progress the effect of (as it were) a free equivalent of the musical structures I was then learning to analyse. The musical analysis seemed to me useless – just identifying formulae; though I had a sense that, if the analysis were less formulaic, it might help deepen a feeling for the sequence and relationship of emotions through which a movement led. At some point in all this I read *Murder in the Cathedral*, and, trying to get a grip on a work I found difficult to connect with, I read some of Eliot's criticism. I see that in my 1963 copy of 'Poetry and Drama' I marked Eliot's discussion of 'a kind of musical design [in a play] . . . which reinforces and is one with the dramatic movement . . . [that] has checked and accelerated the pulse of our emotion without our knowing it' (Eliot, 1963b, p. 69). I had no language in which to give an account of the sequence of emotions created by dramatic form. But Eliot's comment prompted me to notice how a sequence of tones played a significant part in creating the effect of the whole, though how that worked remained a mystery. As with musical analysis, that sense of major aesthetic effects beyond description gave me a salutary awareness of how much criticism might be whistling in the dark – displacing what was happening in secret with more prosaic things it was better able to bring into the light. And even with those, I recognized that I was not telling my classmates all I knew about why I thought what I thought.

All this contributed to the reading I constructed that allowed *Antony and Cleopatra* both to be fully satisfying in itself and to take me further in the direction of experiences it had opened up for me. I doubt that I recognized the full extent to which the reading was derived from my needs: certainly I found how to give it a quasi-objective location in the play, which I continue to believe it has. But it also gave me a lively sense of how much is going on when one constructs a reading, a sense which issued much later in a book about Blake (Fuller, 1988) in which I tried to give an account of what was in the texts, what was in me, and what was in the relationship between the two.

Antony and Cleopatra was crucial to my beginning to feel how powerful poetic drama might be, but I doubt that I would have become gripped by *Antony* with the same intensity if I had not been reading alongside it a play that dealt with the allure and horror of sexual transgression more directly, Racine's *Phèdre*. Phèdre is possessed by desire for her husband's son by a former marriage, Hippolyte – a desire I experienced as precisely congruent with my own illicit passions. For Phèdre her desire is, though horrifying, irresistible: her declaration causes Hippolyte's death and her own. I was completely drawn in – and particularly to the role as acted with the spoken-sung intensity of Marie Bell. More than with *Antony*, *Phèdre* was a play I could construct to suit my emotional needs. Now I see that, though I responded in considerable part through feelings I brought to the play, my response was at least congruent with reactions engineered by Racine. Despite the illicit nature of Phèdre's desires, Racine does everything he can to retain sympathy for her. She struggles for years to evade her passion. She seeks death rather than declare it. She declares it only when – supposing Thésée dead and her son reliant for the succession on her negotiations with Hippolyte, urged on by her confidante Œnone, and feeling possessed by forces beyond the control of her will – intoxicated by Hippolyte's presence, she finds the allure of release more powerful than the horror of confession. Though Hippolyte is horrified, the audience cannot simply endorse his reaction because Racine parallels him with Phèdre. He too is struggling against a love offensive to his father (for a Princess, Aricie, who must have no children who might avenge Thésée's killing of her brothers). He too declares his love against his will when he comes to negotiate with Aricie about the succession following his father's death. Racine stages the declarations of Hippolyte and Phèdre in immediate sequence. The two 'illicit' loves – though different in many ways – are parallel.

Phèdre is full of the agonies at first of love guilty and repressed, later of love rejected, humiliated, and maddened by jealousy. The excruciating effects of this are heightened by ironies, the common thread to which is that when characters try to act morally so as to evade the consequences of their illicit passions they trap themselves more deeply in circumstances that precipitate disaster. This happens with Hippolyte as well as with Phèdre, but it is with Phèdre that irony, like character and structure, is a source of unexpected sympathy.

Unlike with *Antony and Cleopatra*, I cannot remember that as a teenager I saw consciously at all the sources in the play of the experience I had of it. As I remember it, discussion of the play was largely about fate and free will – the sort of thing you might discuss of any tragedy based in Greek sources, given a special turn towards Racine through his Catholicism (the convent of Port-Royal and Jansenism, with its special views on predestination). It seemed to me entirely remote from becoming Phèdre, and while it might have been made to engage with crimes unknown in Hell, I don't think it ever was. My passions were left in the dark, where to my sense they belonged. There was no chance from this of discovering that the play did to me what I supposed I was doing to it. The sophisticated response, the fundamental tendency of which is to retain sympathy for Phèdre, is dependent on issues about character, structure, and dramatic irony of which I simply do not remember being conscious. I assume I felt this from its sources in the play, if at all, as most people experience drama, intuitively, without being aware of how the play was working on me. But I had no need of the effects Racine so carefully creates to pre-empt condemnation of Phèdre: the experience I brought to reading the play meant that I identified with her illicit desires. Whatever else I failed to notice, Racine's subtle art in the speeches leading to Phèdre's declaration (2.5) was not lost on me: I made those speeches my own. Not that I imagined I could be led to make a declaration to a local Hippolyte, who I would presume had no idea of the seething horrors his beauty and charm were prompting: terror was always as strong as desire. I readily entered into imagining the compelling release of bringing out what had been so intensely dwelt on in secret – though I cannot have imagined even momentarily that that would lead me to lose sight of the disaster of having done it. But so intensely did I interiorize the ban on queer love and desire as a teenager that it was a compelling pleasure to violate it, even surrogately and in secret. Direct identification with Phèdre was what made the play so powerful – more powerful, I think, than if my responses had been under the control implied by their being conscious of having literary critical sources. The play engaged me even more directly than *Antony*; even more than Pamela Brown did Marie Bell give me a sense of the importance to that engagement of the music of poetry; and, unlike with *Antony*, the unconscious ways in which the play worked on me suggested to me later that the conscious modes of knowledge implied by critical sophistication are not a sure and certain good.

All this – the antithesis of prose, the telly, and the kitchen sink – prompted efforts to experience some live theatre. I took myself to see Olivier as Othello (no danger there of a disappointing excess of naturalism) and, also at the National Theatre, an all-male *As You Like It* in which seeing the boys canoodling gave me a sense of theatre as the natural home of sodomy. Olivier I was already aware of from his Shakespeare films, particularly *Richard III*. There I was delighted by the glamour of forbidden energies made attractive by wit and the pleasures of the mask, the ability to play respectable roles with such thrilling panache as a vehicle for the illicit. Olivier-as-Richard's delight in the theatre of assumed behaviours, in role-playing and charming masks of wickedness on film was more helpful to me than the example of Oscar Wilde in books – though I was in accord with Wilde in finding that life imitated art, or at least that art–life imitation was a two-way process. Not that I conceived of Olivier-as-Richard's pleasure in forbidden energies as having any personal application. But in retrospect that seems to me probably what was happening. I enjoyed Olivier's film through a way in that was unconsciously personal – and though partial, not, I would say, tangential to the play.

It was a little later that I became similarly engaged by another play which (like *Phèdre*) is about a love that dare not speak its name – its family names of Capulet and Montague. In a more straightforward way than *Antony*, *Romeo and Juliet* embodies the transcendent aspirations of romantic love. The compulsive sex-consciousness of the Montague and Capulet boys, the more detached adult bawdry of the nurse, the 'wisely and slow' tediousness-as-maturity of Friar Laurence (2.2.94): for me these were frames that emphasized by contrast the luminous quality of the lovers' erotic idealism. The frames were familiar from the world around me. I adored the lovers' love, and learned from it what I felt love should be in the world I was trying to construct. Romeo epitomized boy beauty and its effects as a standard of loveliness by which to judge all aspiration, in art and in life. I had bought my first copy of the Sonnets in 1964, so must already have seen that a sweet and lovely boy could suggest to Shakespeare a range of exalted meanings incorporating the erotic. But the Hippolyte-response remained a more-than-shadow of which this heaven could not be purged.

The standard of loveliness suggested by *Romeo* was not derived unmediated from Shakespeare. Once again pleasure in the play was not separable from pleasure in a particular performance – Franco Zeffirelli's film. Part of the play's erotic charge came from the charm of the celluloid image of Leonard Whiting as Romeo (not to mention his mildly north-London accent – he had grown up near where I lived – which made him seem plausibly like somebody I might know). This was a fascination with boy beauty congruent for me with the forbidden love of the play, the mythic power of which I took to mean that even heterosexual love and desire have about them something inherently antisocial and to be concealed. But though I saw that the play's forbidden love had multiple applications, I experienced my particular engagement as peculiarly illicit and personal. Only later (as with *Phèdre*) did it become clear to me that my pleasure was prompted by a mildly hidden aspect of the film itself. Off the set (as Leonard Whiting told me when I met him much later), it was not Juliet the director was trying to get into bed, and that is evident in the filming. Zeffirelli's bisexuality appears in the camera's gaze at the Capulet codpieces and eventually at Leonard Whiting's naked buttocks. I enjoyed the camera's gaze, but at the time I could not have thought that the heterosexual narrative of the play is complemented by some homosexual presentation in the film. What was forbidden was really forbidden: articulation would have been too near acknowledgement. That a film-maker who shared pleasures I could only conceive of as secret might, even covertly, make them public: I could not think it.

Antony and Cleopatra led me into literature. With *Phèdre, Richard III*, and *Romeo and Juliet* it gave me a sense that poetry could be as passionately engaging as music; and, from the music of poetry, to performance as a mode of criticism, to the mystery of meanings, it did a great deal to create the forms of my literary interests. The values and experiences it suggested led to a discovery of Blake – delight in the passion and wit of *The Marriage of Heaven and Hell* with its Voice of the Devil, which I welcomed as a gospel of beauty and energy, the implications of *Antony* in the form of injunctions. And that discovery was eventually the focus of an extended effort to find my way out of impersonal expectations of scholarship and criticism, underlying which those early experiences of Shakespeare were crucial. Without the discoveries about poetry that *Antony* initiated I would have needed a different form of escape from a dead version of musical education, which at university I soon found tediously disconnected from my actual experience of music. By chance at my undergraduate university (Sheffield) the professor of English was William Empson. Wildly irregular, passionate, intellectual, and funny – and, as I discovered only much later, also queer (bisexual) – he was a living epitome of what I had hoped university education would be. He was an example of the passionately engaged whole person, whose love of poetry was continuous with a large-minded attitude to a spectacular range of interests – in science, religion, politics, and the cultures of east and west. And (though Empson himself would not have agreed to see it in these terms), I came eventually to think that – while his effort was always to locate meaning in objective features of a text seen in wide and various contexts – his often against-the-grain way with text and freewheeling choice of contexts meant that understanding for him also involved a creative-constructive interaction between reader and work.

I seem here to have constructed a narrative in which Shakespeare is the *fons et origo* of everything – life, literary and critical values and experiences. It would be a distortion to report the results of this chaos of secret and often suppressed feelings as though they had issued in confidently held positions I could see clearly. Far from it. I had to flail about in the dark to find means of my own that could articulate ways in which lived and aesthetic experience interact; and with such modes of articulation as I have attempted I am more conscious of their limitations and failures than any successes. As in other spheres, it has been easier to say what is wrong than to do what is right. But flailing around was not all bad. I had a general sense of not belonging to the contexts in which I found myself – wrong in class, in sexuality, and in a difficult to formulate scepticism about confident intellectuality. Though often difficult, however, this had one clear value: it made me properly sceptical about criticism that was too confident about trusting the intellect, which with art is always ready to be over-confident of its abilities. 'Poetry must resist the intelligence almost successfully' says Wallace Stevens (1957, p. 171). I think so. And the obverse is that the intelligence should recognize the resistance and not suppose it can or should be readily overcome.

The excitement of literary criticism is that it is inherently and necessarily anarchic. You never know what might be helpful to understanding – in a text or an author's life, conscious and unconscious; in the suppositions of the first audiences or the history of a work's meanings; in heterodox learning or popular culture; in the relationship of a writer or work to your own cultural situation, your religious, political or ethical views, or – and this is always crucial – to your personal experience. Your personal experience will always be present in the sense-making. The only choice is about how conscious and explicit you want that to be. All this also means that intuitive knowledge that brings you into radical connection with a work may not be able – and may not need – to give an account of itself. It may even mean that being able to give an account may weaken your radical connection with a work – put it into the conscious mind and so give you more control of it. It is not always and necessarily valuable to aim for a critical awareness of art. It has been helpful to me that I have kept a relation to music – the art I love most – largely through performing and listening; and that the analytic operations I undertake with music – because I have long since ceased to perform these in any kind of educational context, or for any purpose other than pleasure – are really those that, for me, deepen knowledge. So they act as a standard by which to judge efforts of understanding undertaken in a context of institutions of criticism.

Finally, all this has also made me sceptical both about how much can be said in writing and how much can be taught. Like all teachers, I have been keen to encourage articulation, and to give people a range of techniques with which to try peering into the mysteries of understanding art. I have nothing to say against this, except that one should not hope for too much from it. Articulation within expected boundaries will often cover up finding out what there might really be to say; the techniques likely to be most prominently on offer are always related to fashion rather than need; there is no guarantee they will have any real connection with what actually happens in engaging with a given piece of writing; and in any case they are of very limited value so long as they remain tools operated by the intellect rather than quasi-intuitive perceptions diffused through the sensibility. It is indeed no use, as Northrop Frye remarked, for literary criticism to be a mystery-religion without a gospel (Frye, 1957, p. 14); but though this is all very well as a wise-crack, unless Northrop Frye is the Saviour it is difficult to see how to apply it. The situation of literary criticism is more like that of Buddhism than Christianity: a multiplicity of texts, none canonical, all of value only when applied through the scrutiny of individual re-creation in meditation and action. Much the best – for which likewise there is no recipe – is for the critic or teacher to help a poem or play give pleasure and then leave the recipient of pleasure alone to work out where pleasure leads and what it means. But with this approach there are no quick results to show the paymaster, and very little that can be made a subject of assessment. It makes literary criticism unlike other areas of education, and gives it a radically uneasy relation to the assumptions of a university about how knowledge is transmitted – a relation so uneasy that it is difficult for literary criticism in a university, in at least some of its aspects, not to become a parody of itself, a homeopathic inoculation against real knowledge of literature.

Chapter 4

Ghosts and Heartbeats

Philippa Kelly

In December 2010 my brother fell in a mountain-climbing accident and was killed. Each morning for six weeks after that, I would awaken and imagine, for a second, that I had only dreamed his death, or that they (whoever 'they' were) had been able to revive him. Within seconds, of course, I would feel again the assault of the new situation.[1]

He was gone, irrevocably dead. I couldn't imagine how my beautiful, vibrant brother could exist in a form other than how I'd known him. It was not enough that he enter a Zen zone of universal consciousness or prepare himself to be reincarnated. It was certainly not enough to believe him instantly extinguished. It was not enough to be told that he lived on in his children or in the people who'd known him. Bugger that, I thought – it is not enough, it will never be enough until they bring him back to life and give unto death instead a slob waiting it out in front of the TV.

I wanted my brother whole, or, at the very least, I wanted to *know* what had happened to him and where he was in the universe. The shadow of his blue eyes and blonde hair, the bulk of his hefty, athlete's body, the echo of his voice. I could only bear to imagine him physically complete, looking at us all from another place.

Before there were even words in the world, there were ghosts. Ghosts tread on clouds. It's the ghost, falling, who clutches at grass as it sticks uselessly, unnaturally, to the hand. Yet it's also ghosts who can come to the rescue. Originating from the words 'gast' and 'geist' (breath, spirit), ghosts have always provided a vital way of imagining and exceeding the dimensions of our brief time on this earth. They indicate – but tread the unknown reaches of – that place to which we go when, as Hamlet puts it, we shuffle off this mortal coil. Ghosts provide the breath of continuance – bitterly insufficient, but at least something.

My brother was always the closest one, eagerly crowding the finish line, his hands reaching out to his children as they threw themselves over the wide red tape. He adored them and embarrassed them and he was their shining light. 'So excellent a king. . . so loving to my mother,/That he might not beteem the winds of heaven/ Visit her face too roughly! Heaven and earth,/Must I remember?' (1.2.139–43). In *Hamlet*, we never get to meet the young man's father: we can only be witness to the ghost of a father bitterly mourned. This ghost is seen by others, but is audible only to Hamlet himself. He is, in this sense, his son's special ghost.

His son's special ghost. 'The hour is almost come', the ghost tells Hamlet, 'When I to sulph'rous and tormenting flames/Must render up myself' (1.5.2–4). It is Hamlet who must imagine alone the flames in store for his father. Hamlet's mother has clearly shelved her husband in the recesses of the (briefly) mourned. No one else can hear, no one else can feel the apprehension of what lies in store for this ghost – the flames and fumes. Old Hamlet's memory and the fear of flames are entrusted to Hamlet's capacity to *feel*. His body *is* his son's. But not his body either. Hamlet is on earth. The ghost is, for all intents and purposes, gone from the busy world of Denmark, remaining only in the shadows of the night.

My brother fell and he was gone. He couldn't float or fly enough. All that is left is my body, and the bodies of those who loved him. We feel the ache in a way that he can no longer ache, with the physical assault of a grief he can no longer suffer. When my brother died, I lay in bed, thoughts spinning in a busy, illogical way. The only thing we know is what our minds can imagine. Ghosts force themselves into (or out of) our bodies because these bodies don't know how to live without them. A constitutional impossibility, yes. But the rage of water isn't enough, the ache of unknowing isn't enough. We have to have them.

> Grief fills the room up of my absent child,
> Lies in his bed, walks up and down with me,
> Puts on his pretty looks, repeats his words,
> Remembers me of all his gracious parts,
> Stuffs out his vacant garments with his form;
> Then have I reason to be fond of grief. (*King John*, 3.4.93–8)

I went to the mortuary to see my brother. They had put a body in the satin lining of the coffin for us to look at. A clenched expression on one side of the face, a massive contusion on the other.

I find myself endlessly puzzling over my brother as if he has, today, a body and a brain. I try to assess his character, alone or with other members of my family. 'I think the rot set in,' my mother said to me, 'when Dad got ill. Then John died. He was taken, actually.' When my mother says such things, I understand her perfectly. Tomorrow we will turn it over a different way.

I try to bring some sense to John's departure, his busy ghost ripped untimely from his life's work. How did he feel about the constraints of corporate life? My brother was the living form of love, brimming with it, throwing it around, occasionally kicked in the stomach for his gift, quick to recover and gallop on. I think about his family life, his passions, his wife in whose body his own heart had its back-up beat. I think of him as my mother imagines him, walking without headphones for miles, breathing in the morning air, with a graceful, easy posture and long strides. Or as she recalls his childhood days, workmanlike, his joy at getting a new toy or new shoes, and the way he would take them to bed with him in their new box. I obsess about the mountain-climbing hobby, inhumanly difficult, testing his body against the strength of nature. I wonder what he thought as he climbed, the release from time, or the special kind of intimacy this thoroughly extroverted man might have found with his climbing partners on the quiet slopes. I imagine how he felt at that moment when the ground fell away. And so I preserve him as he was, whole and athletically present, or a simulacrum in satin. He is so close to me that I can see his honest, salt-blue eyes; yet he's also reassigned to another place in the universe just as, before, he lived in a house across the Pacific from my own.

Whether they are dead or still living, those who have accompanied us – our own custom-blend ghosts – create, for us, the most potent of places. My brother is an un-plumbed part of myself, and when he fell he took with him (and with the fruitlessly grabbed-at pieces of grass) whole chunks of our shared childhood, the windy winters and the weeping willows, the old rickety boats we rowed on the creek.

Hamlet's ghost, in all its ambiguity, embodies the adaptive nature of ghosthood. The ghost is 'real'; it walks around. It talks – but only to Hamlet. In its very nature, then, it is both actual (others see it) and a haunting from the subconscious, just as Banquo, later in Shakespeare's life, would emerge from that tortured region of Macbeth's mind, a symbol of mental wounds inflicted, as well as of the multitudinous seas that Macbeth's one hand has painted, rendering them 'incarnadine' (2.2.57–61).

We might feel that our ghosts are driving us mad; we might try to bury or banish them, to consign them to a place beneath the floor-boards or to the cool sanity of a therapist's office. But ghosts won't stay there. They come out because we need them. They are always never enough – but these ghosts are what we have. Am I Hamlet for a moment, imagining his father's upcoming purgatorial stint? Am I Imogen, weeping indecorously – but who cares about that? She feels, she has the permission of grief – over Cloten's body? But how could this happen to her? A Princess! How could it happen to me? This unnatural thing should have happened only to David. It was accepted and understood, the story of little David who was killed when I was four, a screeching car in the pouring rain and eternally ever after in our family prayers, placed at the head of the list of those who came in good time to lie next to him, Grandma and Grandad and Aunty Clarrie with pacemakers and cancers and so on. Unimaginable for John. For me, and for John's wife. For Simon, born before John, gentle and beloved, come with our brother Ben to the leafy afternoon to tell our mother that John had had an accident. 'Which hospital's he in? Quick, quick, tell me.' 'Mum, he's gone.'

Somehow, we have to live with our ghosts, just as we have to live without the bodies they inhabited. They stir in our bodies, they hurt us.

I have always wondered whether Shakespeare needed ghosts as structural elements of plot, or whether he shared the prevailing beliefs of his time that ghosts were sent from the world beyond: the Catholic ghosts who came from purgatory to remind us of their virtues and frailties, or the Protestant ghosts who were demons sent from hell to tempt humans to their spiritual destruction. I think that the physicality of ghosts – like the belief in witches – began to fade with increased social understandings of the workings of the universe and the human body. When the handles on the nature of human existence became more secure (never as firm as the handles on a coffin), there was, in other words, less need for ghosts.

But the ghosts still stay with us, whether there's room for them in the rational world or not. More than anything, the ghost of old Hamlet highlights his son's *own* incapacity to act, his *own* incapacity to name the apprehensions that bear down on him so immensely. Hamlet suggests that he can't express an outside that mirrors an implied inside, nor does he really know what this 'inside' is, or should be. He delivers himself to us in the shadow of a ghost, and, therefore, in the shadow of mysteries. Mysteries about the universe, a place so very much altered in the decades before Shakespeare started writing: mysteries about the body, which was, following Andreas Vesalius' studies of cadavers published in *De Humani Corporis Fabrica* in 1543, a subject of new knowledge, especially in terms of the regions of the heart; mysteries about the human soul, voiced by Sir Thomas Browne when he wrote in *Religio Medici*: 'if the soul of man be not transmitted and trans-fused in the seed of the parents, why are not those productions merely beasts . . . Nor, truly, can I peremptorily deny that the soul . . . is wholly, and in all acceptions, inorganical . . . in the [human] brain, which we term the seat of reason, there is not anything of moment more than I can discover in the crany of a beast' (Browne, ed. Martin, 1964, pp. 35–6). In the haze of such mysteries, there is Hamlet's bewildered ejaculation: 'I could be bounded in a nutshell, and count myself king of infinite space, were it not that I have bad dreams.' (2.2.248–50)

Such mysteries, the aching vein of unknowing in *Hamlet*, are in other Shakespearean moments beautifully, if momentarily, and thus for ever partially, resolved. In *Othello* the soldier, bewildered by a wound that can't be bandaged, looks at the creature he believes to have betrayed him:

> Put out the light, and then put out the light.
> If I quench thee, thou flaming minister,
> I can again thy former light restore
> Should I repent me; but once put out thy light,
> Thou cunning'st pattern of excelling nature,
> I know not where is that Promethean heat
> That can thy light relume. When I have plucked the rose,
> I cannot give it vital growth again.
> It needs must wither. I'll smell thee on the tree. (5.2.7–15)

Othello's words are a cry for miracles: putting out the light, smelling the rose, hoping for the light to relume and for the rose to keep her scent; but heavy with the dreadful knowledge that this cannot be and that, for him, there is yet no choice but to act – to snuff and pluck. No miracle will clear his vision, nor save him from his injured vanity, nor cure his injured heart; and no miracle, therefore, can save Desdemona from his murderous deed nor bring her back. But in those moments of incantation ('Put out the light, and then put out the light') we experience Othello as a hero bent on the mission he must accomplish; and so, for that instant, the miracle of ritual cleansing hangs over the stage. We know it will last only as long as it takes to say the words and do the deed; but it is there.

Shakespeare is a play-maker; he re-creates the world. He can give people back the miracles they thought they could never expect, even if, as in the case of Othello, they are absurdly broken fantasies. Then think of Lear, awakening from the sleep his doctor has induced in him after his terrible living nightmare: 'I know not what to say./I will not swear these are my hands: let's see;/I feel this pin prick. Would I were assured/Of my condition!' (4.7.54–57). In this state of un-knowing, both asleep and awake, half-alive and half-dead, Lear is visited by the vision of his daughter, Cordelia: 'You do me wrong to take me out o' the grave:/Thou art a soul in bliss . . . Do not laugh at me . . . I think this lady to be my child, Cordelia' (4.7.45–6, 69–71). In the old man's vision is his hope, his sorrow and repentance, and, as he comes into wakefulness, he realizes that this is not in fact his death or his dream or even his ghost: Cordelia, his daughter, is here again, and she *can* repair all harms in a single kiss. Cordelia comes out of the realm of spirits and brings her father out of the grave. The two are whole again, their love is complete, and there is, after all, a second chance.

Shakespeare possibly himself knew the longing for such a miracle. His only son, Hamnet, had died in 1596 at the age of 11, and his father, John, died in 1601. And if Shakespeare hadn't experienced the urgency of such feeling, he could evidently imagine what it was like: the scene between Lear and his daughter shines with the simple capacity to live again – to have one's loved one back again – as a magical mystery that can redeem the human horrors that are inexorable.

Those who are lucky, or not yet old enough, might be innocent of that moment after the loss of a beloved, when they are briefly, safely with us again, untouched by whatever brutal force has ripped them away. Shakespeare permits us this moment in the beautiful redemptive exchange when the father discovers that all is not lost and his daughter not gone for good. In *King Lear* this moment is the return to life itself, the fulfilment of the hope we were taught to abandon when we left behind the world of fairytales. Shakespeare restores the fairytale, he makes the dream come alive; he gives us back, in other words, the childhood world of miracles. It's a world that has actually never left us, because when we really need it, there it is, safe and sound. There was my brother, only five days dead – surely they could revive him? Cordelia *has* come back again, Lear is *not* dead; all is not irrevocably lost. This dream is secured, a glimpse, and then gone – both daughter and father are dead. But the very fact of the dream's existence, played out on the stage before us, is an affirmation that sometimes, just sometimes, the light can be relumed.

For me, Lear's 'Look there! Look there!' (5.3.310) shines a light on those hundreds of moments when I think my brother lives because I need to. It's perhaps testimony not to life, to the rise and fall of the chest, but to the power of the mind itself. The fugitive penumbra between sleep and wake, a single note from Luka Bloom, the way a person stirs a coffee, thumps down on a chair – this is where one can say, with Lear, 'look there!'

'Why should a dog, a horse, a rat have life,/And thou no breath at all?' (5.3.306–7) Yet the tiniest body, like the most vital of men, the most regal of kings, holds, as a miracle, the immensity of death. The pit of despair, too, and the glimpse of transcendence.[2]

Notes

1. In memory of John Kelly, loved, we discovered, beyond measure. 24/3/1960–30/12/2010.
2. My thanks to Simon Palfrey and Ewan Fernie, whose generous minds inspire my best thoughts.

Chapter 5

Going to Shakespeare: Memory and Anamnesis

Peter Holland

> Anamnesis *is a figure whereby the speaker calling to mind matters past, whether of sorrow, joy, &c. doth make recital of them for his own advantage, or for the benefit of those that hear him*
>
> (Smith, 1657, p. 249)

Peter Holland Goes to Shakespeare

I remember it happening every time we went to the Aldwych Theatre. My father would drive up to the 'No Parking' sign-board placed in Drury Lane, the narrow road running up beside the theatre. The uniformed doorman would look at him, move the sign, beckon us forward, put the sign back in the road behind our car so that we were parked right by the main entrance, and then stand waiting for his tip. While my mother went in to the cramped foyer, my father and I would walk quickly down the Aldwych, past the Waldorf Hotel, to the little chocolate shop, buy some rum truffles for my mother and me and some chocolate orange sticks for my father, walk equally quickly back, meet up with my mother and head down the stairs to the auditorium, with that still strange experience of finding that the Stalls were/are below street level. Whatever Royal Shakespeare Company (RSC) show it was that I was being taken to see – Peter

Brook's *King Lear* with Paul Scofield, Ian Holm as Richard III in the last part of *The Wars of the Roses*, Scofield and Patrick Magee in *Staircase*, Peggy Ashcroft in *Days in the Trees* – the process of arriving seems, now, always to have been the same.

And why, oh reader, should you care for a moment about my 'mak[ing] recital' of these memories? Is it 'for [my] own advantage' or 'for the benefit of those that hear' or read me? For me, there are many conflicting emotions even in this brief narration of a sequence of memories, however flawed and reconstructed they most probably are. I have no doubts that I did see those productions but the details of parking and chocolates might have happened only once or twice, for all I now know. There's a certain boastfulness about these memories: I saw these productions and, most probably, you didn't. The pettiness of my still glorying in my father's securing the ideal parking-space for the price of a tip is almost – but only almost – embarrassing. There was that sheer delight in the expensive chocolates, so much nicer than the usual Cadbury's. There was the pleasure, the unmitigated and still profound pleasure, of going to the theatre, to the liveness of the performative event. And, above absolutely everything else, there was the thrill of being out with my parents. But why would you care about any of that? Why should I fill in more of my autobiography to explain why that thrill was so special? What business is that of yours?

There is much here about class and wealth. Did you notice how I dropped in the information that we had seats in the Stalls (and not at the back of the Stalls either)? And, before you get the wrong idea, we were not particularly well off: it is just that theatre was my parents' one real indulgence, a regular escape that made up for their rare holidays. And I have said nothing yet about the productions beyond the mere fact of having seen them and who was in them, information that confers bragging rights but is not much of a basis yet for analysis of performance practice, say, or acting style or scenic design or even cultural meaning. As a young boy, I was excited enough by seeing this *Richard III* (well, I'd already seen Olivier's on film) to have kept safe the memories of a few details of Ian Holm's Richard, especially the unnerving sounds of his whimpering inside his armour on the battlefield at Bosworth, wielding a sword impossibly large for such a small man. But there are no traces at all left of Peggy Ashcroft's Queen Margaret. The photos of the former are infused with the particularities of recollection, that sharp alteration in perception when there is recognition derived from the experience rather than simply recognition of a well-known shot, but the ones of the latter have no resonance, as distant for me as the images from dozens of shows I never saw, however familiar they have become for me as a scholar of Shakespeare performance history.

It's the sensation of the chocolates that is strongest, just as memories of mid-week matinees in the West End are also of the interval wooden tea-trays being passed along the rows, with tea for my mother and weak orange squash for me. The madeleine here is in the hard chocolate granules around the soft centre of the rum truffles. And there are evocative sounds too, equally firmly implanted in my memory, like the endlessly repeated cry of 'Stalls on your left, Circle on your right' called out far too loudly by the commissionaire at the Golders Green Hippodrome, our nearest theatre, where we saw *Chu Chin Chow* on its umpteenth tour and the out-of-town try-out of Arnold Wesker's *Four Seasons* and, every year, Gilbert and Sullivan performed by the D'Oyly Carte Company. At the Hippodrome, the National Anthem was played before the performance on a piano while at the Aldwych there was an eighteenth century arrangement – and I remember my father once excitedly pointing out in our row one of his heroes, the left-wing Jewish MP Sydney Silverman who refused to stand for 'God Save the Queen'.

As I write about these thoughts, there is exactly the sorrow of their pastness, mixed with the pleasures of their relics of immediacy. Each thought, formulated for the first time now into words worth typing, leads to others and this chapter might wander off to many shows, theatres, experiences of parking and tastes, shouts and sights, which have even less to do with Shakespeare than some of the other ones I've mentioned so far. But the mixture is precisely the point. Histories of Shakespeare in performance are more interested in *Richard III* than *Chu Chin Chow* but, for me, the two co-exist (and one day I must find out what happens in the second half of the latter since I had to be taken home at the interval, ill with a terrible migraine). Because we saw the RSC more often in London than in Stratford, the Shakespeare productions were comingled with the new work that was central to Peter Hall's vision for the RSC as a company playing in two locations, London and Stratford-upon-Avon. Ashcroft as the world's worst mother-in-law voraciously consuming the choucroute in *Days in the Trees* or Scofield as a camp, gay hairdresser in *Staircase* or transformed into the most exquisite dandy as Khlestakov in *The Government Inspector* are as immediate as – and often for me more memorable than – their Shakespeare work. The RSC as company and ensemble, working in a single London theatre, was far more various than in its work at the Royal Shakespeare Theatre (RST) where Shakespeare was only leavened by the occasional play by one of his contemporaries, like Middleton's *Women Beware Women* or *The Revenger's Tragedy* (I saw the former in Stratford but the latter in London), while the work in London was continually interspliced with plays by some of our contemporaries and a classic European repertoire.

And, beyond the RSC and the local theatre, there were the frequent visits to the Royal Court Theatre, seeing Edward Bond's *Saved* at a preview, before the reviews made such a fuss, and always feeling the rumble of the tube trains below our feet. There was occasional Shakespeare at the Royal Court, like Bill Gaskill's searingly brightly lit *Macbeth*, with set and costumes made of the same rough hessian, and with Alec Guinness starring opposite Simone Signoret whose English was horribly approximate, a 60s version of 'O weederdee'.[1] We went often, too, to Olivier's National Theatre at the Old Vic where there were no parking problems but no chocolates and there was Feydeau's *A Flea in Her Ear*, still the funniest show I have ever seen, as well as Olivier in *Othello*, Robert Stephens in *The Royal Hunt of the Sun* as well as in *Black Comedy* – and in *Much Ado* too with its chattering statues and its attempt by Robert Graves to modernize some of Shakespeare's language, with a programme note that is another fragment stuck in my mind, explaining why one needed to do *something* to Borachio's 'Being entertained for a perfumer, as I was smoking a musty room. . .' (*Much Ado About Nothing*, 1.3.46–7). As I write this, I have to stop myself from running to the basement and opening long-closed boxes of papers in search of those programmes I brought home, stacked up in ordered disorder and often reread, with no distinction made between theatre, concerts and my other great childhood love, the annual military show of the Royal Tournament at the arena at Earls Court with its massed military bands and the intricate riding of the King's Troop, Royal Artillery (and no, no-one else reading this is going to be remotely interested in that but I could take you step-by-step through the intricacies of the nightly race of the field-gun competition).

There were also productions I was not taken to see. I remember my father's pleasure in the performances in the RSC's production of Weiss's *Marat/Sade*, not the stars like Patrick Magee and Glenda Jackson but the 'chorus' of the mad at Charenton who, he described to me, never stopped their obsessive neurotic tics. He came home in the middle of the night from going on his own to the RSC's late-night reading of *The Investigation*, Weiss's docudrama from transcripts of the Frankfurt Auschwitz trials, and was still deeply shaken by the experience the next day, though or perhaps precisely because the Holocaust was so immediate in our home, for most of his family had died in the camps.

Turn to any history of British theatre and drama in the 1960s like Dominic Shellard's (1999) or Michael Billington's (2007) and most of what I've described will be there (except the Royal Tournament), analysed subtly and with proper attention to the formative post-War cultural contexts within which Hall's RSC, Gaskill's Royal Court and Olivier's National Theatre co-existed. But what I have been sketching is not an academic's view nor a theatre reviewer's, not even a proto-academic's as if I had some idea then what career I would follow, how much of this experience would turn out to be the basis for writing about Shakespeare in performance decades later. It is a child's view, through to my early teens, and it was part of family life. As often as my parents went to the theatre and as often as they met friends of theirs there, they didn't book tickets to go with their friends; theatregoing was a family outing, a domestic activity, something that they seemed to do more often than their friends did. It was not part of other cultural activities either: we never went to art galleries or museums, except the Science Museum and Natural History Museum to amuse/educate me; trips to the opera with them waited for my enthusiasm for it a few years later (Verdi's *Falstaff* at Covent Garden, Peter Pears as Peter Grimes at Sadler's Wells, and, my very first live opera, Richard Rodney Bennett's *The Mines of Sulphur* in 1965); concert-going was something they did because I was excited by classical music, not because they really enjoyed it; we rarely went to films *en famille* (so that a trip to a West End cinema was a change from theatre) and never to art-house films, though, of course, I went to the local cinemas almost every week with my friends and the Ionic, Golders Green, or the Hendon Odeon was as familiar as the Aldwych or the Old Vic. Theatre was, I see in retrospect, oddly isolated from anything else as culture to be consumed.

Theatre stretched outside London to Stratford and here, too, the performances are inseparable from the experience of arriving or leaving. Which matinee performance was it that we were so nearly late for, my father driving unwontedly fast through the countryside to get there in time but my mother insisting on his stopping for us to eat the picnic she had packed? And the precise recollections of going to David Warner's Hamlet in 1965 with my older sister and brother-in-law, the performance images aligned with the view from our seats in the Dress Circle, are enmeshed with the drive back home to London through thick fog, with my half-lying in the back seat chattering about what I'd seen and Ruth complaining, not entirely unreasonably, that we seemed to have been at different plays. It would be about thirty years before she and I went to the theatre together again.

Those rare Stratford excursions once or twice a year apart, we were enmeshed, to a very remarkable extent, in the theatrical life of London and it was done out of sheer pleasure, for the immense satisfaction we all derived from it. My delight led my parents to take me often but they would have gone anyway. Theatregoing was intellectually demanding, of course, but it had to be a form of entertainment: as my father used to comment damningly on the way out, 'That was very interesting but I wasn't entertained.'

What now matters most to me as a professional academic, the Shakespeare productions which underpin my research and teaching, that rich repository of decades of productions seen, actors followed and directors admired, none of that is separable either from the non-Shakespearean events which were as, perhaps more, frequent. Nor can it be divided from the social circumstances, the family meanings attached to going to the theatre. Where seeing Shakespeare productions is now the dominant part of my theatregoing, then Shakespeare was only a part of it. Shakespeare's presence outside the liveness of theatre or Olivier's films was limited too: there was no copy of the *Works* at home on the family's bookshelves until I wanted one and, though I listened to an LP we owned of Olivier reading speeches from *Hamlet* and *Henry V* so often that I still read 'Once more unto the breach' in the rhythms of his delivery that I had learned by heart and passably imitated, I have no idea quite why my parents had bought it. Of the tedium of Shakespeare in school, of the lack there of anything of the excitement that theatre brought, I could say much but will say nothing more.

Elisabeth von Ephrussi Goes to Shakespeare

The urgency of the activity of memory resists any careful sorting, especially when the memories have not been carefully and repeatedly structured into forms of narrative. The welter of fragments above is a recollection of a practice of playgoing, remembered for the particular purposes this volume has suggested to me. The 'I' is a childhood, teenaged person, someone for whom those experiences of theatre have come to be seen as profoundly formative of the professional academic but whose experience then was familiar in the particular, buried sense of the word as implying that connection with 'family', the context within which the familiar is, usually, most immediately and earliest formulated. The materials of seeing Shakespeare at that time have repeatedly been selected and used: I have often mentioned productions I saw then in class, in conference papers, in articles and in academic conversations. I have rarely discussed *Staircase* or *Chu Chin Chow*. I have a long-held secret wish to write one day about Gilbert and Sullivan, precisely because of that early delight in *The Mikado* and *Ruddigore* I began to experience then. But the Shakespeare memories, the 'I' that went to Shakespeare, are far more dominant, to the extent that the specific placing of Shakespeare within other kinds of theatre performance has rarely been visible, even to me.

But the more we look at others' records of their experiences as members of theatre audiences, research their evidence of their social activity of playgoing as something we are fascinated by as curious scholars of social history and of the cultures of consumption, the more aberrant our professional theatregoing appears to be. And our use of the records of our own experiences is usually isolated from the social contexts within which the event occurred. In *The Hare with Amber Eyes*, Edmund de Waal's brilliant account of his family's history, there is an illustration of an opening from his grandmother's 'little green book in which she records the concerts and theatres she attends', the pages covering the first few months of 1916, when she was seventeen, a young woman, living with her extremely wealthy Jewish family in Vienna (de Waal, 2010, p. 191). It is not, as the phrase might seem to suggest, simply a journal, a diary in which theatre might have taken its place among the other fragments of a life recorded. Instead it is a book designed specifically for the purpose with printed columns with headings for 'Title of the dramatic or musical works', 'Author or Composer', venue, date and a space for notes (p. 192, my translations). De Waal selects the page because on 11 May Elisabeth went to Wagner's *Die Meistersinger* at the Opera and noted 'Heilige *Deutsche* Kunst', 'sacred German art', with 'German' 'patriotically' underlined (p. 191).

I am, of course, intrigued to find that, as well as Lessing's *Nathan der Weise* (an appropriate play for a Jewish girl to see) and Delibes' ballet *Coppélia*, Elisabeth went to *'König Richard der Dritte'* on 1 February and *King Lear* on 8 June, both at the Burgtheater. But I am even more pleased to find that, for every single trip, Elisabeth von Ephrussi notes exactly whom she went with: she went to *Richard III* with 'Daisy, Arthur, René, Leo' and to *King Lear* with 'Mama, Papa, Gertrud Sturmer'. The group of cousins with whom she listened to Wagner was the same group who took her to Lessing. Her parents took her to Adolph L'Arronge's *Doktor Klaus* and to Friedmann and Kottow's comedy *Onkel Bernhard* premiered in Vienna that year as well as to *King Lear*. Mama but not Papa was part of the group that went to Schiller's *Maria Stuart*. The groupings suggest patterns of taste, networks of relationships, cultural positioning that one could investigate for their significances, their definitions of the highest echelons of Viennese society in the midst of war. In contemplating that search, work I will not be doing, I wonder whether Daisy and Arthur are English or American rather than Austrian, people who might know their Shakespeare in a different language, in a different social context. And I find myself speculating that the two Shakespeare productions were part of the celebrations of the Shakespeare tercentenary that was equally vigorously supported on both sides of the War's divide, though, of course, Viennese theatre always had Shakespeare in its repertory and his name appears alongside the great German and Austrian dramatists on the Burgtheater's façade.

Of her visit to *King Lear* Elisabeth notes two pieces of information beyond the usual. The first, bracketed after the title, simply says

'Wüllner'. This is Ludwig Wüllner (1858–1938), the extraordinarily versatile singer and actor, who played Lear and whom Elizabeth had heard giving readings from Goethe, Schiller and Rilke on 20 March and Goethe, Schiller and Lessing on 2 May (she thought the Rilke 'grossartig', 'brilliant'). He had sung Wagner's Tannhäuser and played Shylock and Hamlet. He was a favourite star, noted simply for his presence. The second, after the list of playgoing companions, is her overwhelmed, deeply moved response to the play: 'das Wortversagt, den Jammer zubeschreiben', 'there are no words to describe the misery'.[2] It resonates with a reader's famous response rather earlier, Dr Johnson's comment that 'I was many years ago so shocked by *Cordelia*'s death, that I know not whether I ever endured to read again the last scenes of the play till I undertook to revise them as an editor' (Johnson, 1765, vol. 6, p. 159). Dr Johnson reads (for he could not have seen Shakespeare's ending); Elisabeth watches. Both are distraught at the ending. A middle-aged scholar and a teenaged girl are equally affected. Elisabeth here cannot forbear to record the performance's emotional affect on her. There is almost a tone of astonishment in her comment and I hear an inevitable echo: 'If aught of woe or wonder . . .' (*Hamlet*, 5.2.307). Elisabeth, in that note, performs her anamnesis, calls to mind 'matters past', here of sorrow, and 'doth make recital of them for [her] own advantage', noting because she needs to note, feels the pressure of the experience forcing her to note, with excitement as well as astonishment, both the emotion and the failure of language, overrunning the printed space for her notes as she does so.

Samuel Pepys Goes to Shakespeare

Elisabeth's visit to *King Lear* survives in a series of records that deliberately places the groups of playgoers as that which is consistently, for her, noteworthy, something to be noted. Not only does she always note her companions but also that is most often the only item recorded under 'Notes', 'Bemerkungen'. Nothing else seems to have mattered to her as much as this marking of the social event, the sociability of going to the theatre with friends, relatives, parents. Turn to another passionate theatregoer who left detailed accounts of his playgoing and the presence of the social is even more emphatic.

As soon as he can assure himself that he can afford to indulge his pleasures with a reasonably clear conscience both with regard to cost and to his moral scruples about pleasure itself, Samuel Pepys goes to the theatre with striking frequency. Between 1 January and 31 August 1668 he visited the theatres seventy-three times. Of those, twenty-six were made by Pepys alone, even though on many of them he met people he knew, perhaps pre-arranged but, if so, not noted as such in the diary. Twenty-one of those solitary afternoons were during April and May when his wife was out of town staying in the countryside. In all, during April and May 1668 he was at the theatre thirty-three times, only twelve of which were with friends and colleagues. So, for instance, he went with Lord Brouncker four times, with John Creed twice, and four more with Mary Mercer and her friends. While Mrs Pepys was in London she usually accompanied her husband: of the forty theatre visits he made while she was in town during these eight months, she went with him thirty-two times, on thirteen of which she was accompanied by her maid Deb Willet and on ten more by Deb and Mary Mercer. On 7 January, for instance, Pepys went to Whitehall to wait on the Duke of York but, the Duke being away, he took a coach to the Nursery, a theatre where young actors were trained,

> where I never was yet, and there to meet my wife and Mercer and Willet as they promised; but the House did not act today and so I was at a loss for them, and therefore to the other two playhouses into the pits to gaze up and down to look for them, and there did by this means for nothing see an Act in *The Schoole of Compliments* at the Duke of York's House and *Henery the 4th* at the King's House; but not finding them, nor liking either of the plays, I took my coach again and home . . . and by and by they

came home, and had been at the King's House and saw me, but I could [not] see them. (Pepys, 1970–83, vol. 9, p. 14)

The trip is arranged in the morning but it is not a response to seeing a playbill advertising the performance. Pepys has simply assumed that there will be a performance at the Nursery and, in the absence of cellphones, he can't think what to do when he finds the theatre closed. Given that there were only two other theatres in London he heads first to the Lincoln's Inn Fields Theatre where they are playing James Shirley's pre-interregnum comedy. Pepys had seen the play on 5 August 1667 with his wife and his colleague Sir William Penn, 'a silly play; only Mis's dancing in a shepherd's clothes did please us mightily' (vol. 8, p. 375). Mary Davis, 'Mis', was a favourite actor for Pepys but his pleasure is shared by the others: her dancing 'did please *us*'.

Looking for his wife, Pepys has taken advantage of the custom that one could see one act of a play for free, only paying if one stayed. He does not like *School of Compliments* and he has not found his wife and so he moves on to the Theatre Royal, Bridges Street where Shakespeare's *Henry IV Part 1* is on – and, as usual, he does not note the name of the playwright, only the play's title, just as playbills did not carry the author's name. In the diary period, he had seen it three times before and would see it once more. The first visit was on 31 December 1660 when he bought a copy of the play in Paul's churchyard (probably the most recent edition, the 1639 quarto) and went on to the Theatre Royal in Vere Street

and there saw it acted; but my expectation being too great, it did not please me as otherwise I believe it would; and my having a book I believe did spoil it a little. (vol. 1, p. 325)

As usual, Pepys records whether he enjoyed the play or not, here affected by anticipation and by having the book – perhaps he was reading along with the performance. When he saw the play again on

4 June 1661 he thought it 'a good play' (vol. 2, p. 115). He did not see the play again until 6 November 1667, this time with his wife and her maid: 'and contrary to expectation, was pleased in nothing more then in Cartwright's speaking of Falstaffe's speech about *What is Honour?*' (vol. 8, p. 516). Unusually, he picks on a speech to mention as the highlight of the performance – more often he only notes a dance or a song that particularly pleased him, as with Mary Davis's dance in *School of Compliments*. He also notes something striking about the composition of the audience: 'The house full of Parliament-men, it being holiday with them', since Parliament had adjourned. On his final visit to the play on 18 September 1668, he turns up late, 'at the end of the play', not to save money but because he had planned to 'have gone abroad' (i.e. out on the town) with Elizabeth Knepp, an actor in the company and a close friend, 'but it was too late, and she to get her part against tomorrow in *The Silent Woman*' (vol. 9, p. 310). Knepp's day is not over: after the end of the performance, she needs to work on her role for the next day as the title character in Jonson's *Epicoene*.

Henry IV Part 1 was a popular play in the post-Restoration repertory of the King's Company, which owned the rights to most of Shakespeare's plays by claiming descent from the pre-War King's Men. But Pepys never gives a sign on the five occasions he sees it that he has seen it before. There is no particular consistency in his response. On two occasions he only watches part of it, catching it by chance because he is looking for his wife or thinking to spend the evening with Knepp. Indeed, more often than not, Pepys goes to the theatre without any indication that he is going to see a particular play, that he is responding to advertising or the buzz about a performance. Only occasionally is his visit directly the result of some such response. On 19 June 1668 his wife goes to the Theatre Royal to look for him and sees Dryden's new play, *An Evening's Love*, 'which though the world commends, she likes not' (vol. 9, p. 247). On 20 June both of them go to see 'this new play my wife saw yesterday; and do not like it, it being very smutty, and nothing so good as *The Maiden Queen* or *The Indian Imperour*, of his making, that I was troubled at it'. What is more, 'my wife tells me is wholly (which he confesses a little in the epilogue) taken out of the *Illustr. Bassa*', i.e. Madam de Scudéri's novel *Ibrahim* (vol. 9, p. 147). So, the next day, a Sunday, after dinner and between the day's two visits to church, his wife reads 'in the *Illustr. Bassa* the plot of yesterday's play, which is most exactly the same'. On Monday he called at Dryden's publisher, Henry Herringman, who informs him 'Dryden doth himself call it but a fifth-rate play' but nonetheless he goes to the theatre with his loathed colleague Creed and 'saw an act or two of the new play again, but like it not' (vol. 9, p. 248). Pepys and his wife each see the play twice and she shows him the source (and note how Elizabeth, of French descent, recognizes the source and reads it to him).

Playgoing for Pepys is something that he prefers to do with his wife. On 18 February 1668 he saw Richard Rhodes' *Flora's Vagaries* with Sir William Penn, a frequent companion to the theatre, but thought it 'a very silly play; and the more, I being out of humour, being at a play without my wife and she ill at home, and having no desire also to be seen and therefore could not look about me' (vol. 9, p. 78). Pepys does not want to be seen because he does not want word to get back to his wife that he has been at the theatre when she has been ill for days with stomach pains, partly the result, they think, of a bad reaction to 'some physic' she has taken. When he gets home after the theatre, he goes 'up to my wife, not owning my being at a play'. The play, her illness, his embarrassment and secrecy, all mingle together with her showing him that evening a ring 'of a Turky-stone set with little sparks of Dyamonds, which I am to give her as my valentine, and I am not troubled that it will cost me near 5*l*- she costing me but little compared with other wifes, and I have not many occasions to spend on her' (vol. 9, p. 78).

I have been exploring Pepys' theatregoing in a fairly arbitrary and random way. One fragment leads to another. A reference to one visit to a play can be read across the diary in terms of the other times he saw or would see the same play or in terms of his companions or his relationship to his wife or to his contacts with the people who worked in the theatre industry. Pepys frequently talks with Sir Thomas Killigrew who ran the King's Company as well as with actors. After the first night of Etherege's *She Would If She Could* on 8 February 1668 when the theatre was packed and the King present, Pepys cannot find his wife to go home with her and, 'it being dark and raining', he 'stayed going between the two doors and through the pit an hour and half I think, after the play was done, and the people staying there till the rain was over and to talk with one another'. He hears Etherege complaining about the actors 'that they were out of humour and had not their parts perfect, and that Harris did do nothing, nor could so much as sing a Ketch in it', and he hears 'all the rest did through the whole pit blame the play as a silly, dull thing' until 'At last I did find my wife staying for me in the entry, and with her was Betty Turner, Mercer, and Deb' (vol. 9, p. 54).

Here is Pepys listening to the playwright, spotting celebrities ('here was the Duke of Buckingham today openly sat in the pit'), picking up on others' opinions, all while it rains and he goes to and fro in the auditorium in search of Mrs Pepys. As the diary entry unfolds, his own view of the play – 'how silly the play, there being nothing in the world good in it and few people pleased in it' – changes, for while he now notes that all those waiting out the rain 'blame the play', he has moved on to find that 'there was something very roguish and witty; but the design of the play, and end, mighty insipid'. It is his trying to find his wife that creates the space in which his gathering responses to the play is achieved. Pepys records the excitement of the premiere, noting it as an act of fairly immediate memory as he writes up his diary but also creating in the diary itself, in its bound volumes part of the superb library he bequeathed to Magdalene College, Cambridge, something that is a record of his response that he 'doth make recital of . . . for his own advantage' but which, being written in shorthand, is also private and secret even while visible on the library shelves, for it is long before the diary is able to be read by others, transcribed and edited, and selectively published in 1825.

I have deliberately not concentrated on Pepys' visits to Shakespeare, even though, for example, Helen McAfee's still useful sorting of the diary's materials on theatre and drama puts all the references to Shakespeare in the first chapter that arranges the entries by topic, before 'Other Pre-Restoration Plays' or Pepys' comments on contemporary drama (McAfee, 1916, pp. 65–78). For her as an early twentieth-century scholar and for us as twenty-first century Shakespeare scholars, it is Pepys on Shakespeare that matters most. Pepys on *A Midsummer Night's Dream* – a play which 'I have never seen before, nor shall ever again, for it is the most insipid ridiculous play that ever I saw in my life' (29 September 1662, vol. 3, p. 208) – is quoted more often than his comments on any play by the new Restoration dramatists.

Yet, in the maze of interconnections that any one entry begins to trace (from wife to maid to playwright to celebrities and so on), Shakespeare really does not figure. Shakespeare is hardly constituted as an author with whom Pepys might define a relationship. Pepys really has no 'and' to place between Shakespeare and himself, his 'I'. I think (though I cannot be quite sure) that he only mentions Shakespeare by name twice in the diary. The first is on 15 August 1665 when, after dreaming that he had Lady Castlemaine 'in my armes' and dreaming that he was dreaming it, he reflects on the fact of dreaming:

> But that since it was a dream and that I took so much pleasure in it, what a happy thing it would be, if when we are in our graves (as Shakespeere resembles it), we could dream, and dream but such dreams as this – that then we should not need to be so fearful of death as we are this plague-time. (vol. 6, p. 191)

The passage from *Hamlet* comes to mind, from a play he had often seen but from a speech that he has learned a few months earlier when, after dinner on a Sunday, he 'spent all the afternoon with my wife within doors – and getting a speech out of *Hamlet*, "To bee or not to bee," without book' (13 November 1664, vol. 5, p. 320), perhaps something he did because of his great admiration for Thomas Betterton's performance in the role. Now, movingly, the lines come to mind as he meditates on dreams, because the virulence of the plague creates a terrifying immediacy of death against which the concept of sleeping perchance to dream is a comforting thought.

The second comes on 7 November 1667 when he goes with Sir William Penn to see *The Tempest*, 'an old play of Shakespeares, acted here the first day'. Pepys' wife and her maid and his friend Will Hewer were also there, sitting separately, but Pepys and Penn are 'close by my Lady Dorsett and a great many great ones'. Pepys thought it 'the most innocent play that ever I saw', particularly noting 'a curious piece of Musique in an Echo of half-sentences, the Echo repeating the former half while the man goes on to the latter, which is mighty pretty' but deciding that 'The play no great wit; but yet good, above ordinary plays' (vol. 8, p. 521–2). Though Pepys defines it as 'an old play', it is the adaptation by Dryden and Davenant, *The Tempest or The Enchanted Island*, that he is watching, just as the performance of *Macbeth* he saw the day before was of Davenant's adaptation. What he identifies as Shakespeare's is, for us, 'not-Shakespeare', more Dryden-Davenant than Shakespeare, of more interest to us for the ways in which it is not Shakespeare's play than for the ways in which it still is. Its difference is what counts.

This is the only time that Pepys goes to 'Shakespeare', heading off to a play with Shakespeare's authorship in mind. Elisabeth von Ephrussi and I as a child always knew when we were going to Shakespeare but in a manner that places us close to Pepys, for our visits, however powerful, however firmly lodged in our emotional memories, were embedded in a continuum of theatregoing in which Shakespeare may have figured significantly but certainly neither exclusively nor dominantly.

And why do these records of three moments in the history of practices of theatregoing matter? Why should the particular ways in which Pepys and Elisabeth and the young I perform our versions of anamnesis count? In part because of the ways in which they each allow the event of theatre to connect with emotion, with family and friends, with excitement and pleasure. But, not least, because of the difference from the practice of playgoing that dominantly figures for Shakespeare scholars, however much or little they are engaged in performance, whether they are thinking of or writing about their own or others' acts of watching Shakespeare.

In a recent article, I argued that my own act of watching a production of *Coriolanus* at Shakespeare's Globe in London was contained within a group of parameters: as editor, as pre-performance lecturer, as participant in a number of economic transactions, as erstwhile teacher of the director and leading actor, and as critic (Holland, 2007). Strikingly I never mentioned in the article that I went to the production with my wife Romana, that my theatregoing is bound up with her presence in my life (the professional academic life as well as the private one). We go to the theatre together even more habitually than Pepys and his wife. Nor had I noticed that the title of the autobiography by the show's director, Dominic Dromgoole, could have applied to me too: *Will & Me: How Shakespeare Took Over My Life* (Dromgoole, 2006). For nearly all my playgoing now, unlike my trio of earlier playgoers (young self included), is to Shakespeare productions, the professional responsibility dominating over everything else.

What I do, what most Shakespeare-in-performance scholars do, is out of the run of most theatregoers' practice and we forget or ignore the difference, the unusualness, the aberrancy. One remarkable exception to the norm is Gordon Crosse, whose extraordinary theatrical diary covering 1890 to 1953 he excerpted for a published collection but which, read at length, volume by volume, records in fascinating detail his frequent, nigh-on obsessive Shakespeare theatregoing, without discussing any other plays he may have seen.[3] Crosse was a church historian, not a Shakespeare scholar, and his account is that of a true amateur, noting addictively what he liked and disliked, what pleased him or irritated him, from performances to the pronunciation of particular names: hence, for example, he notes in 1924 with relief, 'I was glad to hear them pronounce Coriol*ah*nus, not Coriol*ai*nus'. Even among professional theatre critics the privileging of Shakespeare is unusual, with J. C. Trewin's account of eighty-five productions of *Hamlet* an exception (Trewin, 1987).

Shakespeare performance scholars are as nerdy as trainspotters. Our relationship to Shakespeare productions suggests we should be wearing anoraks and sandals. We speak in the same codes as other such obsessives, swapping names and dates and castlists, data as precious as a sports fan's knowledge of his team – at least it seems to me that the statistical obsession is that of male sports fans, not female ones. Our Shakespeare productions are 'call[ed] to mind' so that we can 'make recital of them . . . for the benefit of those that hear' us, our colleagues, our students, our friends in the subcultural club of Shakespeare performance addicts. Our 'I' is neurotic and aberrant in our charting our connections, the links between 'Shakespeare' and our selves. Like many neuroses, we are unaware of just how neurotic we are being, how odd our behaviour is. Remembering my childhood, reading Pepys' diary, encountering an opening of Elisabeth von Ephrussi's theatre journal startlingly reminds me that 'Shakespeare and I' is a definition of an illness that has unhealthily dominated my professional career. But it is an illness of which I have no wish to be cured.

Notes

1. The phrase comes from a famous 1936 review of Leontovich as Cleopatra, turning her attempt at 'O, withered is the garland of the war' into 'O weederdee degarlano devar' (4.16.66). See the edition of

Antony and Cleopatra by the aptly-named Richard Madelaine (1998, p. 294).

2. My thanks to Jessica Ritter-Holland and Angela Ritter for help deciphering, translating and contextualizing de Waal's reproduction of a page from Elisabeth's journal.

3. See Gordon Crosse, 1953; for the full diary, see Crosse, 1986, reels 8–10.

Chapter 6
Stand Up for Bastards

Richard Wilson

'Marshall McLuhan thinks the world's a global village. Shakespeare would say he doesn't know what a village is!' The Welsh accent gave this gnomic pronouncement a chapel lilt. We had been imitating its indignation since the time of the Cuban Missile Crisis, when our teacher John Davies perched on a radiator to distract us with *The Hobbit* and shaggy yarns about the 'National Elf'. A D.H. Lawrence look-alike, John's lessons harked back to 'Sunday evenings at home, with winter outside/And hymns', as 'The business is to live really alive', he would quote from 'Hymns in a Man's Life', 'And this needs wonder' ('Piano', Lawrence, 1932, p. 188). So when he came across a James Bond his reaction was comic contempt: 'I throw it out the window!' Instead he stocked our school library with village classics: Edmund Blunden's *Cricket Country*, George Sturt's *The Wheelwright's Shop*, and George Evans's *Ask the Fellows Who Cut the Hay*. And handily portable, the little red volumes of Dent's New Temple edition lined up squarely on these oak shelves as reader-cheeky invites to pocket Shakespeare, so I will forever associate the plays with Eric Gill's stark naked woodcuts. Gill's paradise of Ditchling was a short ride away by Southdown bus. But the paradox of John Davies's hymn to the Shakespearean village was that this was Thomas Bennett Comprehensive School, in Crawley New Town.

'Uniformity is the New Town shortcoming', recorded Pevsner of Crawley, 'even if it is a friendly, cosy uniformity. What is needed is every time identical: a row of shops, a pub, a church, a chapel', and 'finally there are the SCHOOLS, of which THOMAS BENNETT is specially good (1959–61)'. Of Crawley's shopping plaza Sir Nikolaus clucked that he would need to visit 'when it is swarming with people to see the point'. The only thing he liked in it was a bandstand shoved from its lost village by Gatwick airport. But the way the clean Bauhaus lines of the school named after the New Town planner 'taper off into countryside' evidently appealed to the Weimar émigré as a solution to the *rus in urbe* contradictions of the 'garden suburb' (Nairn/Pevsner, 1965 repr. 2003, pp. 201, 204). In her *Romantic Moderns* Alexandra Harris explains how Pevsner was chronicling a post-War England 'caught on the cusp' between the modern and the medieval, in 'the years when the village bus ran regularly into town', but it still seemed necessary to reaffirm that 'the English had done well in avoiding revolution' (Harris, 2010, pp. 134, 169). Tony Judt has similarly spoken of the Green Line buses, which wove a blitzed London back into the Home Counties, as comfy coaches for the reproduction of both deference and entitlement, on board which everyone felt pleased with themselves: 'I remember thinking that the bus *smelled* reassuring, more like a library or an old bookstore than a means of transport' (Judt, 2010, p. 61) And this was a country journey on which I had also set out from Crawley, with, in my pocket, John Davies's chosen edition of Shakespeare.

Under its saintly ascetic head Tim McMullan, Thomas Bennett entered the Guinness Book of Records as the largest school in Europe, and TV cameras generated the illusion of a permanent revolution. McMullan would lead his team on to the even more unstructured Community College of Countesthorpe in Leicestershire. But in Crawley, after assembly readings from *The Rainbow*, the only truly mixed-ability activity was drama, so hundreds would be drilled in vast Reinhardt-inspired pageants, with titles like *Pilgrim*, energized by a human dynamo, John Challen (see Challen, 1973). English, with its Oxbridge exams, was a Green

Line, I can now see, connecting this mass movement to an older country of inheritance and tradition. Even its common-room had apparently been barricaded by Hobbits, to secure a snug book-lined hideaway from plateglass transparency and conformism. The Comprehensive image has since changed so much that it is hard to credit the spirit of *election* Davies was allowed to brew in this crafty corner. Here we prepared for the superfluous 'S' level, pored over *Peter Grimes* in *The Listener*, and revered Edward Thomas 'for his scrupulosity', as I was loftily told by another sixth-former, today an eminent critic of Pope, no less. So, if I remember 'Adelstrop', it is as a key to an English subjectivity which might not have had a clue about sex, drugs, or later, the Village People, but was certain of its title to 'The World We Have Lost'.

In the New Town Comprehensive of the 1960s the ideological function of English was to run the Green Line of literary inclusiveness into the land of cultural exclusion. How Shakespeare instilled deference was plain to the school when actors of the RSC made their Tudorbethan songs sound quaintly condescending. By then we had been offered entitlement by Lawrence Lerner of nearby Sussex University, opening his poems like a living Shakespeare. 'I have come back to tell you all I know', grinned the wandering professor, 'I know nothing, but I tell it rather well' (see Lerner, 1980, p. 61). This was, perhaps, the day I identified with charismatic bald writers. But John Davies's production of *The Winter's Tale* was my epiphany. This was not the first of the plays in which I acted. That was *As You Like It*; and it would be followed by sixth-form assaults on *Measure for Measure*, *Troilus and Cressida*, *King Lear*, *Cymbeline*, and a *Tempest* I directed. We had lost all sense of our own limitations. But it was the religious seriousness of John's *Winter's Tale* that made us believe our efforts were essential. Because it was itself so young, the Comprehensive ethos was always about Lawrence's 'glamour of childish days' (Lawrence, 1932, p. 1). Peter Coveney's *The Image of Childhood* was a set text. And while I only played the lord Antigonus, with a Bostik beard, I could glimpse in his *Winter's*

Tale that John's teaching was offering a lifetime of the same other-worldly self-importance:

> What we changed
> Was innocence for innocence. We knew not
> The doctrine of ill-doing, nor dreamed
> That any did. (1.2.70–3)

When I saw the film *Goodbye Lenin* I recognized the traffic-free Crawley of the 1960s in the GDR and its idealistic Pioneer Corps. The town was, after all, twinned with Eisenhüttenstadt (Stalinstadt), and at Thomas Bennett the most enthusing teachers were still Communists. So after I led our *TV Top of the Form* team, 'The captain would grace Eton', crowed the *Crawley Courier*. Into this class-less utopia John Davies's *Winter's Tale* seemed, however, to bring the continuities of the village England celebrated in the play's Bohemian pastoral. This was partly due to the fact that rehearsals were held at John's beamed cottage in Ifield, an actual village not yet eaten up by Crawley, where like the mysterious man in Mamillius's ghost story, he 'Dwelt by a churchyard' (2.1.33). It was also because John punctuated the play with a darkly lugubrious cello version of Mozart's Masonic Funeral Music, the repetition compulsion of which was meant to lead us back to somewhere authentically agrarian, like Eliot's loamy field where 'on a summer midnight' you can see them dancing in 'Mirth of those long since under the earth/Nourishing the corn' (Eliot, 2002, p. 185). I cannot now recall how all this organic rootedness was represented, except that there was a lot of foliage, and that the show was stopped by the lyricism of Perdita's aria about flowers Proserpina let fall 'From Dis's wagon' (4.4.118), which in the programme-note G. Wilson Knight informed us connected ethereal European culture to earthy English horticulture:

> You might call Perdita herself a seed sowed in winter and flowering in summer . . . Note the fine union, even identity, of myth and

contemporary experience. Dis may be classical, but his 'wagon' is as real as a wagon in Hardy. (Knight, 1965, p. 106)

'O, master, if you did but hear the pedlar at the door' (4.4.182): our budding Pope scholar did a side-splitting bumpkin, but the laughter had a lot to do with the double-take the play explored, of a peasant performed by a patrician. The planners had given aspiring New Towners the dream of growing beyond their neighbours, to just such 'an unspeakable estate' (4.2.35). But if I winced, it was because I could indeed hear the pedlar at the door, in the songs of my father, a commercial traveller like Autolycus, who had cycled the Sussex lanes in sun and rain, his hamper packed with trinkets in all the colours of Betterware. He had sung in the choir when *his* father swept the church before the War, and might have followed him as a gardener, growing prize carnations on one of the bankers' estates that fenced the forest when Crawley was a village. But he never kept up with a New Town, and instead poured life and soul into Crawley Ramblers, a cricket team that toured the Weald, capped with a rambling rose, before dropping dead at forty-four of athlete's coronary. 'Shiner Wilson' died content, claimed the *Courier*, having 'finally arranged a fixture at Arundel Castle'. My father was the last man I ever saw tug an imaginary forelock to imagined betters; yet decades later I was still hailed in 'Old Crawley' as 'Young Shiner', in tribute to this 'very good bowler' (*Love's Labour's Lost*, 5.2.573). They told me the fellows who cut the hay had driven their tractors to the Palace to try to stop the New Town. But if *The Winter's Tale* taught me about the 'ancient'st order' that kept the Duke in his castle, my father's wandering life ought to have alerted me to Shakespeare's equal insistence that once uprooted, these ramblers would never grow back: 'I witness to/The times that brought them in; so shall I do/To th' freshest things now reigning' (4.1.11–13).

When our Perdita wished she had told the king 'The selfsame sun that shines upon his court/Hides not his visage from our cottage' (4.4.432–3), I should have been struck by the irony that these lines were said by a daughter of an ambassador, and niece of a Greek film star famous for also playing peasants, who lived in one of those bankers' mansions. So was the beauty of her voice nature or nurture? As the courtier said, the 'report of her' was 'extended more than can be thought to begin' from such a setting (4.2.37–8). Camillo is 'reared' from 'meaner form' himself (1.2.315). But together with inhibitions, our Bohemian schooling had suppressed all awareness of class, race, or religion. My fellow actors had surnames like Levi, Steckelmacher and Wasserberg; not to mention Hughes, MacLean or O'Rourke. I will therefore never forget the shock on opening night of the concentration camp number on a father's arm. Yet we all shared the determination of Shakespeare's sheep-shearers not to darken the mirth of the feast with 'these forced thoughts', to 'Apprehend/Nothing but jollity' in our Sussex smocks. 'Golden Apollo' had become 'a poor humble swain', lectured the prince in the play (4.4.21, 24–5, 30). If Shakespeare's drama about opening up a stagnant, suspicious society resonated for us, can it have been, then, because we saw how its pastoralism chimed with the Apollonian dream of inclusion in a New Town? And if I overreacted to John Davies's Dionysian version, was that because I sensed Shakespeare was warning us this post-War accident of equal opportunity might be nothing but yet another Cinderella story of blue blood revived?

'We are, I think, forced to recognize a universal mystic significance in these final plays', intoned Wilson Knight in one of his Druidic sermons we recited at 'A' Level, as 'They represent symbolically the resurrection of that which *seems to die*, but is yet alive. . . there is not only loss in the tempest: there is revival, resurrection, to the sounds of music' (Knight, 1967, pp. 66–7). It was Knight's belief in rebirth which made him the uncritical critic for my generation, a literary Stanley Spencer, whose naïve nudism and unscholarly spiritualism could be read as prophetic of Flower Power. So, while the 'global village' erupted in the spring of 1968 with the thousand blooms of a different little red book, in Crawley we were rooting for daffodils that 'take the winds of March' (4.4.120). After such strange gods the Green Line might have carried us down some dark roads. It led me, for instance, to where Hilaire Belloc sang his anti-Semitic Sussex songs with men that were boys when he was a boy, at King's Land in the village of Shipley. I arrived at dusk, and the decrepitude of the poet's relics framed by candlelight cured me of his reactionary Catholic Distributism. Another trip was to Newbuildings, near Horsham, where an ancient Lady Lytton regaled our English Society with the legend of Ezra Pound's 'Peacock Dinner' for her grandfather, as she talked us through woods to his huntsman's tomb. *Et in Arcadia Ego*: Wilfrid Scawen Blunt's Byronic anti-imperialism was more to my political taste. But it was a pilgrimage to Virginia Woolf's Downland village of Rodmell that gave me my bearings on all this significant blood and soil.

Leonard Woolf had been dead a year when I walked into the garden of Monk's House one late summer afternoon. The scene was from a Woolf story, as children of the tenant (Saul Bellow, I later read) played Red Indians in a bonfire's smoke. An aged gardener was tipping papers on the flames, and to my surprise carting these from the sacred summer house. 'Mr Quentin Bell's taken all he wants', he coughed, 'the rest is rubbish'. I rescued a diary auditing every painting Leonard ever saw; but watched stunned as his wife's straw hat fell into the fire. Then, in roots where a tree had blown down, I wiped slime from some broken slabs and pieced them together. 'Beneath this tree lie the ashes of Virginia Woolf', read the reassembled tablet. These, then, were truly those 'Orts, scraps, and fragments' the novelist took from *Troilus and Cressida* (5.2.158–9) in *Between the Acts*, where she gave her character Lear's line: 'I fear that I am not in my perfect mind' (*Lear*, 4.7.64). Woolf's last novel was grounded in contemporary Sussex, and the pageant she had her Miss La Trobe direct was a response to the county's high-minded cultural Keynesianism, which was moving the pacifist Bishop Bell to commission her sister to daub murals in its churches, and would shortly infuse its schools. Glyndebourne lay in the background. Yet if *Between the Acts* was a fantasia on the country house culture that

had survived in these parts ever since the Earl of Southampton and
A Midsummer Night's Dream, what I experienced that September
day was the other Shakespearean process the novel described, when
words 'sank down into the mud':

> 'Mrs Manresa, if she'll allow me my old man's liberty, has her
> Shakespeare by heart.'
>
> 'Shakespeare by heart!' Mrs Manresa protested. She struck an
> attitude. 'To be, or not to be, that is the question. Whether 'tis
> nobler. Go on!' she nudged Giles, who sat next to her.
>
> 'The weariness, the torture, and the fret . . .' William Dodge
> added, burying the end of his cigarette in a grave between two
> stones. (Woolf, 1953, pp. 42, 147)

'Digging and delving', like the pageant in *Between the Acts*, John
Davies's *Winter's Tale* was devoted to 'the roots that clutch' (Eliot,
2002, p. 57). But in Virginia Woolf's ruined garden I had my les-
son in cultural uprooting. As Harris writes, Woolf describes a village which seems to be 'untouchable in its longevity', yet Mr Haines
'goes off home in his car to the "red villa in the cornfields"' (Harris,
2010, p. 190). And when I came back to this garden many years
later with Julia Briggs, she told me the novelist had herself thrilled
to the violence of 'Guy Fox [sic] days' in Lewes on November 5 (my
parents were 'Bonfire boys'): the pageant was both 'old and new:
its roots were in "the old play the peasants acted"', but it had to be
reinvented, because Woolf found the 'ancestral voices both seductive
and inhibiting' (Briggs, 2005, pp. 384–5). It had never occurred to
us in our country dancing that the bucolic sheep-shearing in *The
Winter's Tale* was similarly integrated into global history and the
cycles of world trade. Yet what I had stumbled into was a politics of
language that would shape my own work, its attempts to analyze a
Shakespeare both local and universal by combining 'high theory and
low archives'. In an episode itself cut from *Orlando*, Woolf, who read
the plays via the stream of consciousness in Montaigne, imagined

the prudish scholar burning 'Shakespeare's own account of his relations with Mr W. H.' (Briggs 2005, p. 201). But it was not until I
went up to York University, a few days after this Rodmell *auto-da-fé*,
that I began to feel the force of the critical storms that swirled about
these Pentecostal fires and fundamentalist roots.

My teacher John Davies preceded me to university, having been
appointed by York to a Lectureship in English and Education, so I
would have the odd Oedipal experience of observing the same tuto-
rial father-figure from eleven to graduation. Great was the grief at
Thomas Bennett when John was replaced by a chain-smoking Jim
McCabe from elitist Latymer Grammar, whose Elizabeth I impressions were considered no substitute for Elizabethan authenticity.
At his funeral, however, actor Alan Rickman praised Jim as 'clear-
sighted to the tumults of Shakespeare' (Rickman, 2007); and not for
nothing was his defining poem 'The Naming of Parts': 'The readi-
ness is all. How can I help but feel/I have been here before?' (Henry
Reed, *Lessons of the War*; quoted in Stallworthy, 1984, p. 257) So
the irony of the outsider was what this Peter Grimes brought to a
Comprehensive; with the realization which came with our loss of
innocence that we were part of something with a name, and this was
F.R. Leavis. Generations of York interviewees have quailed outside
the door bearing his initials; but Leavis's presence on campus was
heralded annually in the 1970s by student panic over the emaci-
ated tramp that police would then wryly identify as the illustrious
critic. This scarecrow fright was in keeping with York's claim to be
a Leavisite Cambridge in exile. The great discriminator had recently
announced he was no longer 'a loyal backer of the Liberal Party' due
to its support for Comprehensives; and his idea of a university in the
north was apparently as the 'Athens of the English-speaking world'
of which he dreamed.[1] But if he saw himself as a Socrates surrounded
by grammar school youths, it was strange that no less than eight
pupils from the despised Thomas Bennett were studying English at
York when I got there, including both Perdita and Camillo, and that
my first sighting of the embattled foe of Comprehensive education,

in the autumn twilight of 1970, was beside the plastic-bottomed lake on the arm of John Davies.

'Now you needn't be so *craven*', was how John greeted me at York. He was surely irked by the deference bound up in my sense of entitlement. But with his Welsh background, he had perhaps misread the 'badge of servility' which still defined the rural working class of Sussex, where my grandmother, born in Ringmer, might easily have gone into service in nearby Rodmell, and so contributed to what nettled Mrs Woolf about 'the problem of Nellie': that 'servants were affronted by change', and 'missed their old privileges and borrowed esteem' (Light, 2007, pp. 184 and 241). Such internalized paternalism was at odds with Keynesian meritocracy. But my family's feudal forelock-touching equipped me with a sharp angle, I now recognize, on the cringing contortions of Shakespearean theatre, in which 'Our bending author' (*Henry V*, Epi.2) is forever bowing and scraping at the door of the big house, yet 'our good [W]ill' (*Midsummer Night's Dream*, 5.1.108) ironizes himself as 'a gentleman born' (*Winter's Tale*, 5.2.116). 'You'll die apologizing', my teacher warned; but 'You've still got sap in you', he also liked to encourage, without noticing how this organicism affirmed 'The constant service of the antique world' (*As You Like It,* 2.3.58). Perry Anderson has described Leavisism as the product of just such a 'culture in contraflow', conflicted between reaction and revolution, as John personified, and that Q.D. Leavis betrayed when she sneered at Raymond Williams's *The Country and the City* for being typical of 'the scholarship boy who bites the hand from which he feeds' (Anderson, 1992, pp. 96–103).

In his elegy 'Seeing a man running', Raymond Williams described the sense of betrayal when Leavisism split between its Left and Right tendencies, as its leader tore off on his lone fight against a rootless 'mass' culture, 'his face set hard in the effort' (see Williams, 1984, p. 122, and Anderson 1992, p. 103). The great critic of organicism admitted he had been slow to see Leavis's rightward lurch, since it was driven not by any constructive program, nor even nostalgia, but *despair* over the lost organic community. Likewise, Michael Bell has argued that perceptions of Leavis as a conservative were belied by 'his support, during most of his life, of the Liberal Party' (Bell, 1988, p. 54). Bell obviously never met the Poujadist wing of the old Liberals. But I had just endured precisely this regressive fraction, canvassing Sussex villages with a pig-farming Liberal candidate to the right the National Front, and knew its *ressentiment* to be fixated on Comprehensive schools. Soon it would realign around another flinty East Midlander named Thatcher. So, while others have spoken of Leavis's York period as a tranquil coda, I recall my horrified fascination as he railed against the BBC, the Welfare State, the Open University ('an exalted subsidized correspondence college'), Sunday papers: the entire Keynesian 'Technological Benthamite civilization', in fact, which had made me what I was. Suddenly I understood I was one of those, like William Dodge, who in the Cambridge phrase, 'would not do'. I was now an extra in this epic psychomachia, as with kamikaze mischief Leavis denounced his own disciples, mumbled compound imprecations against his discipline, and hacked the branch on which he sat. Although only those squeezed on the front row at his lectures could hear his waspish asides, I got close enough to be stung, therefore, by his appropriation of Shakespeare:

> Shakespeare had an immeasurably great influence upon English but couldn't have done so had he not inherited in it a rich, supple and exquisitely vital language . . . (although Shakespeare was notoriously *not* a classical or an English don) . . . a subject on which a first year man reading 'English' could write at least a page or two. (Leavis, 1969, pp. 41 and 67)

When I played Timon for York University Drama Society, my gold loincloth was justified by Wilson Knight's homoerotic reading; but it was Leavis who cued my rant as the Athenian who turns his gifts to stones. For the rhetorical trick with which he simultaneously invited and refused discussion, with 'This is so, is it not?', was the switch to a critical closed circuit, which seemed to offer communion only to snatch it back by dictating what the community should be. From *The Waste Land* and I. A. Richards Leavis had absorbed the modernist shock that *language speaks*; but also the anti-modern backlash that its meaning can be fixed by the response it generates in the 'right reader' (Richards, 1924, p. 87). Harris links his resulting 'back to the village' mentality, with its invocation of a country life in which craftsmen were drawn 'ever closer to England', to the folksy ruralism of the Studio Pottery he collected (Harris, 2010, pp. 179–82; Leavis/ Thompson, 1932, p. 85). But it was his assent to Oswald Spengler's lament that civilized man is 'homeless' which prompted his angst in his 1932 *Culture and Environment* that 'the organic community has gone. Its destruction (in the West) is the most important fact' (see MacKillop, 1995, p. 204; Leavis/Thompson, 1932, p. 87). And this cry of existential homelessness suggests a more troubling framework for his reactionary modernism, with its anti-intellectual jargon of authenticity, cult of manual labour, and mythology of the purified group. Leavis's affinity with that other long-distance athlete Martin Heidegger is discussed by Bell as if sharing essentialist notions of language can be separated from politics (see Bell, 1988, pp. 35–54; Storer, 2009, pp. 26, 40, 132). Yet either could have written 'Why Do I Stay in the Provinces?' (see Sheehan, 1981). And their kinship is pungent in the English critic's *Sprachmystik* about Shakespeare in his polemic 'Joyce and the Revolution of the Word', which he published in the ominous year of 1933:

> The study of a Shakespeare play must begin with the words; but it was not there that Shakespeare – the great Shakespeare – started: the words matter because they lead down to what they came from . . . he incarnated the genius of the language – to the utmost. And what this position of advantage represents . . . is the general advantage he enjoyed in belonging to a genuinely national culture . . . A national culture rooted in the soil (Leavis, 1933, pp. 194, 199).

'He gives new meaning to what it is to be provincial', glinted John Davies, as we emerged from one of Leavis's jeremiads. Yet, with what 'wily strategy he used the term "provincialism" in a positive sense', as Adorno observed of Heidegger's similar ideology of the earth (Adorno, 2003, p. 43). In fact, Dr. Leavis had written his thesis on journalism in seventeenth-century London, where his golden world was *urban*, focused on the coffee-house as 'a nerve-centre of communication' (MacKillop, 1995, p. 72). But by the time I sat in on his chilly dawn seminars at York, often with just a Shelley-like ephebe destined for Orders ('my best students are all Jesuits'), we were required to scan his dreaded dating-sheets for morbid signs of 'coffee-house tittle-tattle'. The Savonarola of the Ouse had long perfected this method of 'textual harassment' to discriminate authentic Shakespeare 'from the Shakespearean-ish' (see Armstrong, 2000, ch.3; MacKillop, 1995, p. 76). Indeed his biographer traces his hostility to the metropolis, and conversion of Shakespeare into a horny-handed countryman, whose 'strength belongs to the very spirit of the language – the spirit that was formed when the English people was predominantly rural', to his trauma of 1931 when he lost the Cambridge promotion race to the Bloomsbury thespian Dadie Rylands. But the call to order in all his titles – *Mass Civilization and Minority Culture, New Bearings in English Poetry, Revaluation, The Common Pursuit* (of *true* judgement) – was in lockstep with the graver turn in European politics. And read in the light of Heidegger's concurrent Nazification of Hölderlin as the originary national poet, in whose 'word, unveiled being is placed in the truth of the people', Leavis's ruralization of Shakespearean language takes on an alarming *völkisch* flavour:[2]

> The countryman's life and language grow together: they are like flesh and bone ... And how much richer the *life* was in the old, predominantly rural order ... When one adds that speech in the old order was a popularly cultivated art, that people talked (so making Shakespeare possible) instead of reading or listening to the wireless, it becomes plain that the promise of regeneration by American slang,

popular city-idiom or the invention of transition-cosmopolitans is a flimsy consolation for our loss. (Leavis, 1933, p. 200)

'One would like to know the farmers' opinion about that', as Adorno tartly remarked of Heidegger's equivalent claims for the 'philosophical work' of agricultural labourers (Adorno, 2003, p. 43). I doubt that the author of *The Critic as Anti-Philosopher*, who scorned theory, ever read *Being and Time*. But Leavis's fantasies about 'lived experience' now sound so like German existentialism they cast a sinister shadow over this talk of rootless 'transition-cosmopolitans'. 'I'm not Jewish', he would protest if his name was mispronounced, which even then seemed odd, coming from the husband of Queenie Roth. More worryingly, I now see, he had shifted Richards's definition of the poet as 'the point at which the growth of the mind shows itself' to make a poet the 'most conscious point of the race'.[3] The myth of the poet as *Führer*, who uncovers the hidden origins of the race, came to Heidegger from the 'Secret Germany' of Stefan George. And Leavis's doxa that the 'leader-poet' is 'more alive than other people', because he enacts the 'sinew and living nerve of English', flirted with similar occultism; indeed his word for such verbal instinct was the German *Ahnung*. So not for nothing was his still centre Sturt's wheelwright's shop, where the oak hub was said to be the swastika-like symbol of 'a mystery. . . residing in the folk collectively'; like that 'wheel of fire' in Wilson Knight's 1930 book on the tragedies.[4] This misty thinking explains the anomaly that while he was constantly gesturing towards 'Shakespearean' language, he wrote so little about the plays themselves, and then mainly on passages: '*Me* – on Shakespeare!' he once exclaimed in disbelief (See Mackillop, 1995, pp. 174, 215; and Newton, 1965, pp. 144–77). For Leavis, Shakespeare remained an invisible *poet*, rather than a playwright, insuring his position as the prophet of national crisis, the role conferred in *Twilight and Italy* by Lawrence himself:

The King, the Emperor is killed in the soul of man, the old order of life is over, the old tree is dead at the root. So said Shakespeare.

It was finally enacted in Cromwell. Charles I took up the old position of kingship by divine right. Like Hamlet's father, he was blameless otherwise. But as representative of the old form of life, which mankind now hated with frenzy, he must be cut down, removed. It was a symbolic act. (Lawrence, 1934, p. 130)

'There *has* been such a change,' Leavis told us in his lectures; 'And is it obviously absurd to suppose that one finds the crisis of it registered in Shakespeare?' (Leavis, 1969, p. 157) 'Hamlet and Lawrence were Leavis's York preoccupations', records Ian MacKillop; and it is easy to see why the sketch of the provincial performance in *Twilight in Italy* proved so powerful in arming his '*crème de la crème*', the 'minority that still matters', with 'tips and propaganda' about 'how brutally political, practical and menacing the realities are that present themselves as zeal for that basic matter: reform in the field of education' (see MacKillop, 1995, pp. 368, 389; Leavis, 1968, repr. in MacKillop, 1995, p. 389). The 'crawling slinking' Hamlet at Lago di Garda is a sad fool in Lawrence's book, 'a creeping, unclean thing' with his 'nasty poking and sniffing'. He is 'the modern Italian, suspicious, isolated, self-nauseated', in contrast to the peasant audience, 'who have the life of the village in their hands', and applaud wildly as he dies: 'a living, vigorous, physical host of men' (Lawrence, 1934, pp. 122–3, 139, 142). So, for Leavis, this village *Hamlet* became an image not just of a threatened folk-community, but of the university itself, as it was being converted into 'an industrial plant'; and to counteract 'the appalling "educational" output' of this academic 'heavy industry', he urged Heinemann to reprint the prequel, where Lawrence depicted Shakespeare 'morbid with fear' of syphilis. 'I *had* thought of writing a commentary, and shall be *talking* one next academic year', he assured his editor.[5] In the event, however, the tricky task of relating Lawrence's theory about Shakespeare's syphilis to British education fell to John Davies, as Leavis' York 'liaison agent'.

When John cited the passage on Shakespeare and King Charles's head in his *Lawrence on Hardy and Painting*, he put it beside another from *Twilight in Italy* about 'Fifty million children growing up with no purpose save the attainment of their own individual desires', due to our 'will towards self-reduction and a perfect society' (Davies, 1973, pp. 5, 163, n.4). Davies had been recruited for York by Harry Rée, Resistance hero and Comprehensive proselyte. Thus the tale-teller of Thomas Bennett became my Personal Tutor. But in his only publication, Shakespeare figured as a witness for Leavis against the entire Comprehensive vision. Perhaps I had seen this coming when John set us Lawrence's *Hamlet* chapter at school, and in an earnest historicist effort, I criticized its 'proto-fascism'. This would not be the last of what he called my 'highfalutin comparisons'. But now, however, his depression at the 'drift of European civilization shown by Lawrence's discussion of *Hamlet*' marked a parting of our ways, not only over the novelist, but the dramatist; itself a sign of alienation from his master's voice in my media-savvy York genera-tion, which included the likes of Greg Dyke, Anthony Horowitz, and Linda Grant (Davies, 1973, p. 2). For Leavis liked to boast how, when Olivier wrote to thank him for his *Othello* essay, he slapped the insolent mummer down. But as he snorted at actors, he seemed una-ware most of us were aiming for TV or theatre, and that under stage-struck Philip Brockbank, York was evolving into a training-camp for Shakespeareans, where every junior lecturer seemed to be editing an Arden. Though I cherish letters about my *Timon* and *Troilus and Cressida* from the great Miltonist Patrides, Leavis never noticed this theatrical life. And nor, to my disappointment, did John Davies.

Leavis famously ended his last Cambridge lecture murmuring Othello's 'Put out the light' (5.2.7), to thunderous applause as he turned off the lamp. At York, too, his lectures remained set-pieces, in which disgust with Hamlet flowed into distaste for Eliot ('A pile of ash this high when he left'), while the soliloquies that passed for semi-nars crackled with the staccato of his machine-gun dispatch: '"Black beetles" Lawrence called Bloomsbury. But then he was not in the habit of soliciting guardsmen. Wittgenstein saw through them. He was a whole man'. 'Don't interpret', the philosopher had, however, barked. And it was interpretation that earned Leavis' rebuke the one time I performed in his presence. The occasion was a concert reading, when his flat Fenland recital of 'Ash Wednesday' – 'This is the land. We have our inheritance' (Eliot, 2002, p. 85) – was followed by 'The Waste Land' done in 'different voices', and he stood shaking his head throughout my rending of the 'Ferdinand' parts. I still see his shaking head whenever I lecture today. For the modernism we were imbibing at York meant taking texts out of such history into a timeless contemporaneity, where they were to be 'set spatially in the mind', as *The Wheel of Fire* prescribed (Knight, 1930, p. 3; see also Grady, 1991, pp. 98–112). So the purest Leavisite approach to Shakespeare was achieved not by any production of Y.U.D.S., in its draughty Drama Barn, I now appreciate, but by the spaced-out flower-child who reduced John's seminar to wondering silence, as she smilingly unfolded her 'presentation' on *The Winter's Tale*: a fantastic origami tree, which as it slowly spread far out, sprung some aptly budding quotation about 'great creating nature' (4.4.88) on every paper leaf.

'O, master, if you did but hear the pedlar at the door': *The Winter's Tale* was confirming Wilson Knight's theory of eternal recurrence, as David Thacker rehearsed us in the Drama Barn. Thacker would become well-known for his mixed-race Shakespeare at the Young Vic. So now a South African postgraduate was coaching us in Zulu dance, as the Old Shepherd marvelled at how 'featly' his daughter stamped (4.4.178). I had been promoted to Polixenes; and was urging Perdita to plant carnations, and not to call them bastards, in face of her high-born distrust: 'I'll not put/The dibble in earth to set one slip.' (4.4.99–100) Autolycus was about to imitate Bob Dylan, who the lapsed Leavisite Wilfrid Mellers told us was a reincarnation of Shakespeare. Instead, the Barn door flew open and John Davies entered, like some Shakespearean constable, to march me off to submit my thesis before I was suspended. Thus it seems prophetic that his final paternal intervention in my life was on behalf of a system John detested, given that Leavis' warnings about the 'industrial university' have all since come true. For who today would deny the critic had been right to rage that 'to debase "research"' with utilitarian 'assessment exercises' is 'to deprive the "community" of an essential element of life' (Leavis, 1969, p. 195)? But even Shakespeare could not underwrite Leavis' idea of a university. And so John would retire early to Wales. 'They think I'm just a Leavisite crank', he protested; yet 'there's more going in Aber than meets the eye'. We heard he threw himself from a bridge. I last saw him, shattered by the 1980s counter-revolution his hero had incited, one raw winter evening in Trafalgar Square. He refused a drink. 'I'm here for Annie Fischer's farewell recital', he murmured wonderingly, as he hurried towards the river and the night.

It had seemed like spring in Bohemia, but it was later than we thought. So, 'Bringing in the harvest, bringing in the sheaves', we sang, as the flower-strewn coffin of Wilson Knight was carried into Exeter's spiritualist chapel. I had invited the great Shakespearean to Lancaster soon after I was appointed there (by predestination, the same day as Crawley's critic of Pope). 'Tarzan of Athens' was eighty-five (see Van Domelen, 1987). But he stayed a week with his performance, in which he stripped to his underpants as Lear, then discarded these for Timon, to strike a pose as Solar Man. Every inch the caped Edwardian actor-manager, he was visited nightly, he confided, by Shelley, with blessings from the Bard. He also promised he would remain forever beside me, as his name was George *Richard Wilson* Knight! 'Richard has graduated to a higher school', the minister at his funeral therefore joyfully announced. Knowing how he was rejected by the Shakespeare establishment, I assume it must be a Comprehensive. For in the end there *was* an elective affinity between this perverse Leavisite pilgrimage and the New Town where we learned the meaning of a village. Both turned out to be far more inclusive than was planned. So the lychgate donated by the poet Blunt which stood beside my grandfather's grave has long since gone the way of the demolished Thomas Bennett. Yet in the church he swept an elderly Punjabi resident tells me about Crawley's roots.

'Like a weather-bitten conduit' (5.2.49), he has lived here since 1970. But now everything has changed, he says: 'We all knew each other then. No one locked their doors. Crawley was a village'. 'I grow, I prosper' (*King Lear*, 1.2.21): who chose the New Town's motto? Perhaps it was Sir Thomas Bennett. Whoever did so surely had a sense of irony, seeing how aptly Shakespeare concludes: 'Now, gods, stand up for bastards!'

Notes

1. Leavis, 1974, p. 98 and Leavis, 1943, p. 11; see also, Leavis, 1969, p. 30.
2. MacKillop, 1995, pp. 72, 76, 128; Leavis 1933, p. 200; Martin Heidegger 'Hölderlins Hymnen "Germanien" und "Der Rhein"', quoted in Faye, 2009, p. 104.
3. Richards, 1924, p. 55; Leavis, 1932, p. 17. This significant shift is noted by MacKillop 1995, pp. 111 and 202–3.
4. See Leavis/Thompson, 1932, p. 79; and Knight, 1930. For the *völkisch* poetic symbolism of the swastika, see Faye, 2009, pp. 108–10.
5. Leavis, 1970, quoted in MacKillop, 1995, pp. 378 and 389; D.H. Lawrence, 'Introduction to These Paintings', in Davies, 1973, p. 129.

Chapter 7

My Language!

Thomas Docherty

The first time I read Shakespeare was in August 1967. The first play was *A Midsummer Night's Dream*. I was twelve, having just entered the second year of my secondary schooling at St Mungo's Academy, Glasgow. The school was run by Jesuits of the Marist Order and its main aim, grounded in a sense of charitable mission, was to give a Catholic education to the under-privileged boys of Townhead, a working-class area of tenements whose people were marked by a high degree of economic poverty. In addition, though, the school also admitted a small number of boys from elsewhere in Glasgow – often, in fact, from even more disadvantaged areas – through a scheme that allowed the Jesuits to cream off what it saw as academic talent at age 11; and these boys were to be given a more advanced academic education. I was one of these, joining the school from the east end of Glasgow initially in August 1966. For those of us who were selected in this way, school was already 'marked' in the sense that it was equated with ideas of escape, primarily the escape from poverty through a good education. Shakespeare, as I discovered in 1967, was supposed to form part of that education.

In what follows here, I want to explore how it is that I moved from what was my initial profound dislike of Shakespeare – more than, and different from, stereotypical schoolboy griping. How did I move from such dislike of *A Midsummer Night's Dream* that autumn, to an entirely different point of view, now, as one who 'professes' literature and who thinks something of Shakespeare probably quite literally every day? The route, insofar as I can reconstruct it from memory however, is rather indirect – or it will at first appear so. We will pass from Parkhead in the working-class east end of Glasgow, via Lisbon and Paris, to my present position. On the road, we will find out what Shakespeare might mean to one who teaches and thinks about English and other literatures: me. The Shakespeare who emerges is different from the Shakespeare of 1967, obviously; and so am I different and still differing, sensing this differing as something that stems from Shakespeare and that is equated in my mind with a kind of freedom.

A Dream of Availability

Why did Mr McDermott, our English teacher, decide to start with *A Midsummer Night's Dream*? What is it that makes this play so often the first play that schoolchildren read or study when they encounter Shakespeare? After all, although a comedy, it is actually a rather difficult play. It involves, among other things, fairies who seem keen on child abduction, a nether-world that parallels the real world, an Indian boy who is stolen by fairies and then fought over, the usual Shakespearean troubled parenthood and childhood, with anxiety-driven relations between fathers and daughters, a queen playing about with ideas of bestiality, a self-reflexive play-within-play motif, gender and class troubles and so on.

Perhaps needless to say, this is not how it is usually presented to a twelve-year-old; or, at least, it is not entirely how it was presented to me. Rather, this play was essentially to be viewed as a harmless comedy, a romp of sorts, through which a moral message about love, duty, and a social order of things was to be conveyed. In this reading, the central character is always Bottom; and he is followed closely by Puck. From the point of view of Bottom, it is a comedy of character: the man is an ass, and Shakespeare is showing him up as such, but in an affectionate manner. Puck is slightly more devilish, or mischievous: a prankster-director whose practical joking makes for comic difficulties in which he finds himself having to resolve complications of his own making.

Who might find these kinds of thing *available* at the age of twelve or so? I think it is fair to say that there were some governing assumptions going on in the distribution of this play to the allegedly academically gifted in a selective intake school. Those assumptions might have held true for some readers, but not for others; and, where they held true, the play would have been more easily and readily accessible than it would be for those – among whom I number myself and my classmates – for whom the assumptions were simply false.

Imagine a certain kind of childhood, where the house you live in stands alone, apart from other houses, and enjoys a good deal of space. Imagine, further, that your parents actually own it and the land on which it stands. Outside, there is a garden, where you have domesticated parts of a wilder nature. Inside, you have your own room. Maybe there are books in your room, for there certainly are books elsewhere in the house. At night, your parents do not seem to be exhausted; but have time and energy to read to you. They read from books of fairy-tales, perhaps, or romances that involve princes whose wealth, while greater than that of your parents, is not different in kind. Here, heritage will be important; for love-relations will probably be tied to land or power, and will certainly be tied to questions of authority. Here, moreover, people may seem to change partners, their amorous commitments being somehow more open, more liberal. In this household, in some cases, children go away from home for long periods, to be cared for by others while living together in a kind of nether-world, the childhood-world, of a dormitory. The child brought up in such an environment has a way in to *A Midsummer Night's Dream* simply in terms of a certain set of expectations of what one does with its story and language.

Now imagine something different, even opposite to that described above: a house in a tenement block shared with seven or more other families; the house rented from the council, not owned; no private space and certainly no garden; noise of neighbours above, below, beside you; not many books, if any; parents working overtime, sometimes in hard physical labour, maybe weaving or as joiners, carpenters and the like, and not having endless reserves of energy to read to their children; and so on. The child of this house, Bottom's house, has to find or make an entirely different route into the play, for there are probably no normative expectations at all regarding what one does with its story, its language, its problems. The play is simply less *available* to this child; or, at best, it is available in entirely different ways. This child reader of the play is 'located' by the norms and expectations that are taken as standard by the more advantaged child described above, in ways that that more advantaged child is not.

In short, then: *A Midsummer Night's Dream* is offered *not* to all eleven- or twelve-year-olds; rather, it is understood that a certain kind of twelve-year-old is the norm; and the play is set in the curriculum for her or him. The interesting issue here is what happens when you take the second kind of child, and treat him as if he were of the first. This is one part of the background to my engagement with Shakespeare. My dislike of Shakespeare was not at all dislike of the play, even if I thought it was: in fact, I couldn't *read* the play at that time. Perhaps I still can't. I do not wish to make the issue of class central to the presentation of my predicament here; yet I will stick with it for one moment longer, to suggest something that I did learn about how we read Bottom.

Bottom is, of course, a hugely interesting character. The play mocks him in some ways for his sense of self-importance; but we are certainly never encouraged to despise him. On the contrary, Bottom is probably the most well-liked of the characters for any audience. Why is that so? The man is an ass, certainly and at one point literally so. Although he has a little learning, he does not wear it as well as the lords and ladies, Helena and Hermia, or Lysander and Demetrius, whose very names indicate that they are at home in the foundational myths of entire civilizations. He is aspirant as well; and, although he shows himself up, it would be wrong – the play seems to suggest – for us to mock such a person. They may be asses, but it is not their own fault that they are thus. My contention is that the point of view that thinks thus sits more comfortably in my first childhood scenario than it does in my second. And, who am I – child of that second scenario – who am I, I think as I read this play? Am I not also an aspirant, not-yet well-enough educated person; isn't my mother a tailor, like Starveling; and isn't my new best friend's father a joiner, like Snug; my neighbour at home a carpenter, like Quince? If I mock this Bottom, however gently, what am I doing in relation to my founding environment? What values am I starting to imbibe here?

When the education authorities set this play as a set text for eleven- and twelve-year olds in the 1960s, they had in mind a very specific audience: the benignly conservative middle-classes. And, when my school set it for us, they were inculcating us into the norms of that audience. For me, it was an exercise in dealing with certain kinds of unfamiliar value-systems. The school streamed and set its classes: 1:A1 was the 'advanced' first-year class; and we heard speak of the legendary 1:Z10 where the boys did not have the chance to read Shakespeare. Instead, those in this 'bottom' set engaged in things like woodwork or joinery and so on while we, in 2:A1, read plays about, well, joiners and woodworkers, Bottoms, Snugs, Quinces and the like. The setting of the play in the curriculum was part of a structure that established a social organization in terms of a stratified, sedimented and layered society.

I don't want to make too much of this, except to say that the educational thinking that lay behind the setting of Shakespeare for us is a mode of thinking that persists and lingers to the present time, despite the many critiques made of it all through the 1970s and 1980s. Education, if anything, has become *more* a matter of socialization than ever before; and its politicization is, of course, now more and more explicit. Part of the shift in my attitude to Shakespeare over the years came about by my realizing – and this is partly due to this first engagement with his work – that the plays might help offer a critique as well as an endorsement of established social orders. That is what I need now to show.

Mr McDermott, then, came into the classroom armed with the books for the year's work. Top of the pile was *A Midsummer Night's Dream*. We knew that this was the serious business, more serious than the J. Meade Faulkner *Moonfleet* that followed. Had I known about Bourdieu, I would have understood issues of cultural capital. If we were indeed to make it in the world (whatever that meant, probably that notional escape from poverty), then we'd need to get on top of this, to get Shakespeare under the belt. The book looked unattractive: the edition was 'the Junior School Shakespeare' edition. To my amazement, when I received my own copy, there was already a familiar name – not just that of Shakespeare – inside it. It was traditional for many pupils to write their name on the inside cover of their books, so that, often, you'd receive a book with about a dozen names all inside, all scored through except the last one. I myself preferred not to do that: I already had a fetishistic respect for the material object of the book which prevented me somehow from writing in it. Yet this copy had obviously been sitting in the school cupboard, untouched, for about a decade.

The name inside was that of my own brother, who had gone through the school ten years before I did. There he was: his name, his class. He had also signed the book about half-way through, with a flashy autograph that he was obviously trying to perfect. He had left a little graffiti on the pages and, tellingly, on the inside back cover, the details of his financial position. It was not good. He owed a friend 6/11d (six shillings and eleven pence: about 35p in today's money, but a huge sum in 1957, when he had the book); he owed my sister 7d (about 3p), my other brother 2/(two shillings: 10p). His total position was a debt of some 9/6 (47p or so). These would have been extremely significant sums for an eleven-year old in 1957. As I sat there, I thought that these figures might help to explain why he had decided not only to abandon Shakespeare and any further midsummer night's dreaming, but also to leave school just a further year on, in 1959, following my father into the shipyards where he could make some money to help clear his debts.

And now, I still have the book in my possession. At the end of that year, Mr McDermott was more lax than he ought to have been about collecting the texts back in. I could have taken it into school and made sure it was returned; but I didn't. Instead, I kept it. Given that I hated Shakespeare – indeed the whole Shakespeare experience – so vigorously, it is interesting that I nonetheless stole this small piece of cultural capital, which detailed the lack of economic capital that helped determine my brother's life, but which also determined my own life very differently.

Mr McDermott struggled to get us to engage with the opening scene where Theseus tells Hippolyta that 'our nuptial hour/Draws on apace. . . but, O, methinks, how slow/The old moon wanes! She lingers my desires,/Like to a step-dame or a dowager/Long withering out a young man's retinue'.

'Why is it "like to", sir? Why not just "like"?'
'It's needed for the scansion.'
'. . .'
'Scansion,' he repeated.
'What's that, sir?'
'The rhythm of the lines. The beat.'
'Rhythm?'

'Yes: five beats to the line. Pentameter. Hasn't Mr McConville started you off on this in the Latin class yet?' We were beginning to 'read' Virgil's *Aeneid*, Book 2. 'You know,' he went on, 'dactyls, spondees, trochees, all that malarkey.'

We groaned. But two things were being driven home: first, the ostensibly unwelcome news that English could be as foreign as Latin; and secondly, more positively, that there was a semiotic aspect to language – rhyme, rhythm, sound – that helped carry the semantics. Needless to say, we hadn't a clue what was going on – yet.

Mr McDermott had to demonstrate, putting the stresses in, in an exaggerated fashion: 'Four DAYS will QUICKly STEEP themSELVES in NIGHT,' he sang, his hand cutting the air with each beat or stress.

We started to sing along, making fun of the text and emptying it of whatever semantic content it had had under our steady beat. We could make neither head nor tail of the text; but it sang to us in some way. Then, scene two comes along, and we're in prose, not singing. This, of course, is the realm of the workers. This is where the complications start for us. These workers are recognizable, given that we are all from such working families. Yet, the play is presenting them as odd in some way, as an anomalous deviation from certain norms that have been set up in the opening. Above all, this is a question of language: while the opening scenes were incomprehensible semantically to us, we at least found a solace in the regularity of their semiotic aspects. Here, we are among people whom we should recognize, but it is their language that is alienating us all the more, now that we have been given a means of grasping the opening scene with its rhythmic verse.

It is not the case that we had some strong class allegiance that made us feel insulted or anything of the kind. Rather, the difficulty is that we understood so little of what was going on. We also knew that we were in the presence of high art, a high art that was to become part of our identity through our acquisition of it as cultural capital. Thus, the linguistic difficulties that we have here become redeemable, in that we see that we are not yet adequate to the text. In short, what is going on, as I now understand (but at the time only vaguely felt), is that we are about to become mildly alienated from our backgrounds: we were to start to become the norm, singing along, five beats to the line, as we prepared ourselves to assume the commanding roles of the normative verse-speakers. The singing was more important than it had first seemed after all: it gave us a solidarity, even the identity to be found in a mindless solidarity, such as we knew and recognized from Saturday afternoons at football matches.

Yet I resisted. The play was about fairies, but my objections to it had nothing to do with the subject-matter, which I simply didn't understand. My objection, voiced loudly in class discussion, was about the language, which I described as 'flowery'. Why did Shakespeare have to go all round the houses in saying whatever it was that the characters had to say? I had so little understanding of the operations of poetry, so little awareness of the history of the language, that I simply would not believe Mr McDermott when he suggested that the language I was reading here was somehow readily understood by an earlier audience. He conceded readily that ordinary folk didn't speak like the characters in the play – not even those working weavers and joiners. The language was contrived, certainly – 'poetic', he called it, even in the prose passages. However, he maintained that the language did not occlude the sense for Shakespeare's audience, for his contemporaries; and that it should therefore, in principle, be understood by us.

To the extent that we did manage to glean some understanding of the subject-matter (admittedly not much), again we found reason to object. The driving force in our education – why we had given up our friendships in our locality to attend this school – was aligned to a sense of growing sophistication. We were about progress, especially progress as achieved through the intellect and reason. We were certainly not at this school to read fairy-tales or to be seduced by the irrational world of this play. The play was rank with superstition: by contrast, we were entering the realms of science and analysis, a realm that rejected the world of fairy as something childish, and unsophisticated.

So we began the process of analysis, admittedly in a naive fashion. We turned to the characters we found interesting, especially Bottom. We knew we were supposed to laugh at him, in his earnest desire to be the most important and the most noticed of the actors, in his keen eagerness to be in a lead role and so to be someone, to be noticed and to feel he *exists*. Yet we already had a double attitude to him, partly given by the language problem. As we tried to paraphrase, we began less to laugh *at Bottom* and more to laugh *with Shakespeare*, we felt, as he encouraged us to laugh *with Bottom*. We looked closely at them as they prepare to rehearse in Act 3, scene 1. There, their concern is about illusion, and about the possibility that they will upset their audience, especially the ladies. In what is actually a sophisticated discussion of the theatrical *bienséances*, we are invited to laugh *with* these characters at ourselves, at the possibility that we can be deluded by mere theatre. Importantly for my present case, the other major element of comedy in this and other scenes is the malapropism. As the characters say the opposite of what they mean, we see their own struggles with language; and we recognized those struggles, for they are the struggles of people who are aspiring to escape from their everyday circumstances, and to identify themselves with another class of people. Like us schoolboys, they know a little; and they strive to know more. The key to their elevation and freedom will be the mastery of a language, of the adoption of a role that is, for the moment, beyond their capabilities. We were watching ourselves. Given this, and given that we were laughing, we were also learning a fundamental rule of critical analysis: the avoidance of pomposity, the avoidance of an unjustified self-assurance, the avoidance – in short – of the kind of judgements practised by the lords and ladies of the play.

Thus, we began to learn that Shakespeare, while certainly a major element in an arrangement by which social order was to be maintained, also gave us a way into criticize that order, even as we were entering it. In a word: he gave us the possibility of difference. Needless to say, at the time, we did not use this kind of language to describe what was going on; but it was important to us that we found such a way to do two things: first, to deal with our discomfort when we saw the rude mechanicals; secondly, to find a means of engaging with questions of language, comprehension and misapprehension.

A detour

At the time, however, we had other things on our minds, things that seemed infinitely more important than all this.

The single greatest event of 1967, as we all know, took place on 25 May that year, in Lisbon, Portugal: Glasgow Celtic, effectively a local team from Parkhead in the east of the city, won the football European Cup, the first British team ever to do so, beating the famed Italian side, Inter-Milan, 2-1. The event was important because it was not simply a game of football. It will sound pretentious to claim, but this match was part of a series of historical and ideological events of some magnitude that would lead to attempted political revolutions across Europe just one year later, in the famed *événements* of May 1968. More locally, it was also a formative event in terms of my relations to culture, to language, to my schooling and to Shakespeare.

We should not forget that Shakespeare himself knew about football, a game that, in his time as in ours provoked strong responses from the public. Dromio of Ephesus, kicked around in *The Comedy of Errors* by Adriana, protests, asking

> Am I so round with you, as you with me,
> That like a football you do spurn me thus?
> You spurn me hence, and he [Antipholus] will spurn me hither:
> If I last in this service, you must case me in leather. (2.1.81–4)

Yet more directly, Kent, in *King Lear*, commits a professional foul or, more precisely, a 'sandwich tackle', with Lear himself, on Oswald. When Lear strikes the brazen Oswald, Oswald objects, saying 'I'll not be strucken', to which Kent replies, tripping him up, 'Nor tripp'd neither, you base football player' (1.4.73–4). Perhaps more relevant to the upcoming revolutionary spirit of May 1968 was Camus, the goalkeeper, who famously asserted that all that he had ever learned that was of value in the field of ethics and human relationships, he learned from football. His Algerian descendant, Derrida, whose own thinking was to prove so revolutionary in the field of literary criticism, also had dreams, like my friends and I in Glasgow, of becoming a professional footballer. Like him, 'we would play until the dead of night, I dreamt of becoming a professional player' (Bennington/ Derrida, 1991, p. 313).

What happened in Lisbon that day in 1967 was part of a spirit of the times; and it was to affect the core of my own literary and critical development. Revolution was already in the air, and the match was a part of it; but, for us in St Mungo's Academy, a very special part and very pertinent to us. As many will know, Glasgow at the time was riven by religious division and bigotry: traditionally, Roman Catholics supported Celtic (a team established by priests in the working-class community in 1888); and Protestants supported Rangers. The boys in my school were, for the most part, passionate supporters of Celtic, football being the main component of our mental and physical activity every day. But what was at stake was not just the destination of the European Cup; rather, what was at stake was an entire attitude to life. Inter-Milan were famous for their extraordinary success, grounded in a system of play that was based on solid defence: the system of *catenaccio* devised by their manager Helenio Herrera. Their back line of four (novel at the time, but more or less standard now), with an additional sweeper, was impenetrable; and they depended on ensuring that the opposition could not score. The opposition, unable to score, would grow frustrated and impatient, allow concentration in their own defensive lines to lapse; at which point the Inter-Milan sweeper would push the ball forward, releasing and launching the solitary attacking move of their game in which they would score. 1-0 was the usual result. It was dull, the dourest and cynical pragmatism; but it was effective, machine-like in its near-industrial grinding-out of victories.

By contrast, Celtic were making a reputation for adventurous play. Their manager, Jock Stein, was a man who saw the romance of ambition. His team were all more or less exclusively born within a couple of miles of Celtic Park (Paradise, as it was known to supporters); and so this was essentially a local team, drawn from the tenements, almost like the scratch-teams that played all over Glasgow on Saturday mornings. They played as if they had nothing to lose, but were willing to risk it all. We identified closely with them.

In the match, Inter-Milan took an early lead and Celtic went in at half-time that dreaded single goal down. What followed in the second half was a relentless assault, attack after attack on that famed defence. It wasn't quite all caution thrown to the wind: the forty-one-year old Ronnie Simpson (known as 'Faither' because of his age), the Celtic goalkeeper, did stay in his own half; but he was virtually the only player there for much of the game (keeping an eye on the dentures that belonged to the Celtic players, apparently all left in his cap behind the goal-posts). When Celtic won, it did not just signal the first ever British team to win this most challenging of competitions; rather, what was signalled was a new future for the game, the validation of an adventurous sense of life's possibilities, a belief in the local people of Glasgow that they were capable of anything, if they could just allow their wild Romantic selves to flourish. 'Total football' and 'the beautiful game' as Pelé referred to it, was just around the corner: and we, in the east end of Glasgow, had turned that corner first. As it happened, Tommy Gemmell, the left-back who scored the equalizing goal, wore suits that were made-to-measure for him by my mother. Starveling's son, as it were, was that close to the match and its adventure.

Had we been more knowledgeable, we would have perhaps cast this as a contest between ruthlessly efficient Enlightenment models of the industrial grinding out of results, set against an untutored Romanticism, full of spirit, imagination – and, crucially, *poetry*. It was also much more than this: it gave us a sense of the aesthetic – the sheer beauty of the Celtic style of play, the very fact that there *was* such play, playfulness, like Schlegel's *Spielen*. This aesthetic adventure was to triumph over the dull but ostensibly successful modes of industrialization: those brought money, but ours brought happiness and joy. Industrialization, of course, was the daily routine for the families I knew from our school: my own father (two years dead by this time) and brother in the Clyde's shipyards; the fathers of my friends working as boiler-makers in the railways; sometimes (if they were lucky), others working as craftsmen (carpenters, plumbers, painters and decorators). Aesthetic play and the play of aesthetics was more than just football: it was politics, and we sensed this, even though we did not have the vocabulary at the time to articulate it.

As a schoolboy in St Mungo's, this game marked 1967 as special. More than this: it marked *us* as special. For the first time, we became visible on a world stage where we were validated, and we were validated through our identification with the spirit of romance, adventure, and a style that could even trump Italy (itself a by-word for style from the 1950s). And we were visible also in Shakespeare: remember, in the following August when we read the *Dream*, we realized that Shakespeare has the audience watching itself. But, at the forefront of our minds was the fact that the summer of 1967 was truly a summer of love: love of football. We returned to the new school year in August of that year, charged with a new sense of ourselves: as Catholics, as working-class boys who were on their way to make good in the world, as adventurers.

It was thus that we approached *A Midsummer Night's Dream*.

The Notes

Struggling with the play, I turned to the Notes at the back for help. Sure enough, my earliest fear – that this is as foreign as Latin – was confirmed. The first note in my edition explains 'nuptial hour', calling it 'wedding hour' and stating that it comes from 'Lat: *Nubeo, nupsi, nuptum*, to marry' (p. 69).[1] So far, so helpful; but foreign. I started to hear again how foreign 'my language' was to me. As a child, in working-class Glasgow, I was aware (actually quite explicitly) of at least three modes of speech, three Englishes. There was the language we spoke at home; then there was the slightly more formal language – polite usage, really, with a slightly modified accent – that I used when speaking to my teacher or to the doctor or priest; and finally, there was the BBC, as it were: a world of televised English. Whenever I watched TV (probably too much), I was aware of the authority of that voice, that speech. I also knew that I would one day be able to speak it, or would need to speak it if I were to accede myself to such authority (the authority, sought by Bottom, that means you count, you exist, you are listened to). The change would come about as a result of my education, an education that was partly built upon that incipient multilingualism. I inhabited different languages, and changed as a person depending on which one I spoke. However, in Shakespeare, there was as yet no question for me of accent or propriety: this was a different kind of foreignness; and it irritated me that I felt excluded.

The feeling of exclusion lingered for some time. However, relatively early on in my engagements with Shakespeare, we read *The Tempest*, another play that I found very difficult, but one within which I found the importance of translation. When Ferdinand meets Miranda, in Act 1, Scene 2, he hears her speak and exclaims, 'My language? Heavens!/I am the best of them that speak this speech,/ Were I but where 'tis spoken' (432–4). He is surprised that this foreign, wild untutored girl, speaks his language. What was important to me, though, was that he claims the language as *his*, that it is a matter of ownership; and that he distinguishes the quality of speakers dependent upon that ownership ('I am the best of them'). My shock at this passage derived from the fact that I have never felt that language is a matter of ownership; rather, for me, it has always been a matter of imagination, something for the lunatic, lover and poet who can inhabit a philosophy undreamt of, in imagination. My attempt to learn French had already shown me that there were things that could be said in French that were, strictly, untranslatable:

to speak French was to 'think' it, to inhabit the mind of a French persona, even to re-mould the shape of one's lips, mouth, and facial expression. Maybe to 'hear' Shakespeare was the same, I realized: a matter of acting, borrowing a persona, standing in the skin of someone I was not.

The note for line 11 put me in my place, telling me how to pronounce 'Philostrate' ('in three syllables', we are told, in case we need tuition on how to speak). But hold, what next? At line 14, we get a note on 'companion', which means 'fellow, used contemptuously'. The note firstly affirms Latinate roots, but then promises something more interesting: 'Originally, one who ate with another. (Lat. *cum*, with, *panis*, bread.) *Fellow* and *companion* have exchanged meanings since Shakespeare's time' (p. 69). What interested me here was that the meaning of a word changes with time, even to the stage where two words can exchange meanings: white becomes black, as it were. This opened up for me the question of translating from this Shakespeare-Latin: it is now a question of how a culture 'lives' a language, lives its words, and how those words can change meanings across time. Suddenly, the play opened to the real world in all sorts of ways, and told me that my language was a living and changing organic thing, tied to communities but open to difference.

At line 69, we are told that 'Whether' is 'to be pronounced "where" as it is still in many parts of the country'. Now, there is a 'correction' of pronunciation, but a correction that allows for dialect variants, that even legitimizes the possibility that those with dialects have an authentic relation to the play and its language. Finally, in this brief introductory section of Notes, we get a note referring to lines 74–5 that tells us 'Elizabeth was unmarried, and nothing pleased her more than to hear praises of a single life'. Shakespeare had a specific audience, then: the Queen, the famed Virgin Queen. Now, we can take our distance from this; but at least we have a place to stand, a language to speak, and a sense that things in this text are not as solidly monumental an authority as we had thought.

Concluding, Beginning

In sum, from these notes, we realized that Shakespeare was a foreign language, that the language required us to change (even to change physically) in order to inhabit it, and that its standing as a culturally authoritative monument was not unchangeable: we could have a relation to that authority, we could make the words change meaning.

We were profoundly aware of the cultural authority of 'Shakespeare'; and yet we resisted it to some extent. It would be many years before I realized what was going on in this preliminary series of engagements with these plays. Hannah Arendt helps explain. When she considers the fraught question of what constitutes 'authority', she points out that 'Since authority always demands obedience, it is commonly mistaken for some form of power or violence' (Arendt, 1993, pp. 92–3). She is adamant, however, that authority in fact both precludes the use of external or coercive force (for then authority as such would have failed), and also that it is incompatible with persuasion 'which presupposes equality and works through a process of argumentation' (ibid., p. 93). Neither Mr McDermott's physical threats, nor his arguments, would persuade us that *A Midsummer Night's Dream* was good or enjoyable; for that, we would rely on Shakespeare himself. Here is the rub: as Arendt puts it, 'Authority implies an obedience in which men retain their freedom' (ibid., p. 106) – or, I might add, in which we *find* our freedom. We can acknowledge an authority here, via this play, that allowed us to gain a freedom, the freedom conditioned by difference, by differing or, as Rilke would have had it, by changing our life. By constantly changing language – that is, by continually reading – it has become possible for me to change my life and its possibilities. Shakespeare has been central to the edification of a self that constitutes itself as differing, as freeing itself from the tyranny of identity; and in that freedom is the sharing of languages.

Note

1. [Editors' Note:] Despite best efforts, we have been unable to locate bibliographical information for the 'Junior School' edition cited here. Professor Docherty's own copy is damaged and enquiries at the British Library proved fruitless, despite the librarians' best efforts. We believe it is a reprint of an 1894 edition prepared by W. F. Baugust.

Chapter 8

Mrs Polonius and I

Julia Reinhard Lupton

Thy state is taken for a joint-stool, thy golden sceptre for a leaden dagger, and thy precious rich crown for a pitiful bald crown!
(*1 Henry IV*, 2.5.346–8)

The concept of the ceremonial chair seems to be as old as the chair itself.
(Graham, 1994, pp. 1–2)

Your furniture's not dead.
Musician Jack White, on his early career as an upholsterer.[1]

Beer is a living thing.
Shirley Landon Lupton, brew master's daughter, 1937–2011

Prologue: Stool Pigeon

Mrs Polonius [seated on a stool]: Things first, people second. That's how the world looks from where I'm sitting – which is on a joint stool, by the way![2] *[She lifts up her skirts, pretending to reveal her private parts, but shows us the stool instead.]* Joining, it's all about joining. If the tenon fits snugly into the mortise, with a nice rail all around, this lowly stool can bear the butt of a king, though you know he'll expect a chair every time. Chairs: don't get me started. *[She gathers up her skirts and stands on the stool.]* First, chairs are tricky to make. It'll cost you a pretty penny to buy one, too. And not very comfortable once you settle into it. In these parts, there are only one or two chairs in a house, and only in the better houses, mind you. A chair is a little stage, a second skeleton, Your Body remade in carved wood and cloth of gold; it may support the rump, like this stool, but it also outlines the head, the trunk, the arms, man's better parts (or so he likes to think). Chairs are the Viagra of home furnishings; they keep the man of the house upright when he'd rather slump and flop. The chair fits right between the two bodies of the king, supporting his mortal ass so that his *dignitas* can shine at court. A chair is not just a stool with a back and arms; it's a bit of holy fuckin' architecture designed to prop up man's precious little difference from animals and things – and from his fellows, and often from women, too. What a piece of work is man? Not much, without a fine chair upholstered in cloth of gold to give him some local habitation and a frame. Stools, meanwhile, are the workhorses of the household; like your nags and jades, they are eminently ass-worthy. The legs of finer chairs end in lion's feet. If stools were beasts, they'd stand on hooves, not paws (Figure 8.1).

Everyone looks grander in a chair – provided, of course, that there aren't too many of them. In your world, I hear that every one's got a chair, or two, or ten. Chairs are the new stools, aren't they? Rows and rows of them, stacked and ready for shipping, moulded out of plastic and fibreglass and metal tubing and wicker and bent plywood and recycled soda rings. No more distinction, no more rank, certainly no lion's feet; like the rest of your world, it's hooves every which way. Well, I'd like to settle myself in a chair one of these days, but it had better be a chair that still *means something* – the stiffer and harder the better, as long as it's upholstered in Turkey work, with purple silk fringe and gilded knobs.

I wouldn't give up my stools, though. You've heard the old proverb, *chairs sink and stools rise*: now put *that* in your bolingbroke and smoke it. There's your tall stool and your long stool, your folded stool and your foot stool; stools embroidered and stools inlaid; and of course, don't forget your close stool and your stool pans. Wherever

Figure 8.1 A joint stool for Bottom. painting by Ellen Lupton, acrylic on paper, 2010.

the stool sits, the fundament is soon to follow. The Reformation? If you ask me, the whole affair boils down to tables and chairs. No more speaking *ex cathedra*; if Jesus was a carpenter, then stools were his thing, and if we're going to have a table at the front of the church, the Puritans won't let you dress it up too much. Did you know that 'banquet' comes from the word for bench? All those objects have their own stories to tell. You just have to learn how to listen to them. But the stool is my soapbox. Sit me down and you'll shut me up. *[She collapses on the stool, and the lights go out.]*

Seeking Mrs Polonius

Mrs *Polonius*? There is, of course, no such personage in Shakespeare. I am slowly inventing her, stool by stool, from the corners, closets and pantries of the plays and the worlds of entertainment and intrigue they harbour with such tact and cunning. Like an Arcimboldo painting, Mrs Polonius is a portrait composed from a grocery cart, coalescing as a roving bundle of attributes rather than a character in charge of a full biography. I take direction from Shakespeare's domestic entrepreneurs – whether it's the she-doctor Helena in *All's Well* or the wormwood-wielding nurse in *Romeo and Juliet,* or the mouthy matrons of *Othello* and *The Winter's Tale.* She's not stitched together from women only: Mrs P. has picked up some entertaining advice from that cot-quean Capulet, and she's as akin to Petruchio as she is to Kate. I am also seeking her out in the inventories, cookbooks, and housewife and husbandry guides of the sixteenth and seventeenth centuries, accidental ethnographies of the *res publica* of things in the Renaissance.

Mrs Polonius constitutes my effort at crafting a link between Shakespeare and me that might operate at the level of objects rather than minds. She reveals not my rational soul so much as my vegetative one: she is a canny trafficker among words, worlds, and things, and between the several chambers of my work and life. For two decades I've been teaching and writing about Shakespeare, psychoanalysis and political theology. At the same time, I've been helping to manage a busy household consisting of two working parents, four children, and a pair of geriatric cats. We interact by family dinner and Jewish law. Ken and I embraced the practice of Judaism together, he as the son of secular Jews and I as a convert with long-standing interests in religion. For fifteen years now, I've been running our kitchen in a 'California Kosher' kind of way: two comprehensive sets of dishes and tableware supported by a few mixed-marriage utensils that seem unwilling to commit permanently to milk or meat, tiny Teflon ensigns of my own ambivalence about God, gefilte fish, and the state of Israel. Meanwhile, a few years ago, I began writing about the everyday life of design with my sister Ellen Lupton, in a mode that allowed me to rant about household stuff, but in a popular rather than an academic mode (see Lupton/Lupton, 2006 and Lupton/Lupton, 2009).

Now, in a plan inspired by Maria Sibyla Merian (taxidermist, botanical illustrator, mother, and Protestant sectarian [1647–1717]) and Hannah Woolley (organic intellectual of the kitchen, the buttery and the boudoir [1622–1675]), I want to address the commerce of things in Shakespeare, but not from a strictly historicist point of view. What does Shakespeare have to tell me about my life with objects now? How might both formal and vernacular design discourses be brought to bear on such topics as the political theology of stools and chairs? And how can I learn to listen for the mute affordances of things in plays rightly organized, Hannah Arendt – rather than Hannah Woolley – fashion, around human speech and action? I cannot venture on such a path alone. I need a partner from Shakespeare's world, a native informant whose knowledge of urine-based hair treatments and the abortificant properties of rue will allow me to follow the strands of know-how linking Shakespeare's environments to my own. And hence Mrs Polonius was born. Half knave, half navel gazer, Mrs Polonius is not the spouse of the Danish counsellor so much as his female impersonation, Polonius in drag: his twin, his madame and his accountant, the consummate fishmonger's wife. Not unlike her masculine namesake, she is partial to aphorisms, which she handles as part of a flexible book of virtues whose outcomes are not always strictly moral. Temperamentally, she is Hamlet's mother-in-law: she would be queen of infinite space (or at least a fierce middle manager) if it were not for the ubiquity of dust bunnies and the nastiness of curly fries.

A voice rather than a biography, Mrs Polonius is able to insinuate herself into several habitats and classes with the dexterous speed of a ship rat or a personal shopper. She has helped me engage the topic 'Shakespeare and I', but the ego she has helped me craft is closer to an alibi or a credit rating than a signature. A casuist of the kitchen and a Machiavel of the bed chamber, Mrs Polonius is, like me, a woman of middle age, but with enough secrets up her slashed sleeves to counter my own mounting inhibitions. Like Hannah Woolley, she knows how to make plates out of sugar and to pickle cucumbers to look very green; and like Hannah Woolley, she is privy to the darker side of household life. ('Most in this depraved later Age', writes Woolley dryly, 'think a Woman learned and wise enough if she can distinguish her Husband's Bed from another's' [Woolley, 1673a, p. 1].) I call her 'Mrs' to indicate her affiliations with the wives of city tradesmen as well as with later household experts such as Mrs Beeton. Like Lady Macbeth, Mrs Polonius has no first name, though she'll answer to Helena, Emilia, Paulina, or sometimes Snug. Mrs Polonius invites me to reread Shakespeare for the pantry, not the plot: to peruse inventories of objects with the eager snout of a cool hunter, and to scan scenes of hostessing and housework as if they were episodes from the DIY channel. She also bids me to index the darker side of hospitality and housekeeping: the poison in the garden, the fox in the henhouse, and the spider in the cup. If Mrs Polonius, like any Renaissance housekeeper, is a kind of curator, an assiduous manager of the life and death of things, the collections over which she presides are both swap meet and cemetery, restless repositories formed by the commerce of objects, persons and pastimes in and between her world and mine.

Moving the Furniture

In her opening rant, Mrs Polonius discloses the Renaissance closet drama of stools and chairs, a tale of kingship and thingship. The remarkable mobility of the joint stool is on display, for example, in the volley of objects and animals exchanged by Petruchio and Kate in their first encounter in *The Taming of the Shrew* (2.1.180–272).[3] Meanwhile, the chair-stool dialectic works its way into the great inventories of the Renaissance, which list chairs first, stools second, and close stools last, assembling a microcosm of the social order out of the status-conscious clustering of forms of seating.[4] Mrs P.'s discourse also tells me a little about our own life with objects: if chairs now verge on universal, it is because they have incorporated the proletarian pragmatism of stools into their stackable, portable, mass-produced frames. Vestiges of the political theology of the chair remain, of course: the head of the table still commands respect while English departments and the boards of companies, prep schools and junior leagues are by and large ruled by Chairs. Mrs Polonius helps me listen to the stories still muttered by furniture in our flat-boxed, land-filled habitats, not in order to wax nostalgic for the world we have lost, but to consider both the costs and the gains of life in the age of IKEA and roll-on deodorant.

Things *sit differently* as a result of these reflections; I consider my surroundings with a more practiced and discriminating eye, and I inhabit my space with a greater sense of attention and care. Mrs Polonius puts the 'sit' in 'situation', urging me to think with my butt and my back. The 'I' at stake here is more dismembered, worldly and distributed than it is introspective or emotional. Like a great pseudo-pod or a roving slime mould, my ego flows among the outposts of intentionality constituted by the swell of the computer mouse in the palm of my hand, the curve of moulded plywood (knock-off Eames) beneath my buttocks, and the optic draw of the two computer screens that stretch like billboards across the highway of my desk. On the wall above and behind the screens, scraps of paper signpost the book and volume of my brain: a fantastical pastel bird drawn by my daughter Lucy, a post card still life of berries and butterflies, a business card flagging a mammogram appointment.

My absorption into the local affordances of writing is broken by the clamour of a child, the ring of the phone, or the looming of the dinner hour. I am: *egg shell, whisk, skillet, faucet, toilet paper, broken cuticle, my son's head, a Lego motorcycle, not an iPhone, a pencil underfoot, circle of breathing cat, gas pedal, Sabbath candles, an exposition of sleep.*

Drama itself is an art of distribution, a parcelling of attention and activity between body and voice, among multiple human actors, and across different classes of actant (persons, props, stage and sets, light and sound, plus clapping hands, candy wrappers and errant cell phones).[5] For the commerce of things on the place made by the stage, I love to read the modest sliver of a scene that opens Act One, Scene Five in *Romeo and Juliet*:

PETER:	Where's Potpan, that he helps not to take away? He shift a trencher, he scrape a trencher!
FIRST SERVINGMAN:	When good manners shall lie all in one or two men's hands, and they unwashed too, 'tis a foul thing.
PETER:	Away with the joint-stools, remove the court-cupboard, look to the plate. Good thou, save me a piece of marzipan, and, as thou loves me, let the porter let in Susan Grindstone and Nell. Antony and Potpan!
SECOND SERVINGMAN:	Ay, boy, ready!
PETER:	You are looked for and called for, asked for and sought for, in the great chamber.
FIRST SERVINGMAN:	We cannot be here and there too. Cheerly, boys! Be brisk awhile, and the longer liver take all. (1.5.1–13)

The kitchen crew shout orders to each other much like the mariners aboard the sinking ship at the opening of *The Tempest,* or my gaggle of children contesting their chores in the terrible five minutes before dinner is served. Shakespeare revels in these scenes; he enjoys the sound and fury of working men trying to create order in moments that reveal the affinity between minor transitions and major catastrophes. Shakespeare delivers us *in medias res,* in the middle of things, and the *res* at stake are not only singular actions as *res gestae* (founding a city, chairing a meeting, proposing marriage) but also repetitive manual activities that involve engagement with physical things (making dinner, clearing the table, kissing by the book). Such activities are habitual rather than monumental, and the forms of intelligence they require concern the improvisational coordination of hand, eye, and the toes of other people in an environment defined by affordances and constraints. Renaissance husbandry expert Gervase Markham (1568–1637) would have discoursed upon 'outward virtues' and 'knowledges' in the plural (Markham, 1615). Universal housekeeper Hannah Woolley would have identified such routines of living with 'usefulness' and 'competent skill' (Woolley, 1673b, from the Epistle Dedicatory). I call it *getting the day going, keeping a lot of balls in the air, keeping my cool, driving, driving me crazy, making a go of it*, and *No, I'm not multi-tasking; you're just interrupting me.* (I am looked for and called for, asked for and sought for, but I cannot be here and there too. Or can I?)

In this little scene, Shakespeare exploits the overlap between *stage management* and *household management*. The servingmen clear space for dancing while recasting the stage itself from street to antechamber to great hall, reminding us of the flexibility of Renaissance rooms and the remarkable mobility of their *mobilia* or home furnishings. In the Revels accounts of the Stuart court, the simple notation 'm/r' ('making ready') covered the duties required to prepare the Banqueting House and other performance and entertainment spaces for the reception of guests, including building scaffolding for seats and stages, hanging tapestry, and of course, like Anthony and Potpan, moving the furniture and dealing with linens, foodstuffs and trash (Malone Society, 1961). By hoping to save a 'piece of marzipan' for the afterhours moment when the porter lets in 'Susan Grindstone and Nell', warm and willing serving girls from down the street, the men carve an ancillary act of partying out of the time, space and resources left over by the main event.

Shakespeare's bit of work with leftovers *gets me thinking*: about the politics of waste, the arts of invention, and why being stranded in Denver on my way back from DC might not be so bad after all, as long as there's a Starbucks and WiFi. (My idea of adultery: texting during a faculty meeting, or zoning out when my son recites episodes from *iCarly*.) As a working mother, I have become not only the emperor of ice cream (Wallace Stevens) but the empress of leftover time: twelve minutes yields one paragraph of prose, or ten emails, or one hot bath, bits often brokered through the strategic use of candy, the carrot without the stick. This is not the time management of Taylorism, however, but a more spontaneous process in which different actors on the scene grab bits of surplus time, space, and brightly coloured almond paste for their own purposes. Architect and urbanist Keller Easterling speaks of 'organization space', by which she means 'an expanded site with physical, temporal and virtual strata' whose valences are constantly rezoned by human use and ecological change (Easterling, 1999, p. 17). I live in organization space, which is also organization time. This does *not* mean I mastermind every second of the day in a total plan that maximizes everyone's efficiency and self-development; I learned early on that for every over-scheduled child there is an overscheduled parent, usually a female one. Instead, organization implies an element of *self-organization* or autopoeisis, meaning that time unfolds responsively, with a sense of improvisation (homework before dinner or after?) around a few fixed needs (absolutely no exceptions: clean underwear at least three times a week). Like a firefly or the daily traffic updates, I am crepuscular: I write at dawn and I cook at dusk, practicing the two forms of invention that become me most, at those times of day when light and darkness congregate together, for better or for good enough.

Christmas in July

Act One, Scene Five sweeps on, leaving behind the gambol of trenchers, joint stools and marzipan in order to make room for the party. Capulet's greeting captures the patterns of speech that accompany flustered hosts and hostesses everywhere:

> Welcome, gentlemen! Ladies that have their toes
> Unplagued with corns will walk a bout with you.

> Aha, my mistresses, which of you all
> Will now deny to dance? She that makes dainty,
> She, I'll swear, hath corns. Am I come near ye now?
> Welcome, gentlemen! I have seen the day
> That I have worn a visor and could tell
> A whispering tale in a fair lady's ear,
> Such as would please. 'Tis gone, 'tis gone, 'tis gone.
> You are welcome, gentlemen. Come, musicians, play.
> [*Music plays, and they dance*]
> A hall, a hall! Give room! And foot it, girls.
> [*To* SERVINGMEN]
> More light, you knaves, and turn the tables up,
> And quench the fire, the room is grown too hot.
> [*To his* COUSIN]
> Ah, sirrah, this unlooked-for sport comes well.
> Nay, sit, nay, sit, good cousin Capulet,
> For you and I are past our dancing days.
> (1.5.14–29)

With minimal stage directions, Shakespeare prompts his harried host to speak in several directions in rapid succession: first to the ladies; then to the gentlemen, presumably Romeo's 'visored' party; then to the musicians; then to the servants ('knaves'), who are ordered to provide more light and take apart the trestle tables; and finally, short of breath, to his aged peer, cousin Capulet, whom he bids sit down with him, presumably on chairs, not stools. The host appears here not only as a greeter of guests but also as a multi-track manager of sound, light, and space, all in the service of shaping the general ambience. To take his seat on the upholstered chair that remains standing at the edge of the cleared room is to catch his breath, but also to confirm his role at the sidelines of the erotic gaming that unfolds before our eyes. Juliet's birthday is Capulet's retirement party. The host is the supervisor, literally the one who looks on and over the events,[6] but he is not the hero (compare Theseus and

Hippolyta in *A Midsummer Night's Dream,* the matronly Venus in Botticelli's *Primavera*, or a cloud server supporting a conversation on these subjects).

Here, Mrs Polonius speaks to me loud and clear: *this* is the flushed demeanour of anyone engaged in high stakes entertaining. Editors have made much of Capulet's command to cool the hearth ('quench the fire, the room is grown too hot'). Since no fire would be lit in July, this reference, editors suggest, may be left over from the tale's original setting at Christmas time. Likely so. Yet Mrs Polonius, my Virgil in Hospitality Hell, conducts us to another truth revealed by Shakespeare's careless editing: is not the heat suffered by Capulet *the sweat and bother of hosting as such,* an inner heat produced upon contact with guests? Is not every host, whether male or female, old, young, or middling, in that first moment of greeting, suddenly and horribly *menopausal,* subject to a seismic sequence of hot flashes, guest by bloody guest? As the guests enter and the scene heats up with its own frantic bustle, suddenly, for old Capulet, it is indeed Christmas in July – too much epiphany, too much advent finally come to term, too much damned good cheer.

Above and beyond the labour of making ready lurks the terror of self-revelation: something of myself appears when I open my house to visitors, releasing unbidden what Hannah Arendt calls the daemon of self-disclosure born in human action (Arendt, 1958, pp. 179–80). For hospitality takes the *activities* of daily life (shopping, cooking, cleaning, setting the table) and raises them to the level of *action* by incorporating the element of risk associated with the presence of other people: not the familiar faces of the immediate *familia,* but personages from outside the *oikos* who bring with them their dirty shoes, their pass-along wines, and their mixed bean salads. Like the stage, the scene of hospitality is defined by entries and exits, zoning the household as an open system, a domestic *theatrum mundi.* Shakespeare's Verona may seem worlds apart from the habitats of middle-class American householders like me. In this country, suburban homes like mine discourage much moving of furniture. With separate spaces for eating, leisure, study and sleep, there is no need to disassemble trestle tables and stack the joint stools after a meal in order to make room for carpentry, tailoring, or sleep. Meanwhile, families of even modest means tend to do their major dancing out of the house, at the rented halls of hotels and community centres. Yet micro-rezonings occur daily: in my house, we sort the remains of the day (the morning newspaper, the afternoon junk mail, this week's homework, plus Daddy's philosophy books, a Playdough kangaroo, and a homeless remote control) that clump and mound on our single collective table in order to make way for the drama that is dinner. And we also rezone for grander functions. In the DIY (do it yourself) *bat mitzvah* party that we threw for our eldest daughter (another Hannah), we pushed the couches against the wall and installed club lighting – strobe equivalents to Romeo's fair torches – in order to gerrymander our house into something equivalent to Juliet's coming of age party. There was nothing 'Shakespearean' in the event, which was teen Orange County through and through, yet the effort to rework house into hall drew all of us into forms of 'm/r' and 'skillful coping', from creating table arrangements out of old books to persuading my daughter *not* to dye her hair pink until *after* the synagogue service. Having the party at home increased the element of self-exposure undergone by every host (people entertain out of house to protect privacy as well as property); but it also curtailed the guest list, and thus exercised risk management at another door. The front one.

For my other desire is not to entertain at all: no more frantic shopping, harried straightening, nervous chatter, endless dishes, or Facebook follow-up. All I really want is more time on the couch watching cable TV with my husband of many sweet and steady years, and more hours on the computer writing essays not like this one. Mrs Polonius' gift is to help me say this out loud, in print, for myself and others – so that I can open my house again, as I always do, for Jewish holidays and post-lecture receptions and children's birthday parties and the occasional dinner party. Capulet's case of nerves lets me encounter the flow of my own hospitality not from the infinite well of the gift-giving virtue, but from a place that gathers shadows along with the light. Because dusk, and salt, and glancing at your watch, are the other side of hostessing. Mrs Polonius is not Martha Stewart. She is Martha Stewart with a red wine headache and a yeast infection.

Hospitality is an interface: a threshold between the *oikos* and the outside world, but also a script that bridges activity and action, our daily life with things and the drama of our encounter with neighbours, strangers and mothers-in-law. Hospitality is a *design for living*, a set of protocols that organize human beings in a social and natural world striated by existential vulnerabilities, including the terror of small talk and the ubiquity of UTP (unidentified Tupperware). In drama, hospitality knits the things of the plays (stools, cupboards, marzipan) to dramatic interests (love, rivalry, betrayal) in a single network of action, activity, and concern. Chairs play a role here. To offer a visitor a seat is to disarm him as well as to make him welcome. A seated visitor can be poisoned, strangled from behind, or forced to watch home videos while drinking cucumber tea. To prefer to remain standing signals that I am not your friend, and that I am prepared to bolt to the door with your signed edition of *Specters of Marx* in my messenger bag.

Hospitality is also an interface between Shakespeare, me, and my chair-prone bottom, too. Hermione's line to Polixenes, 'My prisoner? or my guest?' (*The Winter's Tale*, 1.2.56) comes straight out of Mrs P.'s commonplace book. Isn't the guest always a prisoner, not fully able to determine his own departure, fundamentally at the mercy of his hosts? And isn't the hostess also a prisoner of sorts, waiting for the guests to leave so that she can finally check her email and take off her bra? Mrs Polonius knows that the darker phantasms of hospitality (cannibalism, rape and kidnapping, instant coffee creamer) are mythic attempts to make sense of the more mundane realities of the guest who will not leave, or the host who won't let you go, or the slow, terrible agony of death by seating plan.

Hermione, *my* Hermione at least, the Hermione I am becoming in my own cooling kitchen, is no flirt or flapper; she is temperamentally inhibited, held back within herself, *already* the Winter Queen long before jealousy takes sudden root in her husband's mind. Shakespeare's women know that every wedding table, and Christmas buffet, and silver anniversary, is furnished forth with funeral baked meats: leftovers with an attitude and an agenda. *Would you like the cheese plate?* Cheese is milk with memory, and not all of them are sweet.[7] *Have you tried chicken?* Boneless breast represents the abstraction of flesh from fowl, of animal protein from its origins in a living creature. *Would you care for some ale?* Beer is a living thing (and your furniture isn't dead, either). Such things of darkness, by acknowledging me as their own, help me get through the terror of receiving so that I can become for one more evening the queen of curds and cream.

Mrs Polonius helps me care about things in Shakespeare, not only in order to better visualize the material conditions of his world, but also to pay renewed attention to my own. Mrs Polonius is the kind of ghost that dwells in the region of shelf lives, date stamps and the bright blue screen of the memory dump. In the environs of *Romeo and Juliet*, she draws her zeal from Antony and Potpan, from the old Nurse, from Nell and Susan Grindstone, and from Capulet, too. She resembles a chair in her spreading bulk and presence, but a stool in her astonishing mobility as well as her talent for making asses of people. Like me, she is an alpha bitch and a beta tester, the consummate 'woman of the house' whose soul is actualized in the assembly of things, the spaces they organize, and the activities they summon. Like Hannah Arendt, Mrs Polonius knows that housework is war by other means, 'a daily fight . . . to keep the world clean and prevent its decay', activities that require not courage but endurance, and whose pain stems not from 'danger but its relentless repetition' (Arendt, 1958, p. 101). 'Screw your introspection', she snapped at me the other day as I was rummaging for reflections of more pitch and moment. 'You should be dusting.' Mrs Polonius has taught me that dust is an ambient cloud of motes and mites gathered from seasons past; settling into the crevices and corners of everyday life, dust gives the lie to our many fictions of smoothness. With so many surfaces to clean, who has time for depth?

In the presence of Mrs Polonius, I want to sip on 'drowsy syrups' and 'feed on nourishing dishes' (*Othello*, 3.3.335, 3.3.79). I find myself writing in epigrams and reaching for words like 'masticate', 'toiletry', and 'sports utility vehicle'. She makes me ruttish for routine. I love her because she doesn't ask me to think big. She asks me to think small, and to think (like a) broad. Mrs Polonius is not, however, a noble model, a feminist *avant la lettre*. A daily ugliness haunts her domestic materialism; a veritable Shylock of dry goods, she tucks old grudges and new disappointments next to her gloves, napkins and handkerchiefs. She harbours the *ressentiment* of a stool who wants to be a chair. She is a closet Machiavel who never compromises her pragmatism. 'The wine she drinks is made of grapes' (2.1.243).[8] When the Nurse, one of Mrs P.'s avatars, in effect abandons Juliet to her own designs late in the play, choosing her own interests over those of her young charge, she reveals the limits of the loves attached to household service. So too, Emilia, another novitiate in the House of Polonia, is quick to pick up Desdemona's fallen handkerchief and deliver it to her husband, putting her own sorry wreck of a marriage before any loyalty to her mistress. So much for female solidarity. The virtues of household management are, in Gervase Markham's phrase, 'outward', devolving into survivalism and care for one's own when the moral stakes shoot even a fraction above the margin of comfort. (Class divisions service those margins. So does fear of earthquakes, mortgage foreclosure, and guests with apps.) In the casual betrayals of the Nurse and Emilia, I encounter my own anxious protectionism of purse and person, my urge to escape existential darkness for the fluorescent light of business as usual, my closet royalism and my high church hang-overs, my inclination towards social media rather than social justice, and my slowness in extending love. Perhaps I can *do better* and *be better* than

Mrs P., but on most days I remain in the circles drawn by the bustle of her busy, self-important skirts. At the very least, though, she helps me reckon the sources of my own attachments and inhibitions. In this, I am her prisoner – caught up in her *claustrum* of objects, duties and outward knowledges – but I am also her guest: free to retool her competencies for scripts not dreamed of in her philosophy, or housed in her panty drawer. With Mrs P. by my side, I can survive anything. Even brunch.

Notes

1. Interview with Jack White, *The Believer*, May 2003. <http://www.believ-ermag.com/issues/200305/?read=interview_white> [accessed July 25, 2010]
2. All seating has been freely adapted from *Of Household Stuff: The 1601 Inventories of Bess of Hardwick* (Levey/Thornton, 2001). No chairs were harmed in the writing of this essay.
3. I develop this reading in Lupton, 2011.
4. My comments on stools and chairs in this essay are developed at greater length in a special issue of the *Journal of Medieval and Renaissance Studies* (see Lupton, forthcoming).
5. On distributed cognition in Shakespearean drama, see Tribble, 2005. On actants, see Latour, 2005.
6. Compare the use of the word in *Othello*: 'Would you, the supervisor, grossly gape on?/ Behold her topped?' (3.3.400–1).
7. 'Virginity breeds mites, much like a cheese.' (*All's Well That Ends Well*, 1.1.132–3).
8. This line spoken by Iago to Roderigo, with reference to Desdemona (but capturing Emilia instead).

Chapter 9

'Who Is It That Can Tell Me Who I Am?'

Graham Holderness

LEAR: I am a very foolish fond old man . . . (*King Lear*, 4.7.61)

Who speaks here?
'I'.
But who is 'I'?
'I' do not know.
It is Lear's own question: 'Who is it that can tell me who I am?'
(1.4.205)

Don't you know? Do you need someone else to tell you who you are, what your 'I' consists of?

There are also other people beyond you, also calling themselves 'I', other persons asking for the same authentication: 'Who is it that can tell me who I am?'

'Sir, do you know me?'
(4.7.48)

It is clearly crucial to Cordelia's identity that her sense of self is shared with her father's perception of her. If he does not know her, he does not know himself.

> LEAR: I am mightily abused. I should e'en die with pity,
> To see another thus. I know not what to say.
> I will not swear these are my hands. Let's see.
> I feel this pin prick. Would I were assured
> Of my condition! (4.7.53–7)

Lear regards himself as if he were another, understands himself as another, as other. He would die from pity to see someone else in the same condition as himself: he regards himself, as it were, from the outside. He does not know if his body belongs to him, or not. He is no longer 'assured' of his condition, no longer a stable identity, no longer 'I'.

And yet he knows himself, understands himself, better than ever before.

> LEAR: Pray, do not mock me:
> I am a very foolish fond old man,
> Fourscore and upward, not an hour more nor less;
> And, to deal plainly,
> I fear I am not in my perfect mind.
> Methinks I should know you, and know this man;
> Yet I am doubtful; for I am mainly ignorant
> What place this is; and all the skill I have
> Remembers not these garments; nor I know not
> Where I did lodge last night. Do not laugh at me;
> For, as I am a man, I think this lady
> To be my child Cordelia. (4.7.60–71)

This wonderful prose poetry of simple, tentative statements, and limpid, common vocabulary, is not the same language formerly spoken by 'King' Lear. Gone are the orotund rhetoric, the long, complex sentences, the subordinate clauses, the Latinate diction. In their place we hear a searching simplicity of utter honesty and absolute self-knowledge that constitutes a heartbreaking authenticity. This is an 'I' of unquestionable integrity, that knows itself only in weakness and confusion. Yet it is 'assured of its condition', since it recognizes itself in the primary relationship of father and daughter. No longer king and princess, lord and subject: just an old man and his child. 'I am a man.' 'I think this lady/To be my child.'

The answer to Lear's question, 'who is it that can tell me who I am?' was 'Lear's shadow' (1.4.206). How is it that Lear can only understand himself, only regain his subjectivity as an integrated 'I', by knowing himself as an entirely different person?

Because he has undergone an experience of conversion so profound that it cannot be understood except via a language of death and resurrection.

> LEAR: You do me wrong to take me out o' the grave:
> Thou art a soul in bliss; but I am bound
> Upon a wheel of fire, that mine own tears
> Do scald like molten lead. (4.7.45–8)

* * *

The story of 'I' is autobiography, but 'I' cannot tell my own story, only the story of another. The writers of conversion narratives, writes John Freccero, construct scenarios that are 'tantamount to a death of their former selves and the beginning of new life' (Freccero, 1986, p. 25). As Rachel Falconer explains, this narrative self-destruction ironically restores the possibilities of autobiography:

> This quasi-deathly experience bestows a special advantage on the narrators of conversion texts. Most autobiographical narrators have a limited vantage point on the meaning and shape of their own lives because they are still in the business of living them. But the converted narrator sees his or her former self as belonging to a prior life altogether; the pre-conversion past is absolutely closed off from the present and therefore open to being authoritatively interpreted. (Falconer, 2005, p. 46)

Jeremy Tambling defines the construction of that pre-conversion self, the old, now repudiated 'I', as a 'fiction', and links it to the 'death of the author'. Conversion writing

> works by its ability to divide up the self's experiences into those of a past "I" whose existence may be completed, destroyed, as the death of the author fiction would suggest . . . and the present self. (Tambling, 1990, p. 20)

The writer 'must maintain the fiction of a past "I" for upon doing so the whole fiction of the possibility of conversion rests' (ibid.). But both the death of the author and the reality of conversion are fact, as well as fiction.

The context here is a discussion of St Augustine's *Confessions*, a work which is credited with inventing the very form of autobiography. No one before Augustine, says Karl Weintraub, had 'opened up their souls in the inwardness of genuine autobiography' (Weintraub, 1978, p. 45). If this is so, then autobiography originated not with the full presence and coherence of a realized self, but with alienation, fracturing, multiplicity, the repudiation of a self now apprehended as wholly other, superseded, dead. When in his garden at Milan Augustine heard the child singing, and eagerly returned to his book (Book VIII, XII.29), it was to Paul's Epistle to the Romans that he returned: 'induite dominum Iesum Christum et carnis prouidentiam ne feceritis'. 'Put ye on the Lord Jesus Christ, and make not provision for the flesh' (Augustine, 1907, p. 171; Romans 13.14. King James Version). 'If Christ be in you, the body is dead because of sin: but the Spirit is life because of righteousness' (Romans 8.10, King James Version). In an extraordinary passage describing the sensations of conversion, Augustine shows unmistakably how labile and iterable was his conception of the self even in the very act of constructing it.

> tu autem, domine . . . retorquebas me ad me ipsum, auferens me a dorso meo, ubi me posueram, dum nollem me adtendere,

et constituebas me ante faciem meam, ut uiderem, quam
turpis essem, quam distortus et sordidus, maculosus et ulcero-
sus. et uidebam et horrebam, et quo a me fugerem non erat. et
si conabar a me auertere aspectum . . . tu me rursus opponebas
mihi et inpingebas me in oculos meos, ut inuenirem iniqui-
tatem et odissem. noueram eam, sed dissimulabam et cohi-
bebam et obliuiscebar. (Augustine, 1908 p. 219, Book VIII,
VII.16)

O Lord . . . it was you who twisted me round towards myself,
dragging me from behind my back, where I had placed myself,
unwilling to observe myself, and setting me before my face, where
I could see how foul I was, how crooked and defiled, bespotted
and ulcerous. I saw, and was horrified; but there was nowhere
I could escape to from myself. And if I sought to avert my eyes
from myself . . . again you threw me across myself, and thrust me
before my own eyes, so I could see my own iniquity, and hate it. I
had known it, but I pretended it was not there, winked at it, cast
it into oblivion. (my translation)

In this construction of the subject as wholly subjected, the impossible physical contortions and the dizzying shifts of vision show
Augustine to be a deconstructionist *avant la lettre*. 'Rehearsing long
before Descartes', said Jonathan Dollimore, 'that most famous proof
of subjective being (*cogito ergo sum*), Augustine wrote: "*Si enim fal-
lor sum*". . . ("If I err I exist"). In other words, Augustine founds his
being upon erring movement.' (Dollimore, 1991, pp. 146–7)

* * *

Philippe Lejeune defined 'autobiography' as

A retrospective prose narrative produced by a real person con-
cerning his own existence, focusing on the individual life, in
particular on the development of his personality. (Lejeune, 1982,
p. 193)

Lejeune admits that there are many problems with this definition, but insists on only one qualifying condition for autobiographical discourse: there must be 'identity between the *author,* the *narrator,* and the *protagonist*' (ibid.). The writer must be telling his/her own story about him/herself.

But this assumption depends on two problematical issues: the status of the writer vis-à-vis the work, and the validity of the writer's intentions. If the writer is, as we now generally believe, no longer sole guarantor of the text's meaning; and if intentionality may be a mere fallacy, at best a distraction; then on this definition autobiography loses its claim to consideration as a distinct literary genre with clear boundaries.

> Poststructuralism . . . by positing language or discourse as both preceding and exceeding the subject, deposed the author from his or her central place as the source of meaning and undermined the unified subject of autobiography. (Anderson, 2001, p. 6)

Paul de Man redefined autobiography as 'de-facement'. When an author places him or herself in the text, he/she produces a persona that substitutes for, and displaces, the living writer (de Man, 1979, p. 919). The autobiographical 'I' is a mask that can purport to realize the author's experience only by fictionalizing it. Roland Barthes further and formally destabilized the subject of autobiography by writing a self-reflexive and parodic autobiography of his own, *Roland Barthes by Roland Barthes* (Barthes, 1977a). First, second and third person forms of address are deliberately confused to fragment any sense of coherent subjectivity or consistent identity between writer, narrator and protagonist. Barthes compares the relationship between author and represented 'self' to that between a Brechtian actor and his/her character. The actor 'shows', without pretending to 'be', the character he/she plays.

Barthes, as Sean Burke has observed, was actually conserving the possibilities of autobiography by recreating its form (Burke, 1992,

p. 189). Jacques Derrida, by contrast, in Linda Anderson's phrase, 'scatters autobiography as a motif or theme throughout his work' (Anderson, 2001, p. 79). In Derrida's work, the dispersive effects of writing negate any attempt to realize self-presence in a text. But at the same time, since autobiography lies between the writer and the work, 'between fiction and truth' (Derrida, 2000, p. 16), it spills over into textuality, rather than remaining outside to anchor the text in the 'real'.

Derrida's most significant contribution to thinking about autobiography was to redefine it (not for the first time) as 'autothanatography', the product of an author who is already dead. The text carries the author's name, but the name has already survived the 'death' of the author:

> In calling or naming someone while he is alive, we know that his name can survive him and already survives him; the name begins during his life to get along without him, speaking and bearing his death each time it is inscribed in a list, or a civil registry, or a signature. (Derrida, 1988, p. 49)

Derrida characterizes Maurice Blanchot's autobiographical story *L'Instance de ma mort* as a 'narrative or testimony – signed by someone who tells us in many ways and according to every possible tense: *I am* dead, or *I will be* dead in an instant, or an instant ago *I was* going to be dead' (Derrida, 2000, p. 45). The author, Blanchot (who admitted to Derrida that the incident narrated in the story happened to him) thus finds a way of saying what cannot be said, the impossible, since 'I cannot testify to my death – by definition, I cannot say, according to common sense, I should not be able to say: I died or I am dead' (Derrida, 2000, p. 46).

'The dead cannot speak; they cannot attest to their own passing, for death annihilates the first-person witness' (Secomb, 2002, p. 33). In the story this 'impossible possibility' (Derrida, 2000, p. 46) is made actual. From the moment Blanchot 'knew the happiness of nearly being shot to death' (quoted in Derrida, 2000, p. 52), 'il fut lié à la mort, par une amitié subreptice' (Blanchot, 2000, p. 4). 'The experience of facing the instant of death means that now he has a death within him awaiting its answering death from without' (Secomb, 2002, p. 41). From then on death was always there with him, only deferred, 'toujours en instance' (Blanchot, 2000, p. 10):

> Comme si la mort hors de lui ne pouvait désormais que se heurter à la mort en lui. (Blanchot, 2000, p. 8)

* * *

A death-destined breath-catching
Bone-brittle ramshackle
Fleshwrapped body, woke
From a sleep of senescence
To a word-web woven
Of cunning contrivance and curious
Craft, mouth-made in another
Tongue, yet sung
By a darkling bird in waste
Night-watches of shivering
Sleep, dug deep
Into pain and praise.

Those are my words. This is my story. Yet they are not, neither. Not altogether.

They are also a translation of the conclusion of Anglo-Saxon poet Cynewulf's epic poem *Elene* (Krapp, 1932, pp. 51–4). The poem treats of the finding of the True Cross by the mother of the Emperor Constantine, Helena. At the end of the poem Cynewulf introduced a brief 'personal' reflection, describing to the reader how his own poetic capacity derived from his conversion to Christianity. Just as the Emperor found victory by entrusting his fortune to the Cross, so the poet has discovered, in the Cross, the means to self-discovery and self-liberation. The parallel thus simultaneously differentiates and connects the two visions, and suggests that what has prompted the poet to compose such a historical narrative is his own life-changing experience of religious conversion.

The 'autobiography' is therefore both inside and outside the poem: it is the catalyst that turns the believer into a maker, and the devotional commitment evidenced by the poetic composition itself. 'Cynewulf' is thus the name of an author, and the name of an author-function; it points beyond the poem to a life lived, but also self-referentially back into the poem for evidence and proof of the autobiographical experience.

The impact of conversion on the poet's imagination is compellingly dramatized. The Cross bestows on him wisdom, understanding, breadth and depth of thought and feeling. The poem's imagery of liberation, of light dawning, of widening horizons, powerfully conveys an experience of awakening, the ending of ignorance and darkness.

> *Me rumran ȝeþeaht . . . on modes þeaht,*
> *Wisdom onwreaht . . .* (Cynewulf, 1977, p. 71, ll.1240, 1241–2)
> . . . learning unlocked me
> And dealt me in darkness
> The blinding blow of a life unpromised . . . (Holderness, 2002a,
> p. 49)

At the same time the imagery of durance and confinement giving way to liberty and freedom of movement realizes the effect of the poet's absolution from the burden of sin.

The verse is remarkable in its weaving together of separate experiential strands. These include the consciousness of intellectual awakening, a sudden expansion of the mind; the freeing from sin, figured in metaphors of breaking, loosening, physical liberation; the unstoppable flow of loving joy that fills the convert's heart with the force of divine grace; and finally the power of inspired speech, the capability of poetic composition that seems to appear suddenly on his lips and in his hands. Even more remarkable is the dialectical rhythm achieved in the poem's oscillation between confinement and expansion, echoed in the subtle play of assonance and half-rhyme. Under the irresistible impact of God's grace, the mind expands, the body is broken open to admit the influx of the Holy Spirit, the caged heart is freed from its prison, and the power of song is unloosed. But then there is a re-focusing of effort and energy into productive labour. Thus the convert's mind is expanded, almost exploded, but its powers are gathered and re-applied in the service of a new faith. The body is fractured, dispersed, occupied, but then re-formed, as the poet finds himself possessed of the technical capability of making something new.

> Dawn
> Upsprung with a far-flung
> Shroud-tearing, chain-shearing
> Bond-breaking brightness
> Of light's laceration, broke
> With a big bang into my
> Bone-box, body with spirit
> So suddenly filled
> To the brim now, full. (Holderness, 2002a, p. 50)

Previously the poet was dead to life, constricted by the bonds of sin, existing in a kind of living death. Now he is dead to sin, in his resurrected body embarking on a new life in the service of the spirit. Thus we find enacted in Cynewulf's brief autobiographical interpolation nothing less than the great drama of Christian redemption itself: 'as sin hath reigned unto death, even so might grace reign through righteousness unto eternal life by Jesus Christ our Lord' (Romans 5.21). Devotion to Christ means death, the death of my old 'self' and the birth of a new. 'For if we be dead with him, we shall also live with him' (II Timothy 2.11). The death of Christ on the Cross permanently transvalued both death and life, setting them into a new relation. Christ's death releases us from the death of sin, so that, from the everyday perspective, living towards Christ can appear as a death. 'Now if we be dead with Christ, we believe that we shall also live with him' (Romans 6.8). St Paul meant this literally. We are 'dead with Christ from the rudiments of the world' (Colossians 2.20). Paul's own conversion, forcibly cast to the ground and then raised again, cast into the dark of blindness and then restored to the light, offers an exemplary model of the Christian convert's rite of passage from ignorance to wisdom, from darkness to light, from death to new life.

In *Elene*, Cynewulf's autobiographical confession proves to be another instance of autothanatography. In speaking of his life, Cynewulf commemorates his death; in testifying to the authentic experience of selfhood he describes a fundamental disjunction between the writing self and an 'other' who is no longer here. The subject of autobiography is at once singular and multiple, coherent and fractured, self and other; at once 'I' and 'you', simultaneously 'we' and 'he' or 'she'.

* * *

When I made that translation of Cynewulf's autobiographical fragment, published first in the *European English Messenger* (Holderness, 1999, p. 36) and subsequently in my collection of poems *Craeft*, I was still engaged, albeit in a new way, with Shakespeare. In the course of writing a long-delayed book on Shakespeare's history plays (Holderness, 2000), I found myself brooding on *Hamlet*, and writing a long chapter about the ghost in history. Prompted by these speculations to dig deeper into the *Hamlet* story, I embarked on a fictional sequel to Shakespeare's play, drawing also on the Scandinavian roots of the Hamlet legend (Holderness, 2002b). Wishing to provide a cultural context for a Nordic narrative, I returned to some very early studies, and began to translate specimens of Old English poetry into modern verse, initially elegiac and epic, later Christian devotional poetry. Some of these translations were incorporated into the novel, others into a separate collection of verse (Holderness, 2002a).

This is the version of events that would be supplied by a literary micro-history, were the historian to drill down to so humble a level: source and analogue, imitation and adaptation, tradition and the individual talent. This explanatory narrative however masks the deeply personal, undeniably autobiographical dimension of this story. For what prompted me, after 25 years of publishing critical and theoretical writing, to write creatively, was an experience very similar to that recorded in Cynewulf's *Elene*.

> Grief-grappled, sin-shackled,
> Pinioned and paralysed
> By fault-fettered manacles
> Of my own making,
> Till learning unlocked me
> And dealt me in darkness
> The blinding blow
> Of a gift unpromised,
> A gift half-grasped,
> When freely God's grace
> On my dry face dropped
> As a dew. (Holderness, 2002a, p. 49)

I would not have written this if it had not happened to me. I returned to those ancient words because I found that Cynewulf was speaking of something I had known, felt in the blood, and felt along the heart. I can testify to the authenticity of this experience with all the seriousness and sincerity required for a traditional categorization of autobiographical writing; I can assure the reader of a complete and indissoluble identity between author, narrator and protagonist.

A testimony is always autobiographical: it tells, in the first person, the sharable and unsharable secret of what happened to me, to me, to me alone, the absolute secret of what I was in a position to live, see, hear, touch, sense and feel. (Derrida, 2000, p. 43)

And yet, notwithstanding the unassailable veracity of the witness, my poem, 'The Awakening' is as clear an example of *autothanatography* as Blanchot's *L'Instance de ma mort*. Can this be so in any way but rhetorically, since I so obviously live to tell the tale? Yes: but only by means of the theological truth embodied in the mystery of Christ's death and resurrection. The 'self' I recognize, or remember, as mine, the 'self' that entered that labyrinth of translation, adaptation, reconstruction, is now literally, that is to say ethically and linguistically, dead. The 'self' that emerged from the labyrinth was a resurrected self, wholly disengaged from its predecessor. The poem is the record of that transaction. But though it was the old, corrupted self that entered the activity of the poem's making, it was only the new self that was capable of making anything at all, since the gift of expression came to that new self, as it came to Cynewulf, as a free gift of grace.

I say 'wholly disengaged', knowing that physically and psychologically this cannot be entirely true. The old superseded self can present itself as other, as deceased, as capable of being reinvented to play a role in a retrospective autobiographical drama. Yet that rejected, unwanted otherness remains part of the new self too, as a cry of reproach, a shameful reminder, a wound that can never truly be healed. Derrida suggests that all mourning is doomed to failure since mourning involves the interiorization of the now dead other. Only the living can mourn only the dead, and what is dead is wholly other. Successful mourning however is that which assimilates the other(s), making them a part of us, and thereby destroying their otherness, their 'alterity'. Such mourning 'makes the other a part of us . . . and then the other no longer quite seems to be other' (Derrida, 1989, p. 35). If, however, that which is other is that which was once me, 'my self', 'myself', then mourning is an essential distantiation of the living self from its now dead counterpart. Such mourning can succeed only by failure, since to succeed would be to re-assimilate the other, and thereby threaten the achieved viability of the self. Secomb is correct in her paraphrase of Derrida's paradox: 'A failed mourning may succeed' (Secomb, 2002, p. 36).

* * *

She's gone forever!
I know when one is dead and when one lives;
She's dead as earth. Lend me a looking-glass;
If that her breath will mist or stain the stone,
Why, then she lives. (*King Lear*, 5.3.258–62)

Thoul't come no more,
Never, never, never, never, never! . . .
Do you see this? Look on her, look, her lips.
Look there, look there! He dies. (*King Lear*, 5.3.306–7, 309–10)

What does Lear see in Cordelia's lips? The distinction between life and death, the living and the dead, is here proposed as absolute: Cordelia is 'dead as earth'. Yet having pronounced her dead, Lear looks for signs of life, for the faintest traces of breath, invisible and inaudible, that yet may mist the mirror, 'stain the stone'. If it be so, 'she lives'. The second speech repeats exactly the same paradox: 'thoul't come no more'; yet some motion about her lips, some stirring of breath or speech, seem to imply vitality.

But 'life' may mean something different within the symbolic language of the drama from a pulse, respiration, continuing cerebral activity. What Lear feels from Cordelia's dead lips may be a breath that mists no mirror, a quickening spirit that transcends mortality, a sign of life everlasting. As Bradley and many critics after him have shown, the language of the play's closure overtly hints at redemptive, sacrificial, even specifically Christian meanings.

This feather stirs; she lives! If it be so,
It is a chance which does redeem all sorrows
That ever I have felt. (5.3.264–6).

'. . . if it be so', then Lear may die, as Bradley describes him, in 'unbearable joy' (Bradley, 1904; 1905, p. 291).

My first encounter with *King Lear*, at school in the early 1960s, was very much in the context of that optimistic Christian hermeneutics. Though I absorbed Christianity through literature (Dante, Donne, Hopkins, T. S. Eliot) rather than religious practice, I thought of myself as a Christian. Cordelia's resurrection was as real and authentic to me as the confident affirmations of the service for the burial of the dead: 'sure and certain hope of the resurrection to eternal life'.

Naturally that confidence and certainty faded, with a fairly standard intellectual development, through my early twenties, from spirituality to political commitment. I studied the Victorian writers, and followed them from religious confidence to secular humanism and social mission. My teaching and writing became philosophically and politically Marxist, and had no place for faith. I wholeheartedly embraced the supersession of those old redemptive interpretations of *King Lear* by bleak and nihilistic readings. I knew when one was dead, and when one lived.

Cordelia at the end of the play is probably already dead, and the evidence of life merely the delusion of a mad old king, himself on the point of extinction. She may be still barely alive, her actual death perhaps coinciding with that of her father. Lear's perception could hardly be trusted, if one were looking for a reliable clinical diagnosis; and the silence and inactivity of Edgar and Albany and Kent, who make no move to resuscitate her, seem to tell their own story. Lear's desire for Cordelia to survive, his yearning 'ache' for a romance resolution to the tragedy, is all that creates these imaginary vital signs. At the beginning of the play Lear looked to Cordelia's lips to speak a public declaration of love. But he did not listen, either to her speech or her silence; he was unable to grasp that Cordelia's lips would inevitably speak differently, that 'woman's desire would not be expected to speak the same language as man's' (Irigaray, 1985, p. 25). Now it is too late.

My father never became an old man. He died, in 1980, at the age of 52. Though I knew when one is dead and when one lives, the impossibility of accepting that he was merely 'dead as earth', would 'come no more', ignited in me a spiritual fuse that took fifteen years to burn through. His death enabled me to rediscover the fundamental symbiosis of the greatest poetry with the surest faith. Call it conversion, or reversion, by January 1997 I was confirmed in the Church of England and reconciled to the Christian faith. Dying to sin, and awakening to new life, I found myself speaking a new language, a language of poetry and revelation.

> Racked on the Cross
> A ghost, upgiven, received
> This songskill, craft and art,
> Exuberant eloquence, manifest
> Mastery of word and wisdom,
> Service and song. (Holderness, 2002a, p. 50)

I looked again on Cordelia's lips, and I saw, again, with 'unbearable joy', what was there.

> Do you see this? Look on her: look, her lips.
> Look there, look there!

* * *

To realize the self it is necessary first to apprehend 'the caesura which severs present from past selfhood' (Falconer 2005, p. 1). And here the death of the past self and the death of the author join hands. We know our former selves in the same way as we read texts. We cannot know the past as it knew itself, and we cannot know ourselves as we were at an earlier age. We cannot re-live our past experience, we can only recall it; we cannot recover the past, we can only read it. We are absent from both. Yet memory throws light on present being, and the present consists largely, as T.S. Eliot observed, in reading the past:

> For the pattern is new in every moment
> And very moment is a new and shocking
> Valuation of all we have been. (Eliot 1963a, p. 199)

The author is dead, yet lives. I am dead, yet I live. He is dead, yet he lives. Autobiography and autothanatography both

> Point to one end, which is always present. (Eliot 1963a, p. 190)

Chapter 10

Hierophantic Shakespeare

Philippa Berry

> *Many are the thyrsus-bearers; few are the Bacchoi.*
>
> (Plato, *Phaedo* 69c)

The subtle threads of meaning that I have found in Shakespearean texts have enabled me to navigate some dark and challenging times, revealing unexpectedly complex yet delicate patterns amid the maze-like disorder of human life. Only very gradually, however, was I able to accept that the inspirational and instructive role being played in my life by our elusive native poet had a strongly numinous character, and that the unfamiliar beauty of many Shakespearean tropes was directing me to look both at and beyond the shadowy simulacra of mundane reality, in order to explore the deeper mystery of human existence. Because it is now so well adapted to empirical forms of intellectual investigation, modern English is almost denuded of words to describe heightened experiential states and the modes of cognition associated with them; as a result, I will be raiding the more nuanced lexicon of ancient Greece in my attempt to describe Shakespeare's formative impression upon me. For, during my almost life-long study of his extraordinary and riddling art, he has generously offered me access to a mode of consciousness qualitatively different from the rational, discursive knowing that is sometimes termed *dianoia* by the Greeks.[1]

The unfamiliar mode of knowing shown to me by Shakespeare is not exclusively aesthetic, even though my induction into his bardic mysteries began by focusing on the 'inky' materiality of Shakespearean representation. Gradually my intimate critical engagement with his 'millions of strange shadows' directed my attention otherwise, as I sought to understand their origin and 'substance'. In the process, I encountered two closely related types of cognition, both defined by early Greek philosophers as functions or expressions of *nous*. *Nous* was equated with the intellective faculty in man, sometimes termed the higher mind (its Latin equivalents, *intellectus* or *mens*, enjoyed a high status in medieval philosophy and theology, where this form of cognition was clearly differentiated from *ratio* or reason.) This quasi-spiritual faculty does not acquire knowledge via sensory perceptions but intuitively, in a manner described as related to the higher properties of soul. Such properties were held by early Greek philosophers to mirror, albeit imperfectly, the ordering principles of the cosmos. Plato conceived of *nous* as 'the eye of the soul', while Parmenides urged his followers to 'look with the *nous*' in order to apprehend an immaterial or spiritual reality. Aristotle defined *nous* as equivalent to Mind or universal reason, which conferred on humans the capacity to apprehend Truth (see Bremmer, 1987, pp. 48–9).

Closely related to *nous* are the verb *noein* and its cognate noun *noesis,* denoting the ability to apprehend or sense something immediately – to recognize a set of signs through a mental process that is non-linear and seemingly intuitive. According to early philosophers, this was the most accessible manifestation of *nous*, offering intuitive cognitive insights into being and becoming. Writing of Parmenides' philosophical use of *noein*, Martin Heidegger describes this form of 'thinking' as a form of 'non-sensible perception' that involves an 'attentive apprehending', a 'taking-heed-of' (Heidegger, 1984, pp. 79–101). Homer refers a great deal to the mysterious kind of instantaneous cognition that is *noesis*, associating it with crucial acts of *anagnorisis* or recognition (Nagy, 1991, pp. 202–6).

However, it was the more directly philosophical state of *theoria* that was generally understood as *nous*'s highest human expression. The term 'theory' may be extremely familiar to modern literary critics; yet we rarely reflect upon its ancient Greek origins. But in the thought of Plato *theoria*, meaning intellectual contemplation, is the philosophical means of a wondrous vision, associated with the perception of divine truths. By such means the cognitive subject of Platonic *theoria* was said to experience and understand the affinity between human and divine beings. The ritual origins of this term have been traced back to the practice of pilgrimage to religious sites and sanctuaries in archaic Greece. Thus, long before its philosophical adaptation, *theoria* meant 'seeing the gods'.[2] *Theoria* recovered some of this original meaning in early Neoplatonism, where it was used to denote 'epiphany' by Proclus and Iamblichus.

In my explorations of Shakespeare's works, whether as reader or spectator, my impression is that I have experienced both these aspects of *nous* – *noesis* and *theoria* – at least to some degree. In other words, I consider that I have experienced Shakespeare as both *mystagogos* and *hierophantes*: first as a kindly guide and sponsor in my exploration of his encrypted 'black lines'; finally as an initiator into 'strange mysteries' and 'sacred paths' (*Henry VIII*, 1.3.2, *Merry Wives of Windsor*, 4.4.58).[3]

As a young student, my initial motivation in studying Shakespeare was to gain greater insight into the full spectrum of human experience, in all its joys and suffering, its virtues and vices. But in the process, I was compelled to re-evaluate most of what I had thought obvious about being human. I found in the Shakespearean corpus an extended meditation on human folly and ignorance; a relentless exposure of our comical–tragical habits of solipsism and self-importance. But I also became more and more intrigued by the subtle ways in which the poet-dramatist would dismantle his characters' defensive enclosure within the bounded circle of the self, as he led both them and his audience on strange transformative odysseys of self-undoing. Chief among his preferred instruments in this painful process of metamorphosis was desire of one form or another, most commonly sexual and affective desire, or *eros*. As I tracked the multiple textual traces of this Shakespearean *eros*, I slowly realized that this most exceptional of literary *oeuvres* was not simply dramatizing the dynamic mutability of human identity; it was also hinting at a quasi-mystical view of human potential, in which an obscure and seemingly primordial force of attraction – an Eros that now appeared immense and alien in its wide-ranging powers – played a central shaping role.

Evoked solely through fragmentary and oblique allusions, this barely perceptible Shakespearean vision of man's subjection to and potential transformation by wild and indistinct powers began to pre-occupy me more and more. In my struggle to unravel the seemingly deliberate veils of Shakespearean opacity, two of my earliest guides and allies were Plato and his Renaissance translator and commentator, Marsilio Ficino. From these two intellectual giants I discovered, as yet uncomprehendingly, that Eros is a great *daimon*. According to the Platonists it is *eros*, in the guise of a profound and questing love of beauty, that most powerfully stimulates the mind to go beyond logical thinking (*ratio*, or *dianoia*). While Ficino was careful to use the language of Christianity when he observed that 'love unites the mind with God more swiftly, closely and firmly than cognition', his source for this observation was Plato's Orphic-inspired writings on love (Ficino, 1576, p. 663).[4]

As I puzzled to understand what was signified in any individual Shakespearean text, I was invariably left with a tantalizing impression of almost infinite depth – of numerous hidden strata of meaning waiting to be uncovered, in an untapped reserve of *signifiance* that always exceeded any individual act of interpretation.[5] With the passage of time, however, came more and more moments of elated recognition, of sudden apprehension, which I would now describe as a very imperfect form of *noetic* knowledge. This sensation of delighted, innate knowing during what I gradually came to regard as the receipt of a Shakespearean wisdom-transmission was like being momentarily 'englobed' in an exquisite radiance of golden enlightenment. At such times I would feel myself entering, albeit fleetingly, into a particular bard-given state of grace. Borrowing another term from Greek philosophy, at such times I experienced the texts as possessing an extremely strong and distinctive *dynamis*. This Greek philosophical concept was developed from the word's early meaning of simply 'power'. For Aristotle *dynamis* denoted the invisible potency inherent in a substance or thing that makes it able to 'move': to change or influence another thing or person through its *energeia*.[6] Among Neoplatonists both these concepts became more elevated in their implications; here *dynamis* denoted the generative power of the One and of the Platonic Forms, as well as of the individual soul, while *energeia* was associated with the actualization of this power through the activity of the intellect, or *nous* (see Siorvanes, 1996, pp. 100–1).

Sir Philip Sidney famously observed that 'moving is of a higher degree than teaching . . . For who will be taught, if he be not moved with desire to be taught?' (Sidney, ed. Alexander, 2004, p. 22). I was required to study these words carefully as an English undergraduate; but I confess I did not really understand them. I certainly did not realize that in Shakespeare's work above all I was experiencing the very phenomenon that Sidney was trying to describe, whereby a hidden power or set of powers (*dynameis*), through its manifested effect or enactment as *energeia*, was indeed strongly affecting or 'moving' me. Of course the visible manifestation of the texts' hidden potency used familiar literary forms – not just compelling dramatic narratives, but skilfully crafted tropes and phraseology, clever wordplay, calculated metrical effects. Yet this Shakespearean *dynamis* began to 'move' me subliminally or unconsciously long before I was able to analyse its poetic media or instruments discursively and critically; moreover, it left an impression that always seemed to exceed the combined effect of individual literary tools, along with the rational capacity of the mind to define it.

Why, I wondered, was there always a distinctive luminosity about this process of being 'moved' by a particular passage of exceptional skill or beauty – a feeling of exquisite wordless delight, of being briefly lit up from the inside? An early Greek poet or philosopher might have used the verb *phainesthai* ('to show itself' or 'to be in the light') to speak of such an experience, in order to denote an experience understood as 'a truth-bearing, luminous event,' where something is just 'there', in the light, and some part of the inherent order of the cosmos is briefly 'made manifest in the manifold appearances of the things'.[7] These experiences of sudden illumination seldom occurred when I read other literary works (with some notable exceptions, such as in readings of Dante and Greek tragedy). Not until I encountered and recognized this distinctive feeling in a very different context, through contact with still living mystery traditions such as the teachings of the Vedas, did I conclude that this strange and wonderful sensation of luminosity actually signalled contact with a *mysterion* – with a knowledge that, even while it appeared to be deeply embedded in the material world of the senses, was at the same time otherworldly and *kryphios*, encrypted or secret.[8]

I therefore regard my first memorable Shakespearean epiphany as a kind of *myesis* – a preliminary initiation. This occurred when I was seventeen. I was sitting the entrance examination for Cambridge, in the days when their Admissions process included a formal examination, when I found before me a long passage from the last act of *The Merchant of Venice*. As I looked nervously over the sixty-odd lines I began to grasp, albeit dimly, what I would much later define as the poet's skilful 'intertwining' of human experience with all that initially appears 'other' to it, and to intuit how *eros* or desire constituted a vital link in this quasi-ecstatic process of expansive knowing.[9]

The comedy's last act begins with a nocturnal love scene that is framed by many clichéd romantic devices: moonshine, starlight, wind, sweet music. But it is also invested with a highly charged otherworldly ambience. This is partly effected by the poet's incantatory use of the trope of anaphora, with eight lulling repetitions of 'in such a night'; also by his deceptively simple lexis, here dominated by Anglo-Saxon monosyllables. But it is two lovers' fragmentary allusions to a series of well-known myths and legends that lead us most directly and powerfully into another world and a different experience of time:

LORENZO: The moon shines bright: in such a night as this,
When the sweet wind did gently kiss the trees
And they did make no noise, in such a night
Troilus methinks mounted the Troyan walls
And sighed his soul toward the Grecian tents,
Where Cressid lay that night.

JESSICA: In such a night
Did Thisbe fearfully o'ertrip the dew
And saw the lion's shadow ere himself
And ran dismayed away.

LORENZO: In such a night
Stood Dido with a willow in her hand
Upon the wild sea banks and waft her love
To come again to Carthage.

JESSICA: In such a night
Medea gathered the enchanted herbs
That did renew old Aeson.

LORENZO: In such a night
Did Jessica steal from the wealthy Jew
And with an unthrift love did run from Venice
As far as Belmont.

JESSICA: In such a night
Did young Lorenzo swear he loved her well,
Stealing her soul with many vows of faith
And ne'er a true one.

LORENZO: In such a night
Did pretty Jessica, like a little shrew,
Slander her love, and he forgave it her.

JESSICA: I would outnight you, did nobody come.
But hark, I hear the footing of a man. (5.1.1–24)

Ordinary reality is momentarily suspended here, not just by the poet's rhetorical skills, but also by the haunting combination of moonlight with a strange stillness ('When the sweet wind did gently kiss the trees/And they did make no noise'). Yet although this quasi-magical landscape is vividly illumined by the uncanny beauty of classical myth, it is a tragic, not a comic environment. Like Thisbe, terrified by the lion's shadow, this seemingly enchanted world is itself over-shadowed by unpredictable and 'wild' powers: natural forces of passion and mutability that lead several of its mythic lovers to death, some to rebirth or metamorphosis. The mythic world's loveliness is as fragile and transient as the intense romantic emotions so closely associated with these love stories.

This poignant insight into the impermanence of natural beauty and romantic love relies strongly on the reader's or spectator's knowledge of classical myth and legend. So I was very lucky that my bookish familiarity with such narratives enabled me to weave a convincing interpretation of the scene! Once I had recognized that the recently eloped Lorenzo and Jessica are testing each other by citing tragic love-stories from Ovid and Virgil, thereby revealing their mutual fear of inconstancy and betrayal, the deliberate ambiguity of this skilful prelude to the play's subsequent 'happy' ending became clear. I was struck also by Jessica's close structural affinity with the unlucky or abandoned women from these love-stories (each of which leads to their loss of home or tribe, as well as to personal tragedy). As a Jew, she represents yet another vulnerable outsider who, like Medea in particular, has just sacrificed family and tribe – as well as religion – for her new lover. It therefore seemed to me that the last act of this famous comedy began with a very dark note indeed.

But my pleasure in the sorrowful loveliness of this scene was also due to my partial recognition, at what could be called the *noetic* level, of its skilful meditative movement between different states of consciousness. It opens by inviting us to empathize with heightened emotional states attributed to famous lovers of Near-Eastern and African origin: Trojan Troilus, Carthaginian Dido, Babylonian Thisbe and Colchian Medea. Potent and familiar types of the visceral and affective intensity of passionate love, this procession of unlucky and largely non-European lovers invites the spectator or reader to connect with an 'enchanted' yet dangerously 'wild' state of being that the West has idealized but also feared, because of its intrinsic threat to civility and self-control. Yet no sooner has each of us fallen under the poet's calculated romantic spell than the scene widens its focus to explore heightened states of consciousness of a different kind, in which the passions or animal 'spirits' are no longer excited but subdued. It is now that *eros* works its deeper or higher magic, by deflecting the lovers' focus toward non-human kinds of beauty. Our aural attention is successively transferred from Medea's enchantments to (fictitious) reports of Portia's prayers, then to the 'touches of sweet harmony' made by the musicians whom Lorenzo calls to play outside, beneath the moonlight. Next, the visual focus of the scene is suggestively adjusted, as the poet expands his dramaturgic vision to encompass a vision of the stars. By shining consolatory rays of a subtler light upon our flawed humanity, he now 'sublates' the erotic tensions of the scene. As dramatic sympathy is disengaged from the mythic love stories of Ovid and Virgil, the audience is invited to imitate the lovers' cognitive shift, and participate in a heightened state of ecstasy that parallels the contemplative speculations or *theoria* of Greek philosophers and mystics.

When the eloped lovers gaze upwards to the stars, both their gaze and our own is briefly elevated beyond the sub-lunary realm of mutable nature and tempestuous human experience. Ordinary reality now seems inverted: the night sky resembles a richly ornamented cathedral pavement that is 'thick inlaid' with stars and planets. A classic instance of *theoria,* this awe-inspiring vision is shaped by the Platonic theory of love, whereby the lover may be inspired by the beauty of earthly things – such as a beloved, or sweet music – to contemplate a higher and heavenly beauty.[10] The moment appears to be orchestrated by the musicians who have just entered the garden;

yet it is with subtler kinds of music, non-human as well as human, that the poet is most deeply concerned.

Along with Platonic love theory, Lorenzo is evoking two Pythagorean doctrines at this point.[11] The first concerns the music of the celestial sphere, reputedly inaudible to all save a few. The second relates to teachings on the innate harmony of the soul, which in Plato's *Phaedo* is compared to a lyre by the Pythagorean disciple Simmias:

> Look how the floor of heaven
> Is thick inlaid with patens of bright gold.
> There's not the smallest orb which thou behold'st
> But in his motion like an angel sings,
> Still choiring to the young-eyed cherubins.
> Such harmony is in immortal souls,
> But whilst this muddy vesture of decay
> Doth grossly close it in, we cannot hear it. (5.1.57–64)

We are being reminded that the human music and poetry – in other words, what we can literally hear at this point – is actually counterpointing a vast cosmic silence: according to Pythagoras, this was the sign of our collective failure, as flawed and 'muddy' souls, to hear either the heavenly harmony of the spheres, or our own soul-music.

My seventeen-year-old self grasped only vaguely that ancient philosophy and mysticism had decisively entered the dramatic picture, and that this sudden shift of focus – from sub-lunary emotions to the celestial affinities of 'immortal souls' – was effecting a temporary restoration of harmony. Even today, when I supposedly possess more extensive knowledge of both Shakespeare and classical culture, I find it difficult to write about his Venetian lovers' *theoria*-like epiphany, especially in a largely sceptical and disenchanted age.[12] At seventeen, I still knew nothing of the Platonic love theory that underpinned this dramatic movement from erotic passions to divine contemplation, although it would later be pivotal in my doctoral

188 Shakespeare and I

research. Nor could I have imagined any affinity between Lorenzo's mystic 'showing' and the ancient ritual practices of the Greeks. Now, however, I see this moment of nocturnal revelation as closely akin to the *epopteia* that marked the second stage and culmination of the Eleusinian mysteries. On that most secret occasion, in the darkness of a 'holy night' that probably coincided with a full moon, a 'great light' (*mega phos*) and certain blessed and divine sights were shown to the *mystai* or first-level initiates. These signalled their soul-perfection, and the culmination of their initiation as *epoptai*, full initiates (see Clinton, 2003, pp. 50–60).

Shakespeare is not merely elevating our consciousness at this juncture; he is celebrating the quasi-divine potential of both art and beauty to effect this heightening of soul-attention, through their magnetic appeal to our innate soul-harmony. For when Lorenzo exclaims 'Come, ho, and wake Diana with a hymn' (5.1.65) he is alluding to the Orphic practice of hymning planetary powers and gods, as well as *daimones* or spirits. Admired by Platonists such as Marsilio Ficino and Pico della Mirandola as the reputed source of all the theological wisdom of the Greeks, the hymns of Orpheus were said to harmonize and elevate the soul, moving it from everyday consciousness to a spiritual perception of reality.[13] In this allusion Shakespeare is undoubtedly glancing at the Orphic pretensions of erudite poet-dramatist George Chapman (most probably the poetic 'rival' mentioned in the *Sonnets*).[14] But in the lines that follow, he implicitly claims similar 'vatic' or inspired status for himself. Echoing Ovid's much-quoted account of the Orpheus myth, from the *Metamorphoses*, Lorenzo stresses art's capacity to subdue the passions of our animal 'spirits', and he elaborates further on the Platonic-Pythagorean theme of man's innate soul-music:

JESSICA: I am never merry when I hear sweet music.
LORENZO: The reason is your spirits are attentive,
            For do but note a wild and wanton herd

Or race of youthful and unhandled colts,
Fetching mad bounds, bellowing and neighing loud,
Which is the hot condition of their blood,
If they but hear perchance a trumpet sound,
Or any air of music touch their ears,
You shall perceive them make a mutual stand,
Their savage eyes turned to a modest gaze
By the sweet power of music. Therefore the poet
Did feign that Orpheus drew trees, stones, and floods,
Since naught so stockish, hard, and full of rage
But music for the time doth change his nature.
. . . Mark the music. (5.1.68–87)

What is the normally self-effacing dramatist telling us about himself in this lengthy coda to the lovers' starlit epiphany? Given my teenage unreadiness to engage with the deeper dimension of the ancient bardic role, as played by Shakespeare, I was probably fortunate that this extended Orphic allusion was not included in the passage I had to comment on so many years ago. My interpretation now, however, is that this Elizabethan Orpheus now acknowledges his capacity to elevate consciousness in extraordinary ways, as one who can not only draw 'trees, stones and floods', but who also possesses, like Orpheus, an inspired understanding of spiritual or divine things (see Plato, *Symposium*, 203a). Such a man was termed by ancient philosophers *daimonios*, or more than human, which is how Alcibiades describes Socrates in *The Symposium*: 'strange, wonderful, hardly human' (ibid., 219c).

At this early stage in my study of literature I was by no means ready to recognize the bard of Avon as *daimonios*: as a British hierophant or soul guide from whom I could receive extraordinary teaching. Yet an initiatory door into what proved to be a major chapter in my life was decisively opened for me by Shakespeare's moonlit meditation upon love and soul in Renaissance Venice; when I secured my place at Cambridge, I felt convinced this was thanks to a fairly confident exegesis of the passage from *The Merchant*. What I did not know at that point was that the seeds of a further significant phase in my life were also present in that moment of personal *peripeteia*; some of the unanswered philosophical questions posed by the scene's closing movement would later be fundamental to my research into Renaissance culture. But not until several years later, as my undergraduate degree neared completion, did I find myself struggling to make sense of similarly arcane Shakespearean motifs, this time in *Antony and Cleopatra*, which were once again organized around a strangely ambivalent manifestation of *eros*. The intellectual challenge propelled me unexpectedly towards a new stage in my as yet unknowing passage through the Shakespearean mysteries, by inspiring a spontaneous decision to corroborate and develop an undergraduate thesis through graduate work in the Renaissance.

This quite sudden career decision was to initiate a decade-long attempt to decipher the debt of Elizabethan poets and dramatists to both ancient philosophy and its early Renaissance commentators. But in terms of my Shakespearean initiation, what proved to be just as important about this development were the opportunities it would later give me both to teach the works themselves and to meet and discuss them with other Shakespeareans. Once armed with a Ph.D., and a fraction more knowledge of the philosophical discourses that were circulating in Shakespeare's day, I was privileged to guide a few others along the path through Shakespeare's works, and to enjoy the intellectual companionship of others travelling the same road, as fellow teachers and researchers of Shakespeare. At this point my greatest learning began. Only now did I begin to feel the true weight of Shakespeare's hierophantic wisdom, as a curiously self-effacing revealer of divine secrets, or *arrheta*.[15]

Shakespeare's bardic guidance seldom took the form of substantive, empirical knowledge; instead, it was invariably proffered in the riddling and obscure style of ancient oracles and mystery traditions. As I sifted through the compacted sediments of ideas to be found in seemingly casual tropes, I would frequently chance upon what I would term 'antique' cultural deposits. In such unlikely places the poet appeared deliberately to have laid down choice fragments of 'sacred mysteries', thereby pursuing a secretive practice not wholly unlike the seemingly random burial of ritual caches by our earliest British ancestors. Here could be found suggestive traces of the 'holy antique hours' of Roman, Hellenic and Egyptian wisdom, including Stoic, Pythagorean or Hermetic teachings on the nature of the soul and the universe. Here too were strange remnants of ancient British lore sourced from Tudor antiquarians, and concealed in passing allusions to folk traditions first elaborated by Celts or Saxons. Like half-erased commentaries on ostensibly secular texts, these allusions offered me insights into the anagogical or mystical meanings of the Shakespearean corpus. It felt as if Shakespeare was now benignly extending his hand to me, playing the part of a commentator as well as an inspired poet.

Integral to my induction into these Shakespearean mysteries was my growing sense that they were reconnecting me with what Wordsworth in *Tintern Abbey* called 'the life of things'.[16] The Shakespearean genius for particularity gave me an increasingly powerful experience of the world's pristine *haecceitas* or 'thisness': of the primal singularity of both living and inanimate forms, their inherent *dynamis* and *energeia*. By alerting me to the particular 'virtues' or properties of individual trees, plants, animals and birds – the forgotten potency of oak and sycamore, willow and cypress, of plantain, violet and eglantine, of owl and cuckoo, bear and deer – the mysterious swan of Avon guided a studious young woman into a deep relationship with what still remains of wild nature. Yet not just the elements of the natural world, but any object that might be perceived casually as 'base and vile, holding no quantity' – linen and letters, rings, feathers and pots, candles and casements, calendars and garters – could be mysteriously energized through this poet's art, and invested with 'form and dignity' (*A Midsummer Night's Dream*, 1.1.233).

As my perception of the world around me changed, so did my perception of time; or perhaps I should say rather that it expanded. The rhythmic tempo of Shakespeare's works is shaped by the annual cycle of time as our distant ancestors once honoured this, when due reverence was given to the particular properties of specific celestial events, favoured feast days, and different seasons. In numerous allusions to the potencies of light and shade, of night and day, and to the unique qualities of particular days, he reminded me of the 'sacred radiance' of sun, moon and stars. Strongly moved by the almost otherworldly luminosity of Shakespeare's light-filled tropes, I found myself deeply attracted also by his paradoxical poetics of blackness: this appeared to derive from an Orphic-inspired understanding of Night and darkness as a secretive plenitude, in which extraordinary revelations could occur, hidden rites be enacted.[17] In the process, I began to perceive human life somewhat like the star-struck Lorenzo; not as simply embedded within the material and natural environment, but implicated rather within a vast web of invisible powers, whose profound and pervasive influence on human life our post-modern and hyper-rational era has all but forgotten.

While Shakespeare's dramatic focus often seemed to throw an unflattering light upon humanity's monologic self-absorption, my critical attention was drawn more and more to the narrative and textual threads that interwove with and counterpointed his recurrent theme of human solipsism. These strands of meaning alluded repeatedly to our fundamental affinity not just with other members of our species, but with a multitude of non-human powers, from animals to angels, each possessed of a distinctive *energeia* that implied connection with a pervasive world-animating force. Bridging the natural, human and divine realms, this appeared to be a kind of cosmic *eros* in action. When his cousin Vernon warns Hotspur of the preparation of Hal and his comrades for the battle of Worcester in *1 Henry IV*, his theriomorphic rhetoric metamorphoses this motley crew into a band of semi-divine heroes, whose investment with bird and animal, saintly and planetary forms implies connection to a seemingly infinite source of natural and supernatural energy:

All furnished, all in arms,
All plumed like estridges that with the wind . . .
Baiting like eagles having lately bathed,
Glittering in golden coats like images,
As full of spirit as the month of May,
And gorgeous as the sun at midsummer;
Wanton as youthful goats, wild as young bulls. (4.1.97–104)

In his evocation of a golden energy, radiating and vitalizing, that mysteriously transforms and elevates ordinary human experience, Vernon gives figurative shape to the quasi-electrical current I often feel plugged into by Shakespeare. This shimmering Shakespearean phenomenology seems closely related to the pulsating cosmic circuit understood by ancient thinkers as giving order to the universe, termed *pneuma* by Stoic philosophers, and *spiritus mundi* by Renaissance Platonists.[18] The Stoic *pneuma* was a phosphorescent mixture of fire and air – the same elements into which Cleopatra desires to dissolve on her death. Through soul's highest manifestation, as a vehicle or chariot of light (*augeoides ochema*), each individual was perceived as intimately connected with this animating breath of the world. Ficino observed that:

Whenever you look within at our soul clothed as it were in spirit, perhaps you will suppose that you see a demon, a triple demon. For you will see too the celestial vehicle covered entirely with a fiery and an airy veil, and this veil surrounded with spirit. (Ficino, trans. Jayne, ch.46)[19]

It is my conviction that at its dazzling best, the art of Shakespeare facilitates almost instantaneous connection with this vitalizing force, enabling us to experience, even if unknowingly, the way in which these subtle energies invisibly inform and weave together the entire fabric of planetary life.

A conscious mastery of this individual connection to cosmic energy was said to be achieved only by those possessing exceptional, quasi-*daimonic* powers. Yet Vernon continues:

> I saw young Harry with his beaver on,
> His cuishes on his thighs, gallantly armed,
> Rise from the ground like feathered Mercury,
> And vaulted with such ease into his seat
> As if an angel dropped down from the clouds
> To turn and wind a fiery Pegasus,
> And witch the world with noble horsemanship. (*1 Henry IV*, 4.1.105–11)

The Platonic subtext in these lines on 'noble horsemanship' should have been obvious to Shakespeare's more learned spectators. In Plato's *Phaedrus* the individual's capacity to guide the soul-vehicle is symbolized by a charioteer, who must train his two horses to be led by desire for the highest truth. Only through the faculty of *nous*, in other words, can the unruly energies of *eros* be properly directed. Hal's possession of this quasi-divine faculty, as an exceptional and *daimon*-like being, is implied not just by his skill in a kind of celestial horsemanship but also by his comparison to 'feathered Mercury' and 'an angel dropped down from the clouds'.

I therefore came to see Shakespeare's profound teaching as both phenomenological and metaphysical, a poetic reunification of matter and spirit, of dark and light, that not only connected me with the forgotten lore of the soul, so important to ancient philosophers, but also changed forever my connection with embodied existence on the earth. In the process, I entered into a newly sensitized relationship to the subtleties of place, formerly regarded as the particular *daimones* or *genii* of wood and moor and stream. Shakespeare often gives ephemeral human form to such local spirits or 'shadows': not only as

Puck, the three 'wyrd' sisters, Ariel or Caliban, but also as characters possessed of a distinctive intensity or frenzy – Poor Tom, Mercutio, Autolycus. Through Shakespeare's Cleopatra I first fell under the seductive spell of Egypt, through his strange and charismatic Owen Glendower first sensed the misty and secretive beauty of Wales. And it was likewise because of Shakespeare's shaping influence on my academic life that I found myself propelled into a deeper connection with the heart of England – with Warwickshire and Stratford on Avon. Here, in the course of regular summer stays for academic conferences and theatre going, I made frequent visits to the poet's tomb at Holy Trinity Church. Was I succumbing to the forgotten cult of Shakespeare, so passionately advocated by David Garrick and others in the nineteenth century (see Davidhazi, 1998)? I suppose I was, at least in the sense understood by the ancient Greeks, who offered cultic veneration to the tombs of heroes such as Oedipus. Kneeling tentatively to the left of the altar, I would imagine myself reaching out to the memory of the long dead poet. As I gazed up at the inscrutable expression of his wall-mounted effigy, and pondered the curiously suggestive swan feather that it holds for a quill, I was undoubtedly seeking a kind of benediction. But were my inchoate appeals for guidance amid his enigmatic textual shadows answered? It seemed to me that certain insights were indeed granted – however odd or riddling these may appear to certain of my readers (see Berry 1999)! And did I sense the shadowy spirit-presence of the long-dead bard? All I can relate is that I felt my strongest intimacy with him in a timbered room that looked over the gardens of New Place, where I passed a September night in that strange half-sleeping, half-waking state of stillness the Greeks called *hesychia*. . .[20] For this and many other reasons, I have come to regard Shakespeare as akin to an indwelling spirit of our island – a spirit, moreover, whose extensive *daimonic* powers have by no means diminished with the change of cultures.

It is a literary commonplace that Dante could not have travelled through the many-faceted realms of Hell and Purgatory without his 'courteous master' and poetic mentor, Virgil, by his side. It was Virgil who gave Dante 'eyes for journeying', and who kept the wavering gaze of his pupil firmly focussed on the higher regions to which he aspired. From late antiquity until the Renaissance, there are many comments by the learned that the exemplary poetic art of Virgil bore not only aesthetic and moral fruits, but also arcane or spiritual knowledge. Macrobius commented in the *Saturnalia* *ita suo more velut aliud agendo implet arcana*: 'Thus, as is his wont, Virgil discloses sacred mysteries while appearing to do something else' (Macrobius, trans. Davies, 1969, p. 171). Virgil's Tudor translator, Richard Stanyhurst, made essentially the same point when he observed that Virgil 'doth laboure, in telling as yt were a *Cantorburye tale*, too ferret owt the secrets of Nature'.[21] Yet the comparable role played by Shakespeare is seldom acknowledged in our sceptical age.

True to the spirit of the ancient mysteries, but with an eye also to the particular constraints of his historical circumstances, Shakespeare seems to have elected to play his hierophantic role with exemplary discretion and deliberate self-effacement. Much of his teaching is squarely concerned with the world of the ego – with the moral challenges as well as the delights of mundane human existence. Yet as one who was undeniably *daimon*-like, *daimonios*, he can also act as the inspired revealer of deep strata of archaic wisdom: precious seams of forgotten knowledge that lie buried far beneath the surface of our secular and globalized culture. If I have learnt anything from this wise being, it is that our 'muddy vesture of decay' is most richly dignified through association with the mysterious motions of soul, or *psyche*. And as I approach the end of my long journey with this most 'courteous master', the deeply rooted earth-wisdom expressed in the delicate tapestry of his texts now appears to me to have a single and extraordinary aim: to reconnect us with the subtle soul-fire that animates what we think of as ordinary reality.

Notes

1. I would like to thank Ewan Fernie for encouraging me to address this challenging topic. Thanks are also due to several other companions on the path of the Shakespearean *mystai*, especially Dympna Callaghan, Margaret Tudeau-Clayton, Margaret Jones-Davies, John Joughin and Richard Wilson. My thanks also to Nicholas Mann, for his patient attention to my tangled argument, and to Gerry Ahrens, a non-Shakespearean who played the role of *mystagogos* during two visits to Stratford. In *The Republic*, Plato defines *dianoia* in terms of deductive thinking or reasoning from premise to conclusion, and *noesis* as the ultimate form of true knowledge, which intuitively grasps the Supreme Form of the Good (VII, 1–3).

2. For the early use of *theoria* in ancient Greek culture and society, see Wilson Nightingale, 2004, and Elsner/Rutherford, 2008.

3. For detailed explication of the terminology of the Greek mysteries, see Burkert, 1987 and Clinton, 2003. My references to the language of the Greek mysteries are primarily to the best-documented mystery cult, that of Eleusis.

4. Angela Voss comments that 'the god [Eros] who is the desire to reconnect with one's source . . . leads the mind to abandon its habit of discursive thought' (Voss, 2002, p. 236). In a letter written around 1469 to his friend Giovanni Cavalcanti, Ficino writes of his newly completed commentary on Plato's *Symposium*: 'A long time ago, dear Giovanni, I learned from Orpheus that love existed, and that it held the keys to the whole world; then from Plato I learned the definition of love and its nature.' (See Ficino, trans. Jayne, 1985, p. 179.)

5. 'Signifiance is a process in the course of which the "subject" of the text . . . struggles with meaning and is deconstructed ("lost") . . . Signifiance is "the un-end of possible operations in a given field of a language". Contrary to signification, signifiance cannot be reduced, therefore, to communication, representation, expression: it places the subject (of writer, reader) in the text not as a projection . . . but as a "loss", a "disappearance". Hence its identification with the pleasure of jouissance. . .' (Stephen Heath, summarizing in his prefatory note

the elaboration of this key post-structuralist concept by Julia Kristeva, Jaques Lacan and Roland Barthes in Barthes, 1978, p. 9).

6. See, for example, Plato, *The Sophist*, 247d-e and Aristotle, *Metaphysics*, V, 12, 1019a, 15–19.

7. For a detailed discussion of the association of *phainesthai* with a non-representational understanding of appearances in archaic Greece, see Sandwell, 1996, pp. 42–4.

8. This adjective is one of the titles of Dionysus, a god closely associated with the mysteries, and who as Dionysus Kryphios is hidden or concealed. For the intimate link between the Dionysian and the Orphic mysteries, see Graf, 2008, p. 171.

9. I borrow this concept of 'intertwining' from Maurice Merleau-Ponty's phenomenological account of the *chiasm*, which denotes the intimate intertwining of the visible and the invisible, of nature and the human body, of the human body and perceptual consciousness, and of the natural and the cultural. See Merleau-Ponty, 1968.

10. Although evidence for the influence of Platonism on Elizabethan poets and dramatists is easier to trace in works by Shakespeare's more obviously learned contemporaries, especially Edmund Spenser and George Chapman, it seems highly likely that he read Plato in the Latin or French translations which were widely available at the time. His friend Ben Jonson appears to have owned at least two volumes of Plato's complete works in Latin, including a 1590 printing of Ficino's *Platonis Opera Omnia*. For a recent and detailed study of the debt to Plato across Shakespeare's *oeuvre*, see Rowe, 2010. For the widespread interest in Plato at the Universities, especially in the earlier years of Elizabeth's reign, see Andersson, 2010, pp. 69–116.

11. In Ficino's writings on the subject of the *prisca theologia*, viewed as a genealogy of ancient philosophers that had taught precious doctrines on the immortality of the soul, he often speaks of the Pythagoreans and the Platonists as a unity. See Celenza, 1999. For the Greek sources of Ficino's music theory, see Walker, 1958; 1995, chapter 1.

12. The passage has puzzled many critics; for example, Frank Kermode wrote: 'The whole passage is a beautiful example of Shakespearean excess; why should shady Lorenzo be given this formal *laus musicae*,

this condemnation of "treasons, stratagems and spoils", this hint of the unheard universal order as reflected in the concord of sweet sounds?' (Kermode, 2005, p. 17). Yet one of Shakespeare's persistent devices is to put mystical teachings in the mouths of fools or knaves – Bottom and Falstaff (in *I Henry IV*) being the most obvious examples. His association of this wisdom with a Lorenzo could conceivably allude to Ficino's famous patron, Lorenzo de' Medici.

13. See Voss, 2002, p. 233. Proclus had claimed in his *Theologia Platonica* that 'All the Greeks' theology is the offspring of the Orphic mystical doctrine'. A manuscript of this work was annotated by Ficino, who deliberately borrowed the title of his own *Theologia Platonica* from Proclus.

14. Chapman's first published work, *The Shadow of Night*, was printed in 1594, the same year as Shakespeare's *The Rape of Lucrece*. It was composed of two hymns, to Night and Cynthia, modelled on the Orphic hymns and other Greek hymns by Callimachus and Proclus. Chapman may have found hymns attributed to Orpheus in Aldus's edition of *Hero and Leander* (1517), which he used for his continuation of Marlowe's *Hero and Leander* (in 1598). It is notable that in their 1594 poems, both Shakespeare and Chapman include invocations to the central Orphic power, Night.

15. The Greek words *arrheta* and *aporrheta* refer to what should not or cannot be spoken of. At Eleusis the term *aporrheta* applied to the sacred formulae uttered by the hierophant at the culmination of the Eleusinian mysteries, of which it was forbidden to speak, while the *arrheta hiera* were the cult's most secret and sacred things. On this theme of ritual silence in the Greek mysteries, see Montiglio, 2000.

16. 'While with an eye made quiet by the power/Of harmony, and the deep power of joy,/We see into the life of things' (William Wordsworth, *Lines written above Tintern Abbey*, ll.48–50; cited in Wordsworth, 1997, p. 58).

17. See also Berry 1993, my first piece on Shakespeare's shadows.

18. The Greeks saw the cosmos as a living entity; a cosmos that 'breathes' features in Pythagoreanism as quoted by Aristotle in his *Physics*. The later cosmologies of the Stoics and Neoplatonists combined many

strands of earlier Greek thought; in particular, each owed a major debt both to Aristotle's conception of *pneuma* and to Plato's idea of the world soul. The Stoics shared with the Platonists the notion of a cosmos in which all things, including emotions, thoughts and bodies, were intimately connected. They maintained that *pneuma* was manifested in a high degree of purity and intensity in rational creatures as an emanation from the world soul, itself an emanation from the primary substance of purest *aether*. See Sambursky, 1987, and Wright, 1995, chapter 7. Shakespeare's extensive debt to Stoic as well as Neoplatonic sources is convincingly demonstrated in Weber, 1996, 93–107.

19. For text and translation see Allen, 1989.
20. On the central position accorded to *hesychia* or stillness in the teachings of Pythagoras and Parmenides, see Kingsley, 2001.
21. I am indebted here to Tudeau-Clayton, 1998, pp. 78–112, for a learned and illuminating examination of Virgil's significance in the Renaissance.

Chapter 11

No 'I' in Shakespeare

Philip Davis

No 'I' in Shakespeare? Then how can I be starting with Caius Martius Coriolanus of all characters? He who furiously meets the taunt of being a mother's boy, even as Laurence Olivier is described as doing in a production of 1959 – 'A boy of tears'? Who was it won the name of Coriolanus in the fall of the city of Corioles?

> The *fortissimo* he gave to 'Alone I did it. "Boy!"' left one in no state to speculate about the accuracy of the taunt which aroused it. Olivier may have been subjecting Martius to one of the shocks of recognition he likes to inflict on an audience. But one cannot experience one shock and assess another at the same time. The audience quivered at the sound of Olivier's voice like Avon's swans at a sudden crack of thunder. (Laurence Kitchen, cited in Poole, 1988, p. xi)[1]

Plenty of 'I' there, surely: *I* defeated the Volscians, *I* alone, and none but *I*.

The first *Coriolanus* I saw was not Olivier's but in a television series of 1963 entitled *The Spread of the Eagle*, incorporating the Roman plays, *Julius Caesar*, *Coriolanus* and *Antony and Cleopatra*, and starring in his patrician arrogance Robert Hardy as Caius Martius. It was the first Shakespeare I had ever seen, and my parents, uninterested themselves but encouraging, had let me stay up, a boy of ten, long after they themselves had gone to bed, to see it alone. I did so with that almost physical 'shock of recognition'. The powerful man I watched was still an only child, his mother having loaded him 'With precepts that would make invincible/The heart that conned them' (4.1.9–11). The would-be identification is naively obvious now, but as far as I can recall, it felt like something prior to that, out of which recognition is only subsequently born: it felt like a larger, earlier, first-time language. Coriolanus was the original model of *something*, I didn't know what.

I believe in secret texts: works that appear to know you, or know something in you, better than you do yourself. The psychoanalyst Marion Milner describes how as a young woman she found herself blindly seizing upon certain works that seemed somehow like clues to her own hidden life, certain motifs that half-fearfully attracted her even from childhood – themes such as the killing of a god or the self-sacrificial surrender of a king:

> In Kipling's Jungle Book I had especially loved the story of the Miracle of PurunBhagat, a king who sets aside his riches and embraced poverty, wandering with a begging bowl and – this was a marvel of marvels to me in those days – all the animals had come close to him without fear. Just in the same way the ideas I needed for my work would now come silently nosing into my mind *after* I had given up all attempt to look for them. And then how I had longed to be rid of all my possessions . . . so that I could wander about with no luggage to bother with, nothing to lose. (Milner, 1937, repr. 1986, p. 43)

'*Nothing to lose*,' she concludes: 'How that phrase delighted me.' But she asks herself: was this strong attraction towards poverty and self-abasement merely 'a perverse thing, a morbid desire for failure'? Or was what she as a professional might all so easily have diagnosed as masochism or an inferiority complex, the result of a different sort of failure – the 'failure to understand the *real* meaning of an impulse whose proper expression was something quite different'? (ibid., p. 44).

Whatever the real meaning, it was the ancient pattern of the play that first got itself into me. In the Robert Hardy version Coriolanus died not simply through being stabbed repeatedly by the Volscians but by falling off the edge of a high promontory as a result, precipitated by his own dead weight. The rise of the great hero and then his equally great fall: this last was registered so literally and physically in my very first experience of it. But it was also, I think, the strange feeling that the two movements – all or nothing, winning and losing – were not simply opposites but somehow versions of each other. In the BBC Shakespeare production I next saw in 1984, Alan Howard's Coriolanus, following hints in the Folio direction,[2] actually joins with his own murderers in the repeated cry of 'Kill, kill kill, kill' as by a strange and terrible symbiosis, killing himself in his own spirit. It was *both* movements of the play I loved: the aggressive assertion of life and then that process of simply losing it, of throwing it all away, which Marion Milner describes.

In the first strong motions of the play, it was of course the sense of the exceptional individual that dominated – but an individual felt like a force of nature, a thing of blood, a God of war, utterly careless of what all others thought of him. This wasn't merely a *person*. A person carefully fitting into a tamed and taming social order: that feels like second-order matter. Nor was he simply a spoiled only child, become fascistic military man of action. He was himself like a world, striking Corioles 'like a *planet*' (2.2.110). In the great defiant words of the play, 'There is a world *elsewhere*' (3.3.139), something beyond and bigger than this diminishing place. But it isn't to a world *elsewhere* that Coriolanus is looking, up until his sudden banishment from his beloved Rome: it is *here* that he must will into existence that world of his, through his very being in it. For such a man, inseparable from his body as he is, the world that is within him, in his belief in Rome, must be made existent outside him, in Rome itself, as physical reality and not just mental idea. In the first-order reality of the play then, Caius Martius does not natu-rally think of himself as a separate or separable 'I', does not finally think of himself at all. 'O me alone', he cries but immediately adds, 'Make thou a sword of me?' (1.6.76). I love these beings who appear to be like human content within life's overall form, but actually transcend that form to redeem it from within. Representing from within itself what it should be, they will not simply take the con-ventional shape left for themselves by the institutional version of the thing they incarnate, but burst out with the life of that thing. This man-sword does not want to be given a part, a name, a title, a reward afterwards. Afterwards is no temporal reality to him. The passage of reality from deeds into words is what he fears and hates. As he tells his fellow-soldiers after Corioles, in that inextricable mixture of modesty and pride:

> I have done
> As you have done, that's what I can; induc'd
> As you have been, that for my country.
> He that has but effected his good will
> Hath overta'en mine act. (1.10.15–19)

He throws himself into his act, though his action never entirely exhausts or fulfils all that he throws into it. That is the only mean-ing of character to him: potential arising out of belief. No wonder he does not want to 'act' in any other sense, showing his wounds off in the market place, begging to be made consul for them.

Famously, as Aristotle put it in *Politics* (1276b) and Bacon later repeated in his essay 'Of Friendship', such a figure must be either a beast or a god – as if that range between those two, and not some static taxonomy, were the definition of man living in all the poten-tial space between heaven and earth.

I am not in the least claiming I thought all this aged ten. I am saying there was then created a store of pre-conceptual excitement – characteristic I have found of the great electrical Shakespearean effect – such that when I think about the play now, I seem to go back to that time and its nervous store of felt life.

I loved even his faults. 'You are too absolute' (3.2.40). The absolute contained within the apparently relative, the universal belief disguised as or embodied in a particular person within the universe – that is how I now formulate the secret idea. 'You shames of Rome' he cries, speaking his thoughts directly to their objects, 'You souls of geese/That bear the shapes of men' (1.5.2, 1.5.6–7): *Go home* – or 'by the fires of heaven, I'll leave the foe/And make my wars on you' (1.5.10–11). That he dare say these things, defending the Authentic regardless of those later, conventional considerations diminished by his very utterance! The civilized and liberal adult critic of today will struggle ambivalently to find room for such primitive appeal:

> There is something terrifying but also exhilarating in the very impact of such certainty, something that cuts athwart whatever feelings we may have about the content of what he is saying. The content itself is simple enough: the absolute unreliability of the people whom he is addressing. Yet the very zest with which his speech engages with the objects of its contempt ensures that the speech is not in itself predictable. (Poole, 1988, p. 9)

There is something in 'the very smell' of other people's fear, Adrian Poole goes on, 'that inspires him to exult in his own fearlessness' (ibid., p. 16). The hero/prophet is one who reminds the people of what they were, of what essentially they still should be. Coriolanus does it by his very being, as though he were the essential corrective, the vital memory-element of his world.

It is this Coriolanus, of course, whom the common people with their tribunes eject from that world and expel at the end of Act Three, as though he were a living rebuke. To whom, even as he parts, he responds with that Olivier *fortissimo* almost as mad and futile as it is magnificent and defiant: '*I* banish *you!*' (3.3.127). But the 'I' here is only an extreme utterance of what the ego has always been: a resort and a store for the passion; a default to fall back upon, within the normalized meantime world; a secondary potential, lonely in awaiting fulfilling action.

And so begins the second stage so characteristic of the great Shakespearean experiment. For if I did not have any ambivalence when I first saw the play, it was the *second* movement of the plot that served instead, to represent another side, in action, that I may not have registered in thought. Inevitably there follows upon the rise of Coriolanus a counter-turn which Dryden described as like a violent stream resisted by a narrow passage 'carrying back the waters with more swiftness than it brought them on' (Dryden, 1668, cited in Coote, 1992, p. 36). The neo-scientific experiment here is to test the man of action when he is *not* in action. In 'Of Experience' Shakespeare's great contemporary Montaigne talks sceptically of the great warriors Caesar and Alexander throwing themselves into ordinary pleasures in the midst of their great endeavours. Their aim was not so much to relax as to get relief and thereby gain new strength, he says, by compelling their heavy thoughts and violent pursuits temporarily to take second place to the ordinary usages of everyday life: 'Wise had they beene, had they believed, that that was their ordinary vocation, and this their extraordinary. . . . Alas I have done nothing this day. What? have you not lived?' (Montaigne, 1980, vol. 3, pp. 375–6) But *No!* retorts one such as Coriolanus to this re-prioritization of the ordinary in the act of living. Yet in his multiple points of view, Shakespeare pushes the test even further: he takes the man who *is* Rome *out of* Rome to see what he is then. 'He was a kind of nothing, titleless' (5.1.13).

What is it then for me, most deeply, about this play? It is not war I want, nor is it aristocracy. It is not even the attraction towards massive egoism that is my main interest, nor the hard, hard way to lose it. Like Marion Milner, what I seek is the translation of these things not so much to a meaning deeper than their surface but revelatory of that surface's own true depth. For they point, I believe, to some original dramatic world we have forgotten in our second-order normalities.

* * *

I want to recall that original world – so that it may serve, like Coriolanus himself, as (an admittedly dangerous) corrective to common reality. And I seek to do so by means of what is now, I hope, an adult analysis of my childhood attraction, working inside a language-code quite other than the simple and tame English sense of our day. Text *is* character said John Barton, and actors should not impose psychology upon the language but rather fit themselves within the shapes marked out by it (see Barton, 1986, pp. 61, 143). I think that text in Shakespeare is indeed a prompting script, a sketch-map – but for the making of a world, and not just the characters within it. That world has a dramatic life we have lost, and not just within the theatre.

That is why I want to recommence with the measly ordinary world depicted in this play, intent as it is upon mistranslating the forcible impression of Coriolanus into a merely personal pride and arrogance. It is a distortion not only created by the fickle gossip and the manipulated public opinion of the common people of Rome. Rather, in the aftermath of action the Volscian general, Tullus Aufidius himself tries to work out his great rival, not as a living whole, but piece by static piece in retrospect: 'Whether 'twas pride . . . whether defect of judgement . . . or whether nature/Not to be other than one thing' (4.7.37ff.). What will always lead Coriolanus to fall out with his fellow-countrymen? One of these? all of these? parts of these somehow all together? This method, in its baffled and desperately fascinated need for explanation *outside* drama, is like Shakespeare's creation of anti-Shakespeare matter even in the midst of Shakespeare. Shakespeare at his most dynamic would have used a single word, or the relation between two words, to create the multiform impression. 'One fire drives out one fire; one nail one nail' (4.7.54) is the play's motif – as when our hero repeats his supporters' advice to behave 'mildly' with accent far from mild (3.2.145); or when he re-echoes the resented need for the People's 'voices' (2.3.115–27); or when he mimics the tribunes' imperious 'shall' with bitter incredulity (3.1.92–100). '*Boy!*' he cries, '*Banish?*' But Aufidius's attempted dissection is more like what Rosencrantz and Guildenstern are to Hamlet when he cries back: 'Why look you now, how unworthy a thing you make of me! You would play upon me, you would seem to know my stops, you would pluck out the heart of my mystery . . . 'Sblood do you think I am easier to be played on than a pipe?' (*Hamlet*, 3.2.334–41).

Yet the fact is Coriolanus *can* be played upon. Indeed, you might almost say (consciously or unconsciously) he is *asking* for it, given his heedless disdain for second-order roles, counterfeits and political defences. He lives in *his* world, in the Rome he believes in, and for him there should be no other. But his ideal must be real and not just his own. He would rather die for that belief than live with it in lonely isolation: in that sense the believer is profoundly social, however hiddenly so.[3] Consequently, Coriolanus's intelligent complexity goes on within a fundamentally un-self-protective simplicity. And that means that the crafty tribunes know exactly what they have to do to enrage him into turning on the populace:

> Put him to choler straight; he hath been us'd
> Ever to conquer, and to have his worth
> Of contradiction. Being once chaf'd, he cannot
> Be rein'd again to temperance; then he speaks
> What's in his heart, and that is there which looks
> With us to break his neck. (3.3.25–30)

From the outside he is predictable as a mere character: what feels to him, within, like spontaneous integrity is even thus made externally anticipatable and manipulable. Such is the second-order reality the politicians inhabit, parasitic and predatory upon the soldier's primary nature when translated into that unsoldierly context which exposes it:

> He cannot temp'rately transport his honours
> From where he should begin and end, but will
> Lose those he hath won. (2.1.210–12)

The idea of carrying a beginning unchanged through to its end just bores Shakespeare. But there are even worse betrayals of life than what is unadventurously routine. The tribunes' separation of Coriolanus's behaviour from himself, like the parcelling of his character into component parts, is a denial of Shakespeare's first-order reality.

Coriolanus is *this* or Coriolanus is *that*, say the people around him, for the most part not taking him for all in all, as Hamlet his father – unless it be that with all his faults they love him. Otherwise they ask, like bystanders thinking in undramatic retrospect: Does he do what he does for his *country* or does he do it for *himself*? For *himself* or for his *mother*? Is it more out of *pride* than out of *virtue*? But Shakespeare himself won't write in separate bits, in discrete and static parts. Of if he does so, he does it only by using separate *lines*, on which temporarily to site distinct aspects of thought, before resolving those lines into their completing sentences, re-blurring the aspects into wholes that are more than constituent parts. Menenius, for instance, does not simply explain to the plebeians that 'Coriolanus is not a citizen. He is a soldier', but Shakespeare has him put the two thoughts thus across the *lines*:

> Consider further,
> That when he speaks not like a citizen,
> You find him like a soldier. (3.3.53–5)

Using lines this way is more like simultaneous than successive thinking: Menenius makes the one thing exist *within* the absence of the other and not simply in lieu of it. Hear Coriolanus properly, he pleads; *find* him amidst the misconstructions and within the incapacities. Or again, Coriolanus himself clarifies his own position thus, in relation this time to the patricians:

> Know, good mother,
> I had rather be their servant in my way
> Than sway with them in theirs. (2.1.200–2)

Again it is not just a sequence going on straightforwardly from beginning through to end. The lines are also levels of being, going on within and across that 'rather/Than' structure which holds the present line of thought tensely within a syntactically anticipated future for itself. In this way, by creating a little force-field, words light up in Shakespeare. Even as they pass, they energize each other even a micro-second *after* they are spoken: '*their* servant in *my* way', '*servant* in *my* way/Than *sway* with them in *theirs*'.

It is this Shakespearean alignment of forces that makes for that dynamic world, that sense of a fundamentally different structure of life, we so often dismiss. Ever since the new mechanistic sciences of the seventeenth century, says the theologian Catherine Pickstock, and all the more since the Enlightenment, the world has become a place of nouns and names. 'When we organize the world around us,' she argues, 'we imagine that certain elements are basic. We like to think that these elements can be counted, one by one by one' (Pickstock, 2010, pp. 54–5). But what, she asks, are the basic units of the world? What counts as a separately countable thing?

> Countable things come in different sizes and have different kinds of boundaries. We can count grains of wheat, we can count palaces, we can count events in time, vessels of liquid, we can count the winds, and cities, we can count nations, and gods. But how do we know when we have seized hold of a countable thing?

Blaise Pascal warned us not to hasten to conclude that a landscape is a lapidary edifice, for it would soon proffer an hidden asymptotic analysis: 'A town or a landscape from afar off is a town and a landscape, but as one approaches, it becomes houses, trees, tiles, leaves, grass, ants, ants' legs, and so on, *ad infinitum*. All *that* is comprehended in the word "landscape"'.

Why do we arrange things by assigning nouns or seized nominalizations which conceal their lineaments of time, agency, plurality and continuous aspect? Why do we make things seem like neutral edifices when every arrangement includes an arbitrary moment of decision as to selection or de-selection? (Pickstock, 2010, citing Pascal, 1995, p. 18; paragraph 65)

By imposing nouns and the habit of static explanation upon the multiform flux and vicissitude of things, language – and above all language in its written and then printed form – gives authority to a tamed, falsifying fixity we begin to replicate in our learned behaviour and expectations.

But the Shakespearean text – a language-score for the created performance of life – is not like that. It restores print to voice again, to living time, the lineation finally serving not as a thing seen but as an implicit direction to the actors interior to the text. Otherwise a performance is like the account given in Egypt of Rome's Octavia: showing 'a body rather than a life, a statue than a breather' (*Antony and Cleopatra,* 3.3.20–1). A performance is not about separate 'I's. When Volumnia as mother boasts how ruthlessly she sent her young son to the cruel war whence he returned with brows bound with oak, Virgilia the wife sharply retorts, 'But had he died in the business, madam, how then?' (1.3.16): that creates the angular difference between them on stage like a *third* thing visible only through the language and the arena it generates. The space of life generated between the characters, like a Grecian urn emergent between two facing profiles, is as important as the characters themselves.

And this Shakespearean dynamic is particularly vital in *Coriolanus*. In *Julius Caesar*, before the assassination, Brutus speaks alone and separated, in static Hamlet-like mode. 'I have not slept', he says, because: 'Between the acting of a dreadful thing/And the first motion, all the interim is/Like a phantasma or a hideous dream' (2.1.63–5). In Coriolanus, however, there is no interim, no more than there is temperance in between extremes. In him the inner motion drives straight into outward action, and the man himself is more act than character – or, that *is* his character, a self with more than self within it, that gives itself to action.

In the chemistry and physics of its internal actions and reactions, a Shakespeare play is experimentally protean, after Proteus the old sea-god in the *Odyssey* who must ever change his shape to avoid revealing a truth or foretelling the future. Hippolyta's 'story of the night' near the end of *A Midsummer Night's Dream* invokes and recalls exemplary occurrences of such a process:

> all the story of the night told over,
> And all their minds transfigured so together,
> More witnesseth than fancy's images
> And grows to something of great constancy;
> But howsoever strange and admirable. (5.1.23–7)

By the end of *A Midsummer Night's Dream* we see everything has affected everything else in one great transmutation. But at the centre of *Coriolanus* is an obstinate force who will not bend: 'yet will I still/Be thus to them' is his rhythm of being (3.2.5–6). When in 3.2 his mother urges him back to the market place to placate the citizens and claim the consulship, saying to Menenius 'He must, and will' (97), there follows this sequence from Coriolanus in response: 'Well, I will do't' (101), 'Well, I must do't' (110); but then 'I will not do't' (120); only to be followed by the wry mock-dutifulness of 'Mother I am going to the market place . . . Look, I am going' (131, 134). He does indeed go, but only for his forced nature, his disposition (see 3.2.14–15, 111–12) to recoil upon him in scene 3, and after all create the outburst against the people that provokes his banishment. Bacon knew such forces through the scientific art of experimentation:

> For like as a man's disposition is never well known till he be crossed, nor Proteus ever changed shapes till he was straitened and held fast; so the passages and variations of nature cannot appear so fully in the liberty of nature, as in the trials and vexations of art. (Bacon, 1605; 1962, p. 73, book 2, I.6)

But in the art of *Coriolanus*, the play has to mutate around the defiantly non-protean nature of its eponymous protagonist: 'Let it be virtuous to be obstinate' (5.3.26). The whole play is thus made ripe for internal explosion: 'This lies glowing, I can tell you, and is almost mature for the violent breaking out' (4.3.21–2). Coriolanus himself is always at his worst when he is static, not in action or motion, but (a repeated phrase in the play) left standing here, like a terrible resistant catalyst, inciting the opposition of others and yet frustrated in himself.[4] It is then that he is most in danger of seeming a mere egoistical 'I', standing in ordinary, in memory of himself, without anything in which to put that exposed ego. In search of a place for itself, it makes him go over to the enemy when Rome is no more his friend. By a sort of half-logic and half-magnetism, this is the form life now has to find for itself.

'Martius is the kind of man about whom it would be easier to speak in the past tense' (Poole, 1988, p. 24). It is true: the easiest way, the linguistic norm of understanding, is to seek to establish things in terms of firm, clear and separate boundaries. Yet in so doing the normalizers forget the sheerly present life of time and process. Caius Martius is the man who lives, really lives, only in the present: 'rewards/His deeds with doing them, and is content/To spend the time to end it' (2.2.127–9). In rewarding his deeds only within the *doing* them, he is thus – as Catherine Pickstock might put it – more *verb* than *noun*. So it is, Nietzsche says, with all of us if we could but shed our secondary framework of understanding and behaviour:

> And just exactly as the people separate the lightning from its flash, and interpret the latter as a thing done, as the working of a subject which is called lightning, so also does the popular morality separate strength from the expression of strength, as though behind the strong man there existed some indifferent neutral *substratum*, which enjoyed a *caprice and option* as to whether or not it should express strength. But there is no such *substratum*, there is no 'being' behind doing, working, becoming; 'the doer' is a mere appendage to the action. The action is everything. In point of fact, the people duplicate the doing when they make the lightning lighten, that is a 'doing-doing': they make the same phenomenon first a cause, and then secondly, the effect of that cause. (Nietzsche 1887; 1913, pp. 45–6)

This is the grammar of true Shakespearean being – words not as discrete names but caught in the speed of process and happening. 'The eye sees noun and verb as one: things in motion, motion in things.'[5] So in Coriolanus, 'His heart's his mouth' (3.1.257), his deed's his word, his arm is death: in his speed of motion there are never two things but a blurring into one. Whatever his fault, even at once 'he has a merit/To choke it in the utt'rance' (4.7.48–9) – trammelling it up before ever it is fully spoken.

What this energy means is that Shakespeare's words are not simply inserted into some pre-formed grammar-box; that his protagonists are not just defined by a set name, fixed concept or separate identity; and that his thoughts are not limited to a set agenda in a predictable world. In the classical mathematical physics that Newtonians were to bring to Shakespeare's world, space and time were made external to the entities that make up the universe: those two dimensions served as a fundamental receptacle or frame of reference. A mechanistic universe is one of a separate content within an unmoveable form, of substance in discrete entities and single acts, with clear divisions between within and without; it is a place of distinct cause and effect, of predictable sequences such as subject-verb-object, and straightforward linearity. But in Shakespeare each happening dramatically changes the shape of its world in a moment, Proteus-like. Think of the strange configuration of reality that is Coriolanus: Rome is in *him*, yet at the same time at a different level he is also in *Rome*. It was dynamic philosophers of the late nineteenth and early twentieth centuries such as William James or A. N. Whitehead who recovered what I will call a dramatic world-view. In emphasizing the cosmology of *process* rather than substance, they argued that each occasion new creates space-time in and around itself, minutely shifts the very dimensions of the world as part of its very occurrence.[6]

Creation *before* communication is the law of life in Shakespeare, says the great director Peter Brook. The playwright works at a higher, more primary level than merely 'I communicate my message to you', for he finds a sudden language in which to eschew the pre-established and short-circuit the already known. In the same way, says Brook, the reader, director or actor realizes something better is beginning to 'shape itself' when the response of the ego is not merely to what it 'likes and dislikes', but to what it 'can *discover* through working on the play' (Brook, in Berry, 1989, p. 137). Shakespeare is not a series of set, flat, paraphraseable 'messages' – themes, agendas or names such as we have too often in universities – but the working out of a series of electrical 'codes':

Now to me the total works of Shakespeare are like a very, very complete set of codes and these codes, cipher for cipher, set off in us, stir in us, vibrations and impulses which we immediately try to make coherent and understandable. (Brook, in Berry, 1989, p. 150)

But coherence, understanding and even thinking itself are the second, not the first thing in Shakespeare. The first thing is those minute vibrations which are formative of being, not the interpretation which later explains it. The vibration given off by the language 'cannot take life unless it comes once again into a human organism': it has to be transmitted through an actor (Brook, in Berry, 1989, p. 142). What is more, it vibrates through an actor in imitation of the way in which, within the play, life itself vibrates through a being such as Coriolanus in the creating of him. It is those vibrations, lodged in the very micro-movements and potentials of the language like 'the seeds of time' (*Macbeth*, 1.3.56) which are key, in changing the very pitch of reality.

This is why when Coriolanus finally yields to his mother's entreaty to save Rome even from his own revenge, he does *not* cry as in Plutarch, 'Oh mother, what have you done to me?' Instead, seeing his mother, wife and children on their knees before him like lost or banished parts of himself, he holds his mother by the hand silent in that greatest of all stage directions, and closing the dramatic space that has opened between them, says finally with a quite different vibration in his voice: 'O mother, mother!/What have you done?' (5.3.183–4). All Shakespeare himself has done is cut two words, but two words vital to the argument of this essay, the self-pitying words 'to *me*'. In Shakespeare it is not merely 'I', never only 'me'. The truncation actually makes the vibrations extend further beyond Coriolanus. For as in one dimension the space closes, so in another by Shakespearean physics time opens: the extraordinary intelligence always so implicit in the man now sees and foresees the history of all that will happen to Rome and not just to himself as a result of his death. 'But let it come' (190): the word is not personal or titular; the word is 'it'. In the next scene for a short space Coriolanus will go back down into the present effort of still trying to live, seeing 'it' through again linearly. But at this moment in scene three with the mother, wife and son making him son, husband and father, we as imaginative readers or involved witnesses are

in something of the same impossible position as those Romans who
still love him:

>   for how can we,
> Alas! how can we for our country pray,
> Whereto we are bound, together with thy victory
> Whereto we are bound? (5.3.107–10)

That is to say: at this same massed time when it is as if human nature
itself were at a cross-roads, we do *and* we do not want him to yield.
Do not, but 'stand/As if a man were author of himself/And knew no
other kin' (5.3.35–7). *Do*: and be no longer beast or god but suddenly and essentially (in the word of Ariel in *The Tempest* 5.1.19)
'human'. Yet as soon as it happens – and it *is* a happening – the magnanimity in his yielding feels like pure loss, terrible defeat, sacrificial
death. Yet had it not happened, had he held himself out against the
terrible emotional pressure, you know you would have been argu-
ing the other way, condemning the heartlessness. *Coriolanus* is like
Shakespeare's version of Freud's *Civilization and its Discontents*: there
is in the very structure of life some deep and perhaps irreconcilable
tension between what morality requires and biology urges. In a characteristic Shakespearean formulation, in *Antony and Cleopatra*, what
was undid, did; what did, undid (2.2.211).

A concealed selflessness has long been Coriolanus's life, and now
in another form it is his death. There is no 'I' now, as the 'I' finally
and paradoxically *does* this even to itself – for he has given the self
and its separateness away in the face of earlier, deeper claims of being.
I honour excitedly what we can do both within and to ourselves in
the silently hidden structures of our being. For however loving, those
who are around Coriolanus see only one thing, when silently and
secretly he has done two: it is not that they simply persuaded him,
but the thought of them in him was what made him change himself.
He had tried to hold open a sense of different levels across different
lines: remember, for so he told his mother, 'The thing I have *forsworn*

to grant, may never/Be held by you *denials*' (5.3.81–2). Yet such nice distinctions collapse, or hold only in secret. Coriolanus knows, as she never will, that what he gives way to is not quite Volumnia herself, the person pushing and pushing him, but 'the Mother *in* her' (Sanders in Sanders/Jacobson, 1978, p. 183). That is the passionate idea which, even as he looks at her, is felt despite, as well as because of, its particular personal embodiment. This is the way Shakespeare so densely works, like the dyer's hand in sonnet 111 subdued to what it works in: the personal is an accident nonetheless mortally inextricable from the essential it represents.

Such a moment as this surrender to the human near the end of *Coriolanus* is like the extreme bursting moments of large passion at the close of *The Winter's Tale* which, in their intermixture of the lost and the found, 'dispose permanently of the dichotomy between joy and sorrow' (Sanders, 1987, p. 112). There is no name or concept to unite them, except that in between the two, or with each felt in the other, you feel the range of everything, it seems, that can be felt in a life. Hence even the double movement of the last scenes in *Coriolanus*, when even as Caius Martius is welcomed back to Rome in the person of his mother, almost at the same time, it seems, he is being killed by the Volscians. What Shakespeare wrote, says Peter Brook, 'is not interpretation: it is the thing itself' (Brook, in Berry, p. 133).

* * *

Some of the implications for a life are thus: a celebration of risk through experimental venture in act and impulse; a comparative lack of concern for conventional consistency; a belief in the necessity even of danger to prevent second-order living. This goes with a recognition of the final necessity of defeat even amidst a defiance of it; an acknowledgement of common foolhardiness and egoism mistaking themselves for exceptional courage; and a sense that it is at once great and terrible that life is more than the ostensible I who only for a few moments can be its true instrument. But above all perhaps there remains a commitment to what

William James identified as pragmatism but I call drama – the sudden striking of some vibration regardless of whether it is to be named joy or pain, loss or gain; the sudden lighting-up of some live hot place in the brain, signalling something that one might go with, even blindly, without knowing in advance the macro-consequence for so-called character or story. This is why Peter Brook calls Shakespeare 'the greatest school of living' (Brook, in Berry 1989, p. 137).

Notes

1. Laurence Kitchen quoted in Adrian Poole's excellent *Coriolanus* (1988), p. xi, to which I am gratefully indebted.
2. 'Draw both the Conspirators, and kils Martius, who falles, Aufidius standes on him', where in the truncated idiom 'both' might just mean Coriolanus and Aufidius rather than two Volscian assassins.
3. It is true that before Corioles he cries to his men to 'follow Martius' – but that is *his* imagination of *their* view of him, transporting them into being him, when being him is more than being a self but being Rome incarnate:

> if any fear
> Lesser his person than an ill report;
> If any think brave death outweighs bad life,
> And that his country's dearer than himself;
> Let him alone, or so many so minded,
> Wave thus to express his disposition,
> And follow Martius. (1.7.69–75)

   As soon as they stand 'alone', separate from their usual selves and usual world, then they stand together in embodying one thing.
4. Poole, 1988, pp. 31, 39, 48. See also Oliver, 2005, pp. 1–28 and 179–90 for a discussion of motion moving within as well as without, morally as well as physically.

5. 'A true noun, an isolated thing, does not exist in nature. Things are only the terminal points, or rather the meeting points, of actions, cross-sections cut through actions, snapshots.' (Ernest Fenellosa quoted in Davie, 1976, p. 35). Ezra Pound offered an example in English of the transference of force that he found in Chinese notation: 'dog *attending* man = dogs him'

6. See Witmore, 2008, especially pp. 1–60 on the drama of immanence and on Whitehead in relation to a reading of *Twelfth Night*. See also Oliver, 2005, p. 190 on what follows from the work of Faraday and Maxwell on force-fields: 'In the electromagnetic understanding of the cosmos in which fields constantly interact, and the thermodynamic cosmos in which the energies of natural entities is constantly emanating to others, beings seem to "participate" in each other's motions in such a way that they are intertwined'.

Chapter 12

Real Men Don't Cry

Sarah Klenbort

Inspired by the essay, 'Blessing the New Moon' by A.P. Miller

One

Next door to the Globe, in Shakespeare's time, stood a similar arena featuring bearbaiting. A bear was chained to a pole in the middle of the ring. Angry dogs were let loose to fight the wild beast. Spectators watched from the stands – the same spectators who bought tickets for *Titus Andronicus*, for *Coriolanus*, for *King Lear*. They made bets on who would survive: the bear or the dogs. And when the animals snarled, showing their sharp teeth, extending their lethal claws, the people applauded. As animals growled and howled, clumps of fur and flesh flew through the air and the audience raised their fists, whooping and hollering till death – usually the death of the bear – brought an end to the spectacle.

In *The Lamentable Tragedy of Titus Andronicus*, onstage violence mirrors the bearbaiting across the way. The opening tableau is full of coffins as Titus (somewhat cursorily) salutes his sons lost in battle. Fourteen people die during the play: the final scene is a desolated wasteland. Hands and legs are lopped off. Tongues are carved out. Women are raped. Minced-up sons are served to their mother in a meat pie. With this amount of violence the title word 'lamentable' feels ironic, but the play is not a parody. During Shakespeare's life *Titus* was one of his most popular plays. If you listen carefully, over the bankers barking down their Blackberrys on the Blackfriars Bridge, you can hear the ghostly roar of Shakespeare's crowd. They're still hammering out their applause.

Two

The average American child watches 200,000 acts of violence and 1,600 murders on television by the age of eighteen.

Three

We don't have long to wait for *Titus*' first onstage murder. Just 144 lines into the first scene, Alarbus, a son of the defeated and captured Tamora (formerly Queen of the Goths, later Queen of Rome) is sacrificed. The victorious Romans lop off his limbs. 'And entrails feed the sacrificing fire/Whose smoke like incense doth perfume the sky' (1.1.144–5). The horror is contrasted (palliated? excited?) with the sweet smell of 'incense'. And the regular rhythms of these lines give the ceremony a lulling, ritualistic compulsion. We cannot tear our eyes away. Critics from T. S. Eliot onwards strangely dismiss the play as a mere orgy of violence. But surely this is reductive. *Titus Andronicus* is not a horror movie; instead it probes and challenges our own complicity in horror. It poses silent and incessant questions: why am I watching this play? Why am I drawn to this gruesome scene?

Alarbus' sacrifice sets off the dramatic energy of revenge that powers the play along. Tamora vows: 'I'll find a day to massacre them all/And raze their faction and their family' (1.1.447–8). Tamora is the only mother in the play, and this is from one of her first speeches. From the very start, therefore, *Titus* presents mother-love as inseparable from violence and vengeance. When she tells her sons to torture Lavinia, she declares: 'The worse to her, the better loved of me' (2.3.167). Rape is a filial duty. Mother knows best. The play rejects the conventionally comforting connotations of the maternal womb, likening it more often to a dark pit. This is the mother, after all, who is duped into cannibalizing her own son's flesh – 'Like to the earth' she will 'swallow her own increase' (5.2.190) – in a grotesque reversal of everything healthy, normal, motherly. Aaron the Moor tells the bastard child he fathered with Tamora he is 'enfranchisèd' in birth, 'come to light' 'from that womb where you *imprisoned* were' (4.2.123–4). The pit the dead Bassianus lies in is a 'swallowing womb' (2.3.239–40). Such an 'inmost centre of the earth' is linked to Hell, the underworld: 'Pluto's region' (4.3.12–5). Here, the womb is anything but a comfort-zone: it is as insatiable and engulfing as violence itself.

Four

Four years ago I taught a contemporary short story in an undergraduate Creative Writing class. It was about the parents of a baby who has cancer. One of my students – a young man with a beard, brother fighting in Iraq – spoke up. He said he did not like the story.

'Why?' I asked.
'The husband's a sissy,' he said with a snicker.
'How so?'
'He cries,' the student responded. 'Men don't cry.'

Several girls in the room shot up their hands in protest, while the boys stared sheepishly at the floor. One by one, in Long Island accents, the girls spoke out: 'I'd never marry a man who didn't *cry*.'

'Alright,' the boy in the beard said, '*Real* men don't cry.'

I wrote on the board, *Real Man/Real Woman*. 'I wonder if you could help me define these people', I said to the class. 'Just yell it out.' They did. This is what they said:

Real Man	*Real Woman*
Strong	Likes to clean
Tall	Likes to cook
Rich	Silent
Chops down wood with an axe	Beautiful
Eats red meat	
Fights	

When we got to 'Beautiful' someone said in a quavering voice, 'Isn't that, like, a stereotype?'

'OK,' I said, 'alright. But what's wrong with stereotypes?' And I gave them the first line of a story: Jane meets Joe. And asked them finish the story as if Jane and Joe were a *Real Man* and a *Real Woman* by these, their definitions.

They wrote. The stories were light-hearted, humorous. They were fairytales of sorts, or parodies. It was a fun exercise and perhaps it taught them something about the value of flawed characters. But those definitions haunt me still. The silent woman – not just obediently quiet but uncannily *silent* – has not yet been wiped from the board.

Five

After she is raped, Lavinia in *Titus Andronicus* has her hands chopped off and her tongue carved out. Silenced, she must write what has happened to her. The macabre staging reads:

She takes the staff in her mouth, and guides it with her stumps and writes.

She marks, digging deep into the earth that swallowed her husband, the word 'Stuprum', Latin for 'rape'. One wounding mark reveals another: the bloody holes at both ends of her body are exposed.

Lavinia is what my students might call a 'real' woman. At least, she ticks a worrying number of boxes. And perhaps Coriolanus gives us the best example of what my students might call the 'real' Shakespearean man. Coriolanus is a warrior. He is muscle, strength, perseverance. He is, like Titus, 'Successful in the battles that he fights' (*Titus*, 1.1.66), and his wife is a 'gracious silence' (*Coriolanus*, 2.1.161). He speaks to what it meant – what it *means* – to be a man, a boy, a lover, a son, a warrior and a politician. But like so many who embody such roles, he never grows up. He never becomes a 'man' at all; ultimately, he only ever does what his mother tells him to do.

This bored boy-warrior squirms uncomfortably in the adult world of the Senate. Throughout, he snaps irritably, bored, at the people he is meant to govern. He is pleased only when a messenger announces that 'the Volsces are in arms' (1.1.219): in battle, he's finally freed from the starving, whinging plebeians, the 'musty superfluity' shat out by the body politic. But when he returns, he is easily provoked and outwitted by more experienced and adept politicians. He cannot keep his martial anger under control. He cannot confine it to the battlefield. One of the play's key messages is that physical violence is weaker – less violent, even – than political violence: Coriolanus can excel at the one, but not the other. Another is that violence of one form or another is constant. Like the pit-like womb in *Titus*, it swallows everything up. It aggresses, breaks and breaches any limits set up to keep it in check.

Six

The star quarterback for my hometown team, the Atlanta Falcons, was convicted on charges of dog fighting in 2007. Michael Vick was born in 1980 to a sixteen-year old mother and a seventeen-year old father. He was raised in a housing project in a violent neighbourhood in Newport News, ('Bad Newz') West Virginia (see Minority, 2006). His mother worked at K-mart, raising four children. His father worked in shipyards, teaching his sons to play football in his spare time. He earned the nickname 'Bullet' in High School, running 40 yards in 4.33 seconds. The game suited him. Vick was agile, full of grace. He later claimed football kept him off the streets and out of trouble. Soon he was playing for Virginia Tech, then signing contracts for the Falcons worth tens of millions of dollars.

Everyone was shocked when they found out he was involved in dog fighting, raising pit bulls on his land, and drowning them when they lost. But the only thing that shocks me is that people ever expected this all-American hero to keep his violence to the football field.

Seven

Men in tight uniforms bend over, their firm buttocks in the air. The signal is given. They ram full force into one another, ripping and wrestling each other to the ground. Pushing, pulling, growling, groaning, grunting. One group is victorious. The victors embrace one another, smacking each others' backs and buttocks, holding one another hard, jumping on each other in a rush of exuberance and jubilation.

Eight

Coriolanus greets his friend Cominius like a wife following his victory at Corioles:

> O, let me clip ye
> In arms as sound as when I wooed in heart,
> As merry as when our nuptial day was done,
> And tapers burned to bedward! (1.7.29–32)

The metaphors and images in *Coriolanus* repeatedly worry and weaken the boundaries between fighting and fucking, between friend and enemy. Aufidius – the mortal enemy – likewise seeks to embrace Coriolanus ('Let me twine/Mine arms about that body' [4.5.105–6]), an erotic energy which only intensifies later on:

> I have nightly since
> Dreamt of encounters 'twixt thyself and me –
> We have been down together in my sleep,
> Unbuckling helms, fisting each other's throat –
> And wak'd half dead with nothing. (4.5.121–5)

'Dream', 'down together', 'unbuckling helms' 'fisting' – these are all evocative words, rubbing sexily close to one another in a short, breathless speech. As Aufidius wakes 'half dead', it's hard not to think of the 'little death', *la petite mort*, the orgasm, which leaves you with 'nothing'. A bewildered Aufidius confesses as Coriolanus dies that 'My rage is gone/And I am struck with sorrow' (5.6.147–8): they knew in the Renaissance that sex always preceded a sorrowful emptiness: *Post coitum omne animal triste*.

So far, so straightforward. But – and this is weird – fighting and sex are not just signals for a muscular homoeroticism between classical warriors; they also mark quite strongly Coriolanus' relationship with his *mother*. Volumnia, praising her son, says:

> [Blood] more becomes a man
> Than gilt his trophy. The breasts of Hecuba
> When she did suckle Hector looked not lovelier
> Than Hector's forehead when it spit forth blood
> At Grecian sword, contemning. (1.3.36–40)

Perhaps these connections – blood from Hector's forehead, the milk from his mother's breasts – silently grant a new 'maternal' force to the play's politicized backdrop: perhaps Rome has a maternal duty to feed its famished, rebellious plebeians, much like the wolf at the city's birth suckled Romulus and Remus. But much more important are the eroticized energies that throb and seethe beneath this wafer-thin surface image of war: the ejaculative spitting forth of Hector's blood, the crudely phallic imagery of the Grecian sword, the close comparison of blood and breast milk. The fantasy of Volumnia's son fighting *excites* her. But this excitement is no crude, simplistic incestuous desire: rather, any sexual imagery seems to symbolize a yet deeper, yet more fundamental energy. When motifs of 'nothing' and emptiness mark Volumnia's speech, much as they did Aufidius', they are similarly associated with an eroticized and aggressive imaginative appetite: 'I should freelier rejoice in that *absence* wherein he won honour than in the embracements of his bed where he would show most love' (1.3.2–4, my emphasis). The close proximity of these juxtaposed energies (war, love-making, imagining, rejoicing) imply that the energy-expenditures of each and all are readily comparable. But, as in Aufidius' dream, the *real* (s)excitement only happens when the man himself is not there. In *Titus* the womb is associated with the swallowing earth; in *Coriolanus* nothingness is likewise linked to violent maternal fantasies. Is Shakespeare suggesting therefore that the wound – the inscription of absence or nothingness upon flesh – is the microcosm of the womb?

Nine

He emerges, blinking, into the light. All that violence, all that pain. He's alone. He's screaming. He's dripping in blood. They give him a new name. A new identity. One he didn't choose, one he didn't ask for. Reborn. Martius Caius Coriolanus. Bear the addition nobly ever.

Ten

By the time the top of Baby's bloody head emerged, my husband had been holding my hand for six days straight. Inside the white hospital room, he clung to my sweaty palm while I screamed in rhythmic pain. On the afternoon of the sixth day, I felt his hand begin to tremble inside my own and as afternoon turned slowly into evening, the pain increased, my screams grew louder and my husband's sweaty palm shook hard. When the baby came out crying, he cried, too. Tears ran down his cheeks; he was shaking too much to cut the cord.

When they told us about the bleeding in Baby's brain, the doctor in the neo-natal intensive care unit looked me straight in the eyes and held my hands firmly in her own. *I know, I know,* she said, *we all want our babies to be perfect.* A nurse put her arm around my shoulder. The secretary gave me a tissue. They never looked at my husband, who stood beside me, listening, watching, eyes wide open, clear, unblinking. I knew that he was supposed to play the role of the stone pillar, sturdy and unbreakable, and I knew that his knees were shaking like my own, that his legs too were about go beneath him.

Eleven

At the airport in LA two years ago I met a group of women soldiers, flying to Iraq. They were leaving their babies at home, to be looked after by grandmothers and friends. They proudly rolled up their uniform sleeves, showing me tattoos of newborn baby footprints on the backs of their shoulders. The numbers below gave their birth weights and heights. They'd carry these measurements into battle.

Twelve

This present war in Iraq has seen more female soldiers, many of them mothers, than any previous conflict.

Thirteen

I went dancing once at a club in Sydney. There was a stag night: twenty men spilling over one another in drunken revelry. They were dancing not with other women but with each other, grinding close to one anothers' groins. They grabbed each others' bums; they stuck out their tongues and licked the air in front of their mates' mouths. These men, in their late 20s, early 30s, probably hold jobs in offices not far from the dance club. They no doubt dress in suits and ties for work and sit obediently in front of their computers for most of the day before taking a bus home to their wives and girlfriends, their fiancées. I do not imagine they get out on the dance floor often (their moves did not suggest this). But on that night, after drinks and in the company of men, they allowed their proper male selves to slip off and be trampled on the sticky floor beneath. They grabbed each other from behind, kissed one another on the lips, daring each man to go further than the last.

Fourteen

I imagine from time to time the boys at the very first rehearsals for *Titus* and *Coriolanus* flitting about in Roman costumes with embellished femininity. Older actors slap the boys on their backsides, watching them run. There must have been giggles and teasing, sly looks and winks and – without any women to witness – more than a few clandestine sexual acts taking place off stage.

Women dress as men throughout Shakespeare's comedies, accentuating and commenting on, in all kinds of rich and complex ways, the fact that men were acting as women pretending to be men. Shakespeare thus exposes what we call 'gender' to be a mere epiphenomenon of something freer and more performative. But I wonder: if it *is* free, could it spill off in other, darker directions, too? Do Tamora and Volumnia represent the fearsome potential of a Viola or a Rosalind? Are they the macho old tyrants the comedic heroines might grow up to be?

Fifteen

Volumnia claims that Coriolanus is 'More bound to's mother' than any man 'in the world' (5.3.159–60). In the final scene, Coriolanus caves in, ceding to the Roman Senate he despises, and leaving himself open to Aufidius' mortal revenge, when his mother tells him she 'will home to Rome/and die among our neighbours' (5.3.173–4).

> O mother, mother!
> What have you done? Behold, the heavens do ope,
> The gods look down, and this unnatural scene
> They laugh at. O my mother, mother, O! (5.3.183–6)

A professor in graduate school, G. Whittier, once suggested to me that the 'O's on the page, or in the shape of the actor's mouth, are holes. I think this is right; the 'O's here and elsewhere in *Titus* and *Coriolanus* are differently-inflected voids. They mean the quasi-orgasmic cry of 'nothing', the sudden shift from sex to sorrow and the empty space filled by eroticized fantasies of war. They mean the groans of a silenced Lavinia. They mean the wound, the mark, the gap, that Volumnia's pit-like womb inscribes upon her son and his fragile manhood. They often mean all these things at once.

I did not learn the gender of my baby before it was born. I therefore did not receive any pink clothing at my baby shower. Because she is a girl, she can wear pink or blue, overalls or dresses. She is only three, so now it is OK for her to play with trucks or princesses, or a princess driving a truck. Boys – men – don't have that choice. Our culture gravitates towards maleness, towards violence, no matter who displays it.

Sixteen

The womb and the wound have much in common, but not as much as Tamora or Volumnia would have us believe.

Chapter 13

Ghostly Selections

Simon Palfrey

> *I cannot at will give my past expression, though every gesture expresses it, and each elation and headache; my character is its epitome, as if the present were a pantomime of ghostly selections.*
>
> Stanley Cavell

* * *

Kierkegaard says somewhere that it is crass materialism to suggest that no one can experience death before actually dying. We live a dying life, always. But then to feel this fact, to really know it in our bones, is to recognize that every moment is also a birth. The thought seems worthy of life. But some moments are more birthing than others.

* * *

If birth is a trauma, as I have no doubt it is, then a trauma is also a birth. It is said that trauma repeats on us. We suffer it, suffer for it, but such is its unholy making power that we continue to hunt it down, cut upon cut, long after the immediate conditions of trauma are past. I take from this the thought that those things we most seek out and return to, without clear knowledge *why*, are probably traumas repeating upon us, in more or less disguised form.

Shakespeare is one such thing in my life. I suppose I know his work better than many, but I don't doubt that the reasons I love it are more or less usual – not really intellectual reasons, but to do with passion, an apprehension of life as always imminent, where the public thing is never quite the thing, where the five listed senses are laughably inadequate, where minds and moments are teeming with possibility and with felt impossibility, with shades and strangeness and suddenness, where no emotion, however wild or hidden, is inconceivable, where we immanently feel the fact that we live in time, and that time is past and is passing, and we will die, and that the causes of life, the principles of motion, the forces that prick things into shape or action, are magical, inscrutable, telepathic, ungovernable. . .

Trauma brings us suddenly close, cliff-face close, to the fact that we hang on a thread, or shift as we live from one hanging string to the next, like nimble marmosets, never quite secure in our tree. Most of our traumas are not solely ours. They are shared, more or less inevitable, established by connection. Some are to do with being human, some to do with where we find ourselves. And as for the self – the more I think on it the more I doubt that it, *mine*, is terribly singular. We all get conceived, born, *taken* from one thing to the next. Choice seems very by-the-way.

* * *

Who knows how true anyone's self-recovery is, how much is wishful retro-action and false coherence. Who knows what to choose from the ghostly selection? The question I begin with is mundane enough. How was it that at age twenty-three I came to spend years thinking about the late plays of Shakespeare? I had little idea why at the time. I was in Oxford, I had to find a subject, this one seemed interesting, my angle my own. And maybe there was little more to it than that. But if Shakespeare is or was *true* for me in any but the most casual ways, then presumably his work must connect backwards to events that made me, to more or less decisive traumas. Perhaps I came true, again, in the things I discovered in his plays. Perhaps I was already

there, born but unrevealed, in the untapped spaces of his worlds . . .
Perhaps we all are.

* * *

One birth of mine, I don't say the first, was in the coldest winter
of the century. My mother slipped and fell twice on the ice. She
fell twice, very hard, and she feared that she had killed me. No one
else was there. The first fall broke my peace; the second time I was
awake, every bit of me, albeit it was as dark as hell and formless. I
couldn't see a thing, just some whale-shaped black curve. But I was
present, I swear it. Even writing this I can feel the very same sensation, the one I that I always shut my mind upon: a strange levitation
within, this amorphous eyeless rising, like some awful water monster, without features, discernible only as a dark rotundity, making
my daily sentience, with its confidence of movement, its forethought
and volition, seem like the simplest lie, a carapace of coherence for
the truth to lurk inside, to loom and wait, in some blanketing way
to *refuse*.

Soon I was born another time, ugly visible to others' eyes. The
cord was around my throat, I was bruised to buggery, and I didn't
open my eyes for weeks. Why would I? I don't remember this birth
but I can only imagine the surprise, the indignation, the deep-
browed resistance, as I was shot out into the sickly not-mine light. It
wasn't mine, it smelt wrong. And I've been blinking in it ever since.

* * *

When I was six years old I was taken suddenly to Toowoomba, in
Queensland. 'Palfrey', said my father on arrival. 'G'day Paul', said
our host, and we piled into the panel-wagon and headed west. It
was strange. The flowers were huge and bright. Houses were built
on stilts. Local children walked to school barefoot, their feet effort-
lessly brown. My brother and I tried to achieve the same, leaving
our shoes at home and bathing them in the warm mud puddles that

littered the road to school. Did this portend anything? I doubt it. We were dirt tourists. Or we were aspirant indigenes, without knowing it. Toowoomba had many of what today we call *aboriginalandtorresstraitislanders*, but back then they weren't called anything at all. We wanted to go disguised, little Edgars, with our too-lucent feet, looking for Poor Tom. But disguise is only worth it when it's a portal into appetite and fear. There was plenty of this among the real Toms, who perhaps couldn't afford shoes, or didn't feel comfortable wearing them. The only context for our disguise was awe at native ease, and some abiding feeling of not belonging. The puddles were warm and large and most certainly *noticed*. They weren't ours. The land never was.

I put a garden fork through a bare foot. I stopped hearing about English football. Everyone had short back and sides. People routinely assumed I was a girl, because my face was cute and my fringe like a Beatle's. There were water-snakes close and available. Enormous watermelon pieces sold for two cents in the shop near the school. The desks were bolted to the floor. My sister wasn't allowed to be left-handed. Homework was a hundred full-stops. There was something tight-arsed about the place, fake-decorous, or at least among its respectable folk, caring for their flowers, enjoying their large verandahs. The town was famous for its loony bin; you can only imagine. The place was a pavlova, nothing but the whites of eggs and sugar, whipped up and presented as a prize. People wore suits to barbecues, or crisp shirts with pale shorts and very long socks and shined leather shoes. All alcoholics, I assume.

We watched American television for the first time. I dreamt a lot about dying, or about pretending to be dead while Red Indians or Nazis stalked the field.

* * *

Then for four years I was an active citizen in the sun. This was in Canberra, the nation's capital. There may be a less *Shake-spe-hero-in* place in the built world, but if so I am yet to see it. It is Australia's sub-sub-urban Utopia, strung out for miles on a principle of ever-repeating satellite conveniences, constructed like some IKEA flat-pack, its bywords *parking-space, sporting field,* and *roundabout.* My memory is that everything was above the ground. The streets were clear. I barely remember a cloud. I was school captain, and captain of the cricket team, and the soccer team, and top of the class, & c. I liked the girls with very tan skin, and their dirty blonde hair, and could never understand why they weren't more popular. The ones I liked lived with the Smith Family, which meant they were orphans. They were quiet and felt ashamed, but were always pretty, with big brown eyes. I did feel sad for one of them once when I saw how dirty her undies were. It never occurred to me at the time that they probably weren't really orphans, but aboriginal children who had been stolen from their families, to help make the nation a little whiter.

I was an inland surfer, surfing the wave of effortlessness, when it is always light, you never need to touch the ground, you don't even suffer a subconscious. I teed up a golf ball in the back garden once, and pulled out my father's biggest wood, which I had never swung before, and as my older brother watched I sent the ball sailing over a couple of houses and through the kitchen window of a neighbour. It was a beautiful shot, so crisp and sure, I can feel its surprise and its certainty even now. An Italian-sounding man came running to our fence, shaking, or shaking his fist, and accused me of throwing the ball through his window and nearly killing his baby, who had been eating from a high chair as the glass shattered around it. I didn't throw it, I said, indignant at the thought. It really was a beautiful shot.

* * *

I remember, Daddy wasn't home as I trudged inside, my brother delighted and disbelieving just behind me. Mummy, as I recall, was briskly ironing her shirt, without her shirt on. I always felt slightly repelled by her nakedness, it seemed someone else's, blue and veiny on the beach, hairs in the wrong places, or her exhausted breasts swinging in the vivid lounge-light. 'Oh, who's watching', she'd say, careless of our embarrassment. I can't remember if I told her or Mark did, but either way, exposed as she was, in *her* morning carelessness, she was in no position to play the rectitude-card. An ally, more like, waiting with me, fearing for me, as I sulked elbows down onto the shag-pile and listened for Daddy's step. He always knew when one of us had *done something* – the delicious silence as he entered, the diagonal glances of the Innocent Four. His silence was much worse; better just to deliver the judgement. This time I think he just shook his head. Shook his head, a few times, and walked off. *No more, the text is foolish.* What words can reach to transgression, or fabulous folly, really? It was an event, we all knew it, and ever since we've been happy for the fact. I reckon that, secretly, everyone admired the shot as much as I did.

* * *

I was taken to Hobart when I was eleven years old. It was strange from the moment we were woken up to leave. For unplumbed reasons my brother and I, fifteen months apart, dressed as though we were twins. We hadn't done this since three and four, when posing for one of those fake family photos. And here we were again, two false cards, suddenly stolen from our ease. We both put on new fawn *ironed* Levi Californians, and orange-red checked press stud shirts, and we arrived in Hobart like impostors. The trip from the airport wasn't long enough. I kept waiting for the place to change, to crystallize into the thing I was missing, something bright and sunny. Instead everything was low hung and in an odd palette. All the years on the mainland, the palette had been primary coloured, the number even. Everything here was smudged, its numbers odd. There were no straight lines, no rectangles. Everything waved, or undulated. The sky was very close, and moved the whole time. The clouds seemed ominous and intelligent. The mountain loomed, with its burnt horizontal tree skeletons. The water looked deep, it had no colour at all, and I knew that whales and ships lay buried in its vertical miles. And there we were, my brother and I, in our matching outfits, watching out the window as the car, whose car I have no idea, traversed the curved bridge, with expanses of water to each side, dark hills behind, dark mountain ahead, everything that was manmade tiny and shrinking and sheltering, somehow on loan, gripping like molluscs to the bottom of the world, and hoping without hope that this wasn't yet Hobart, because this couldn't be my home.

* * *

Then it rained, for months. We weren't at school, but the promised home schooling lasted about fifteen minutes. There was nothing to do. The five of us and Mummy sat inside a featureless rented flat, with brown carpet, and waited. We listened to our one cassette, *The Beatles Oldies but Goldies*, and drew the same pictures over and over, as outside in the gloaming it rained. Mummy wept.

* * *

Every night I woke from the same dream. I was inside Mummy, it was very dark, and even as I write this my head involuntarily shakes with my sense memory of the memory. I would get up, every night, and sit in the kitchen on a stool, and Mummy or Daddy – actually, it was at this precise time that we all as one agreed to call them *Mum* and *Dad* – would ask me what it was, what was wrong, why was I up again. . . And I remember refusing to answer, my whole body still trapped in the supra-zone of my nightmare, until one night I said to Mum, 'I *can't* tell you, because it's about *you*'. I couldn't tell her that what I was dreaming about was being *in your bottom*. The very idea, the words that could only fail to convey the experience of the feeling, disgusted me with their wrongness. But I had no others. I was inside her bottom. That was my conclusion, the place curved and dark like the belly of a whale, huge curving walls that forbade egress.

* * *

Meanwhile, every afternoon, Mum wept. I would hover at the door and hesitate over whether to enter. I would ask her what was wrong.

She said she hated the school she taught in, Warrane Primary, a tough school full of the tough kids of tough parents that was newly vandalized every evening. But that wasn't it. I know now why she wept. Is this it, the promised land, the place that at last would be like England? This rain-soaked nowhere land? It couldn't have been less like her dreams if you'd sat down with a sketchbook and drawn the template of alienation.

But nothing of this was spoken. I made her a Nescafe, I tried to make it really nice, I stirred it with love.

Emotions hang in the gaps, thick and wet, no more articulate than a thick wet toad.

* * *

My father was demoralized by Mum's misery. His secretary was there by day, herself a wounded soul, bashed by some bastard first husband and in need of protection, but attentive and very beautiful. Who could refrain, that had a heart, to love. . .?

* * *

My belief is, when my mother fell over carrying me, that these were the first signs of the multiple sclerosis that would kill her. She couldn't prevent the fall. I don't say I caused it, merely that I was in her as it hit. The same thing happened when the MS returned. She felt herself falling in the bath, and could do none of the normal things to arrest it. It returned in Hobart, in this season of rain, as my father accelerated into the loving understanding of his secretary. And again I was in her as it hit, every night, de-spatialized, de-bodied, eyeless in the mothery coffin.

* * *

Soon we found a house to live in and moved to Hobart's Eastern Shore. A big house, directly opposite the beach. The suburb was very close to nothing. To the back were uncut woods; a little further to the left, the north I suppose, the road stopped, the suburb stopped, and there were naked hills. A single road led to the bridge, and so into Hobart proper. On the front side was the River Derwent, *the deepest natural harbour in the southern hemisphere*, a huge estuary spreading out to sea.

Only strangers called such scenes *picturesque* (or *picture-skew*, as we'd mock). Tasmanians generally don't have much time for beauty. Lots of them would rather turn the place into one enormous power station. They say we wouldn't have the stuff – torrents of rivers, magnificent trees – if we weren't supposed to log and dam whatever we need. The most famous dam, celebrated by some, a cause of mourning for others, was Lake Pedder. We went there soon after arriving. It took hours, crawling through a very silent forest, the air so clean and vegetably palpable that it felt like an invasion, an experiential category-mistake, even to attempt entry. It was the classic *are we there yet* family excursion. We couldn't believe it when Dad said yes. We are here. Here it is. All we wanted was a shop that sold something real, like coke. What I remember is a taciturn vendor whose sole line was in fishing tackle, rods and wires, all that stuff that sits spruce around you like a rebuke to your soul, or your competence, or your pretensions ever to belong to a place where metal buckets actually do things. The 'shop' was on a bridge, and the bridge had views of the famous dam. Or maybe it didn't. It would have been perfectly in character, for Dad and indeed all of us, to have got to the vicinity and not quite been bothered to take the extra steps to see the nature-violating wonder. We got the idea, concrete and water, immense silent forests to all sides. We peered over and down, at water stopped by concrete, and then got back in the car and went home, barking with relief.

A few months later we woke up to hear the news that the bridge had been knocked down. This seemed the most impossible, thrilling news, but even Dad confirmed it: some drunk captain, apparently (and a paralytic crew, one supposes). It was like the most perfect teenage fantasy. *The Bridge*. There was only one. Imagine the thrill as the concrete began frittering and huge pillars started to concertina into the black water. I was playing cricket that day at Cornelian Bay school, on their tiny ground almost directly under the bridge. We got there and it felt like the most illicit privilege, to be seeing with our own eyes this gap in nature. It was better than a film. The bridge was so close, and so still, its elegant curve severed about a third of the way across, its teeth punched out, and plunging suddenly into nothingness. I didn't know the word *sublime*, but that is the word for what I felt, as I looked through the gap to the northerner part of the river, always somehow darker and choppier, near where the Zinc Works and Cadbury factories pumped out their mercury, and everything felt startlingly enormous, the broken concrete some presage of nature's stupendous resources. Why didn't it just topple over, all of it? This I didn't understand, and never quite trusted that it wouldn't.

I'm not sure how many cars went off the gap. I know that our local doctor and his family did. It was always such a smooth bridge, and I could hear the silent wonder as Cortinas and Monaros sailed off the bridge and through the air and into the black river. *Would they have survived this entrance, and tried to escape as they sank?* The thought appalled as I asked Mum the question. *So the cars are all down there, now, the families inside them?* I could hardly believe it. They say we're made of water, mainly. But this was no homecoming, surely.

* * *

I started to nurture denials, secret even from my siblings, centred in my difference from the friends I was apparently so absorbed into: praying that they not drop by in case they discovered that my parents had English accents; or that Mum could only keep upright by wildly pushing a trolley, or speak by slurring like a drunk; praying that they never see me naked in the change-room, because (a) I wasn't circumcised like they all were, and (b) because I had as yet no pubic hair, like they all did. Physical childhood was going on too long. My glands should catch up with the rest of me.

* * *

We studied *King Lear* when I was sixteen. Two lines especially I remember repeating with friends, as though from the first true comedy I had ever witnessed.

Let me wipe it first; it smells of mortality. (4.6.131)
Out vile jelly. (3.7.86)

They were endlessly adaptable, and lost all context of tragedy, horror, violation, or pain, and became simple opportunities for trivial deflation. During morning recess: 'Pass that spoon' – *Let me wipe it first, it smells of mortality*; layering a gristle-thick National Pie with tomato sauce, *out vile jelly*. Heedlessness was the thing. In the gap between soccer and cricket seasons we'd drink in the bush on Saturday afternoons, the uncut stuff on the hill where the cul de sacs hadn't yet reached. We'd get quickly plastered, re-enter the silent empty streets, and I'd feel sort of astonished that they were still there, these houses and streets, so peaceful and pointless and as-though eternal. A friend called Adrian, a very fast runner, aboriginal, would start trying to set fire to the manicured nature strips. Of course they were far too trimmed to burn, but still, should the grass briefly catch, with that gassy singeing smoulder, then cue the cry as we hot-footed it, *it smells of mortality!*

We practised a minor key refusal to believe, a sort of constitutional civic atheism. The local shopping 'centre' was a concrete box called the *Shoreline*, mainly an excuse for the eastern shore's best stocked bottle-shop, but also blessed with a Purity (a smallish second rate supermarket), a Scottish barber called Jerome, a pederast real estate agent with a Boris Karloff toupee, a draper's – a *draper's* – and a newsagent who forbade you touching the magazines. And nothing else, not even a takeaway. A place so marooned that even under-age teenagers declined to meet there – unless to scream 'vile jelly', for the sheer bored idiocy of it, at the draper's or Jerome as they shut up shop after another dispiriting day.

Mainly this was all just your normal teenage nothing. But there was something distinctively angled about it, to do with our breezy assumption that we lived entirely without historical weight. There really was for us no such thing as Australian history, let alone Tasmanian. Just as there were no aborigines, they'd all been killed in the last century. We knew the name of one of them, the last one, Truganinni, a short black woman who got dressed up in silly ruffs and went to the governor's mansion once, I think. But that was it. But then we also knew that this was garbage. So at least half my mates were part-aboriginal, just obviously so, but no one called them that or said anything, because there weren't any of them. We were weightless, no past at all. So we all lived in this odd denying impasse, turned away from evident fact, like the commuters at the bus-stop, backs resolute against that grave river with its headstone of hill. Or like us, the five Palfrey kids, and how we all pretended that we didn't know about Dad's other life. We nourished a superstitious refusal to mention it, even to each other, as though it might all just evaporate. I can't say now who I thought should be protecting whom. For a while, for years and years, I really believed in the efficacy of suppression, in the grace of diversions. But wish as I might, every day around 6 pm, Dad not yet home, Mum broke the silent contract. A canker sat sick and big in our guts as we heard her in the kitchen, pretending not to, Mum peeling potatoes in front of the window, rehearsing the same scenes over and over as the knife sliced. I listened, staring vacantly at the telly, and plotted a good moment to bring the resolving Nescafe to them both.

* * *

Of course there was another application. Sixteen years old, all of these *girls* everywhere. What was an aching virgin to do?

> Out, vile jelly.
> Let me wipe it first.
> It smells of mortality.

The two discoveries coincided: the worlds inside words, openings upon openings; and, almost the reverse movement, *ejaculation*. I say the reverse, because whereas Shakespeare seemed to extend into or promise things I had never known, *ejaculation* – it wasn't yet *masturbation* – produced this weird feeling that everything was within, it always had been, and this astonishing *well* had long been inside me, not *mine* but in me all the same, waiting for its moment, patient, unbelievably real and thrilling, reaching back and back into who knows what pasts, and discovered by *me*, me alone, one Saturday morning after my paper run, when I went back to bed and dozed until Turf Talk, it being a time when some sort of avidity in me found expression in horseracing, studying the form and developing morbid affections for specific horses – one called Crepellox, a *rig* (whatever that was, something sexless apparently), a filly called Kapalaran – no doubt the passion was a bridging thing, between being a boy and being with girls – and I recall the nasal knowing drawl of Bert Bryant on Turf Talk, and this *stuff* bubbling up from inside, miraculous and impossibly illicit, and quite conceivably a fault in the plumbing, a body gone wrong, that *only I had*. It was a true discovery, I had zero preparedness for it. I had no idea, none at all, that it wasn't a fantastic mistake. And then, once I realized it could be controlled, could be called upon at will, I did so, as every boy at the same stage does, as often as life allowed.

Quickly it all became routine, and the distancing irony of *quotation* could mediate the move from urgent private transport to visible cool-enough boy. The routine was smooth and silent: slipping into the remotest school toilet; crisply lit visions of the very girls I was moments ago sitting with; inexpert wanking; uprushing effulgence; instantly re-enter the articulating mind, *vile jelly*, *smells of mortality*, *wipe it first*; and back whistling into the daily world. Soon enough (not soon enough) I had a girlfriend to do it for me, and we slipped out each lunchtime, down to the bluff, and we did whatever she would allow. I had to tear out all the front pockets in my jeans, every last one, left and right, they were so soaked with stinking ejaculant. I told mum I needed to blow my nose, some weird allergy to all of those prettifying pot plants, and daily lacked a hanky. Weep your heart out, Othello. Not that I knew the play at all.

The entrances – into world extension, into bodily intension – were pretty much simultaneous. It was nothing less than a birth. Sixteen, a happy trauma, and born again.

* * *

You grow up into whatever awaits. I think now that the single defining thing about my sensibility was Mum's illness – its duration, the long-brewed anticipatory mourning, the daily release from a death-sentence, the fact that you can live simultaneously inside *and* beyond the deepest emotions. We all knew what was coming, always. But sad as it was it was also sort of good. It gave a certain *oomph* to the living.

I suppose something was being marinated, an inward separateness, a feeling that truth was dissident, intense, alert to shifts and difference: it was never lazy orthodoxy. Mum was the key thing, her gradual ossifying the static in my soul that I could always tune into. We never called it her dying. It went on too long, twenty-three years of deterioration. But the thing I most remember is her mouth, open in increasingly silent, increasingly reckless laughter. The sclerosis shreds the nerve cells, but it seemed also to release some sort of serotonin or other happiness hormone. And so irreverence, a relishing of appetites, became our family way. The slow lightning of grief fed into mercurial candour. Likewise with new friends, whom I would tell everything, almost instantly, the shame-free premise of any intimacy. I didn't want to be relaxing, or comfortable, the traits our dickhead Prime Minster claimed for our lucky nation. I wanted to lean forward, into unfinished possibility. Mum's fate was fixed, and yet it was not; she lived daily: defy the auguries.

But always that static, the melancholy that abided beneath the mercury.

One day Mum drove through the large plate widows of the local supermarket, right smack inside it, the bonnet strewn with Mars bars and Twisties. The words buzzed along the street, *Mrs Palfrey's driven into the supermarket!* We all raced up the hill, and there it was, our Datsun 260C, hidden in the dark of the shop like an alien invader. Her foot had spasmed, she missed the brake, the car lurched through the window. Stupid shop anyway, never stocked what you want.

* * *

It can be deadly to know what's coming. A weird number of the blokes I went to school with were killed within a few years, all from accidents. A sawn tree crushed one, another fell from the pier, two drowned, a few smashed into trees or ditches in their cars. Why should we realize that the words in *King Lear* will come true? Or that they have already come true, and that we play our games, like we build our buildings, on the ashes of the fact. Let them be a joke.

I reversed the Datsun out of the shattered shop. Wonderful how the car moved as it should, oblivious and serene. Driving home I welcomed Mum to my little club, where madly smashed windows only nearly kill children who thought they were safe. She snorted through her tears at the memory. You're never safe.

* * *

My intense feeling for Shakespeare was quite slow to develop. But when it did, in a way that had more pressure to it than simply admiring the plays, the moments I loved were these:

Coriolanus to the Romans: *I banish you.* (*Coriolanus*, 3.3.127)
Guiderius throwing Cloten's severed head down the river, *in embassy to your mother.* (*Cymbeline*, 4.2.186)
Autolycus entering, singing, *the red blood reigns in the winter's pale.* (*The Winter's Tale*, 4.3.4)
The drunk Trinculo to his fellow drunks Stephano and Caliban: *They say there's but five upon this isle; we are three of them. If th'other two be brained like us, the state totters.* (*The Tempest*, 3.2.4–6)

My main thought was: these moments are explosive; they are dangerous and prophetic as much as irreverent; they are ignored because literary critics are cosseted and decorous, they think verse means more than prose, that noble characters matter more than ignoble, and they never allow moments to speak for themselves, to have their own gravity and intensity, but instead always pre-emptively discipline events, making them serve an authoritative history that always precedes and succeeds any particular happening.

I still largely think this, by the way.

But now I can see other things in my attractions. It perhaps goes without saying, as much as I didn't see it at the time, that these are family romances, with their lodestone being parents and children, distant and returning. I was far from home, and part of me was calling. But as my favourite bits suggest, my take on these plays was not simply sentimental. Here, I now see, was where other aspects of home kicked in. There's clearly a continuation, temperamentally, from the days of trying to burn nature strips and heckling customers at the draper's. The violence produced by boredom; or the violence generated by being semi-enfranchised, ignored, or anonymous. But also a delight in the idea that feckless, indolent, wasteful energies – the sort that walks in groups around dull suburban streets on early summer nights and rocks roofs, or steals milk bottles, or clumsily tries to finger girls in the sand-dunes – might actually, in some parallel world, take effect, precisely have prophetic capability. That life should not be small, object-sized, forgotten the next moment; that it should instead be *metaphorical*, transporting us from here to elsewhere; that the objects we handle – rock, sand, glass – may through the force of will or imagination carry into futures, promise something, stand for more than themselves. Or rather, be more fully what they are, because the fact that a thing is small and unknown makes it no less real, the thoughts and emotions that carry it no less intense, than the motions of the rich and venerated.

This is what I saw in the plays, through things like Shakespeare's scenic repetitions. Once you see how comedy repeats, we can call it *history*, and not mere romance, or relief, or refuse.

And so maybe there was some sort of faithfulness to Hobart, a repetition of our wayward intensities, in my subject: that knowledge we all had of being distant from any centre that was going, picking things up only via semi-envious media-crackle, as we peered to see over the shoulders of the mainlanders and wish we had four TV stations like they had; the gone-in-a-moment *bark* of our leisures; the bush and the water everywhere, neither to be entered casually, because untracked or too-tracked, either corrupted by pollutants, like the Derwent by the zinc works, or the bush by the loggers, or else simply dangerous, because the wilderness is the wilderness, it isn't a *landscape*, it isn't *picturesque*, it isn't the city or the court bucolically translated, it is its own thing, new and old, and not finally to be possessed. This *nature* wasn't mine, certainly, but I felt its strangeness, and felt the assault on complacency or comfort in it.

Shakespeare's storms and wilds felt right: the sea hits the sky, literally; a bear eats a man, literally; a ship goes down and not a soul is remembered, literally; a spirit is trapped howling in a tree for years, literally; the very island and the state upon it might totter, literally, from the fact that the mind is drunk and appetites reckless and there may be nothing, if no one is looking, to stop you from doing *anything*, literally.

* * *

Speaking of shared traumas: Martin Bryant, the Port Arthur murderer, killed one bloke from my old school, a tall kid, a couple of years ahead of me, who played ruck in the school footie team. Bryant locked him in the boot of his car, took him hostage, and later shot him. Now Bryant is getting fat in Risdon gaol, serving 35 life sentences, but before he murdered 35 people in 1996 he'd regularly be seen walking around New Town, in central Hobart, buying milk and the like, just near where my sister lived. There's not such a long bow to be drawn from one of these things to the next. I mean, in no particular order, setting fire to the nature strips, pretending history isn't, the violence of distant islands, real and imagined.

* * *

Caliban would have been a rapist, he happily remembers the prospect and regrets its foiling; he would have been a murderer, he is *jocund* at the thought and relishes recommending methods of execution. But I turned my mind away from such things. For me, Caliban was the intimate and tender child, my brother in possibility, with all of his past right there at his long-nailed fingertips, as freshly present as the weather, calling for his *high-day, freedom*, playing with his name, *cacaliban*, turning it into a malediction, imaginatively shitting upon his master. I disdained those critics who thought his rebellion a crapulent humiliation. I resented Shakespeare for the hints of innate and intractable servitude. I insisted that the servants were those others, those slaves of opportunity, who had nothing of Caliban's *ontological* openness to possibility – the fact that he *is*, he IS, as nascent and trembling with potentials as the unknowable *young scamels* that he promises to *get* from the rock. I never thought about what Caliban wanted to do with these scamels, serve them up as an exotic pet or nibble. Instead I would dwell on *scamel* as the acme of island incipience. A shellfish? A bird? A *godwit*? A lizard? Some sort of supra-generic scurrier, moving as it lives between mollusc and amphibian and marsupial and mammal, as tender as the flesh of a scallop, as allergic to assault as the naked barnacles that I used to stand over and drop slow saliva upon, in a kind of secret benediction, watching them *shiver like an egg* and retreat deep as nature would allow inside their shelter. . .

* * *

There was a story I traded in, I don't know how true, of an Australian tourist in the Lebanon, or some other war-torn place, getting out of his car to take a piss and seeing a sign by the roadside, 'Danger: Land Mines', at which he duly aimed a high parabola of urine. The ground exploded in front of him. I can't recall if the only thing left of him was his teeth, but anyway the point is clear. Australians of my generation tended to think that history happened elsewhere; that somehow we were liberated from it, on account of growing up in the *greatest bloody place on earth*, and that for us there would be no serious consequences. Most of us had never heard of Thomas Jefferson, but he wrote for us, not for Americans, when he declared a constitutional right to *happiness*.

I was no different. I celebrated Autolycus as the man without a centre, the man with a juggler's hand of pasts, pissing on the hedge as the chosen ones file by, ready to filch what he can and spellbind the girls, sublimely sceptical of attachment.

* * *

Equally, part of me suspects that I was attracted to these *tragi/c/comic* moments for their echo of my own marginality, a kind of cracked, maverick, mock-despairing shout, that hardly anybody hears, that I know is pointless, but which brings a cheer simply from its singularity. Part of me wonders if *tragi/c/comedy* is the perfect correspondent mode of 'my' Tasmanian-Australianness. You don't believe, not really, in the system that you play; you *cacaw* from some askance angle; you bash the drunken drum; and then you submit the work for an Oxford DPhil.

* * *

Not that it matters, but the viva that followed my submission was a laughable, hideous, emptying failure. My examiners were the top-dog professors of Oxford and Cambridge respectively, recommended because it would be good to get supporters with heft.

Question 1: How much of this has Dr. N****** actually read? Blather blather.

I see.

Question 2: How long did you take to write this?

Blather bla--

I see.

Question 3: When are you returning to Australia?

Blather--

I see.

Question 4: on page **, you use the word, 'nubile'. What do you mean?

Blath-

I see.

Question 5: on page **, you use the world, 'visceral'. What do you mean?

Bla-

I see.

Question 6: what year was *Knight of the Burning Pestle* actually first performed?

B--

I see.

Very quickly, it was over. Surely there's more to this than *this*. . .

Did I have any question I would like to ask?

Was there nothing you liked about it at all?

Professor C****: I couldn't possibly tell you; I read it twice, very carefully, and I didn't understand a word.

Professor B*****: It was imaginative.

* * *

The thing is – as much as they didn't see the good things lurking in it, or were blinded to its promise by my frankly perverse delivery – I wrote it such that every sentence was a kind of miniaturized, conceit-ridden allegory of its portent – my examiners were dead right in their judgements. It was a work of deep-hewn, deep-lying, deeply occluded *imagination*. Trying to assess it must have been like trying to decipher the mouth movements of some lost sea-mammal, washed-up on the wrong beach and gasping for breath underneath just-enough water to keep him from actually dying.

But still; it just might have been the truest thing I've ever written. Not passable literary criticism, I don't doubt. But in its own way true to the sources.

* * *

You return to a scene, and its delight or claim upon you has shifted. In some ways my attraction to comic rebellion began as a young man thing, even a boy thing. The fifteen year old, hitting golf balls off the pier into the river, hoping to hear the little *plop* as the tiny white thing disappears. The twenty-three year old, preparing to leave for Oxford and bouncing from port to port kissing my goodbyes. *Let my sheep go*. What's the difference? But life catches up, or you catch up to life. You meet someone who really doesn't believe in careless love. You realize there is no such thing.

I remember, in 1996, hearing about a ship in the Indian Ocean, carrying 60,000 Australian sheep. Now I can't recall if the ship went down, or just the sheep, ushered en masse to the edge and leaping like – well, I could say like lemmings, but *sheep* will do – and sinking in their 60,000 woolly jumpers to their individual deaths. It seemed horrible, grotesque, a kind of absent-minded genocide. But then I suppose such things happen all the time at sea, that capacious, silent grave. I remember thinking about the similar scene in *The Winter's Tale* – I was writing my book on the late plays at this time – and I suppose quietly thinking something like: so many nameless dead; so many unlamented sacrifices; and for what? For trade, or for state, or for some *Romance* hinge-point between *tragi* and *comedy*. In my book, I noted how Shakespeare makes the ship's sinking ('now the ship boring the moon with her main-mast', 3.3.86) echo the conditions of Leontes' delusion ('Affection! Thy intention stabs the centre', 1.2.140). A scenic rhyme, the repetition a proof that violence at the centre reverberates, is not forgotten, is not without consequences. This, I still think, is true. But isn't there also a danger in this kind of clever corresponding? The later scene answers the earlier; it folds into an equation: the specific calamity is sublated into theme. *But of course*, we might object. We cannot truly feel the pain of a ship-full of anonymous sailors, and still less 60,000 sheep. If an art-form is to have ethical and political punch, it has to do so through intimate recognitions. But still. I thought at the time that I was retrieving lost voices. But I didn't in truth *hear them*.

But then perhaps we cannot. Even in the report of these deaths the Clown cannot escape the play's cruel dialectical symmetries: so we hear 'how the poor souls roared, and the sea mocked them: and how the poor gentleman roared, and the bear mocked him, both roaring louder than the sea or the weather'; 'when was this, boy?', asks his father; 'Now, now', says the shepherd-clown, 'I have not winked since I saw these sights: the men are not yet cold under water, nor the bear half-dined on the gentleman: *he's at it now*' (3.3.92–8). Now, now, *now*: this is truly pitiless, multiply pitiless. The history of hearing these lines has been, I suspect, not to hear them. Why is this? Why don't we process a world gone mad with destruction? Perhaps because we can only take on one event, one emotion, at a time. Perhaps because each side of the symmetry subtracts from the other, their existential presence is allayed, and we are relieved of having truly to care. Perhaps because the multiple *mocks* – meaning cruel disregard, meaning teasing with a life, meaning imitation – speak for a play-world that is essentially antinomian in its logic: so, the greater grace of the rescued Perdita waits to claim and redeem our sympathies. We remember and laugh at *Exit, pursued by a bear*, rarely remembering that, as much as the Antigonus-actor never re-enters, *Antigonus* does, named so by the clown, his grisly end happening *now, now*. But what can we do?

We can hear, we can imagine, but we cannot quite see. The men 'are not yet cold under water' (3.3.97). Ponder this for a moment, these still-warm men. They are alive, even *now* they are alive, shouting to be heard, waving to be seen, fighting to reach the surface. But we do not hear; we do not see; the scene shuts down on them, and all we have is the black hole of a clown's mouth. Or – and perhaps as a precise consequence of this sensory *blanc* – they are just this moment *dead*, and even *now* each organ still hums from its usual function, the whole beast is still warm from the living. But we cannot reach them, or give them good burial, or do anything for them. The world is moving past.

I wanted to hear the sailors, and for others to hear. But maybe you can only do so in this snatched, quixotic, slightly self-combing fashion – much like standing at the edge of a pier, in distant Hobart, with that cruel history-laden harbour, heavy with whales and ships and cars, and yelling across its greyness. The waters don't remember, or if they do they speak nothing.

* * *

And what of those other amnesiac wounds, the silent gaps between scenes? There is a scene in *Pericles*, where the heroine Marina is saved from execution by the serendipitous arrival of pirates, who immediately declare their intent (*half-part, half-part!*, 15.143) to submit the lovely fourteen year old child to a gangbang. The scene ends, and we shift to a brothel, where the owners are moaning that their 'stuff', their overworked whores, are all too fucked to fuck. It is only then that the pirates enter with Marina, whom they sell to the brothel as a 'virgin'. Well, they say that Christ can re-virginate fallen women; maybe the romance genre can as well.

What's not to love?

Before I had a child of my own, it never occurred to me to wonder what was happening. It never occurred to me to ask why I didn't wonder about these things, why I didn't simply *believe* the pirates and the would-be assassin when they advertise the fact that she will be raped. What else did I think would happen? The truth is, I didn't think anything else would happen: Marina entered a *blank*. But perhaps I should remember what Milton says of the *blank* space (or as he prefers to spell it, the *blanc*). It is the bleached space of annihilation, of negative ontology, of literal life denial. It is the *blank* other to innocence.

I *saw* Marina in this *blanc* – for some reason I went searching for her in it – when I had a baby girl, two weeks old, and I was in Liverpool and she wasn't. I don't say that was why I searched for Marina, or felt the horror of what no one will ever think can have happened. But the thoughts coincided. Some possibility was born.

* * *

Shakespeare, I think, lives the gaps, he feels their possibility. He always knows how little separates any of us from annihilation or atrocity; how a tiny protective membrane might wobble and detach and suddenly there you are – suddenly born, or suddenly dead, or suddenly raw as sin, no longer some comical monster but an apprentice infanticide, slicing an old innocent's neck because a bearded hag said you might.

* * *

The lonely peril of existing is also its connectedness – with others, or with our former or future selves. My younger mind dwelt long upon Ariel trapped in the tree, or Caliban, the hunkered-down hag-seed in his rock, or upon those scamels, named but never to be known. Now I dwell upon new semi-absences, adumbrated presences: Marina hanging in the gap; Poor Tom, risen up from a 'fathom and a half' down, blindly piloting through ever-narrowing straits, his world's ur-model of *man* and yet, strictly speaking, an ontological and individual *not*.

I don't really call such thoughts *criticism*. I prefer words like imagining, or recovery: or perhaps Cavell's apposite term, 'ghostly selections', in which the selections are not quite my choice, but rather ghost into view, rising half-unbidden from their lairs. Nevertheless, the connections are palpable enough – to the remembered pre-boy, or to the unpermitted homunculi, or simply to the unfinishable 'I' that remains, like most of us do, much younger than it looks. Something in me still casts after the lives unlived, after brothers and sisters, present or possible or not. This is the virtuality, the past and not-yet, that I apprehend in Shakespeare's super-charged breathing spaces – in the worlds inside his words; in the gaps between cue and speech; in the teeming precipices at the end of his lines. I still hear the poor fools who never quite get the audience at court, the little cells who fail to hit the jackpot. I can still hear the ghostly souls, laughing, swearing, screaming, across or from under the waters.

Afterword

'Speak what we feel, not what we ought to say'

Paul Edmondson

After their Midsummer Night adventures the four lovers – Demetrius, Hermia, Helena and Lysander – try to piece together what has befallen them. They all perceive something just beyond their reach.

DEMETRIUS: These things seem small and undistinguishable,
                       Like far-off mountains turned into clouds.
HERMIA: Methinks I see these things with parted eye,
                       When everything seems double.
HELENA: So methinks,
                       And I have found Demetrius like a jewel,
                       Mine own and not mine own.
DEMETRIUS: It seems to me
                       That yet we sleep, we dream. Do not you think
                       The Duke was here and bid us follow him?
HERMIA: Yea, and my father.
HELENA: And Hippolyta.
LYSANDER: And he did bid us follow to the temple.
DEMETRIUS: Why then, we are awake. Let's follow him,
                       And by the way let us recount our dreams.
                                   (*A Midsummer Night's Dream*, 4.1.184–95)

All four of them experience different ways of seeing. Demetrius (who, let us remember, has not had the love-juice removed from his eyes) describes a long-sighted view: are those mountains or clouds? Hermia has a split perspective and sees double. Helena's vision is disconcerting: Demetrius has now become her jewel but one which does and does not belong to her. If marriage is expressive of a physical, emotional, intellectual, and (when celebrated sacramentally) spiritual mutuality, an indwelling, then Helena's words hint at a future of frustrated happiness. Demetrius is still under Puck's spell and will only be truly Helena's by being perpetually untrue to himself. Lysander, the last of the four to speak, seems the most collected. He names their destination: 'the temple', where the two couples 'shall eternally be knit' (4.1.178) alongside Theseus and Hippolyta's own royal wedding. And the lovers exit with the prospect of sharing their dreams along the way, interdependently piecing together a shared truth.

What will they say to one another? Will they agree? Or argue? Will they even be able to articulate their dreams? The newly married Hippolyta later describes the effect of their story:

> But all the story of the night told over,
> And all their minds transfigured so together,
> More witnesseth than fancy's images,
> And grows to something of great constancy;
> But howsoever, strange and admirable. (5.1.23–7)

The lovers' dreams are now recounted as the memories of the night passed, which transfigure their minds in the telling, and take on their own imagined and intangible reality, 'something of great constancy', that can neither be grasped nor described fully. Hippolyta's vague report describes the effect it has on her: ''Tis strange, my Theseus, that these lovers speak of' (5.1.1); Theseus dismisses it as the unreliable product of 'seething brains' (5.1.4), nothing more than 'antique fables' or 'fairy toys' (5.1.3).

Just after the lovers' waking exchange takes place, the audience hears someone else trying to recount his dreams, Bottom, who struggles to communicate the incommunicable:

I have had a most rare vision. I have had a dream past the wit of man to say what dream it was. Man is but an ass if he go about t'expound this dream. Methought I was – there is no man can tell what. Methought I was, and methought I had – but man is but a patched fool if he will offer to say what methought I had. (4.1.199–204).

Bottom cannot tell what he was, but his experience has crept into his language with his reference to 'ass'. It is 'a dream past the wit of man' – but the audience has just shared Shakespeare's wit with which he has portrayed the dream. Bottom's dream is a motley experience and can only be understood by a fool – but that's precisely what Bottom, and the actor who played him for The Lord Chamberlain's Men, are. There is ample scope for different gestures with: 'Methought I had . . . methought I had'. How far might these relate to what the audience has already seen? Bottom's ass's head, ears, nose, penis? In one moving interpretation the actor tinged his speech with melancholy and recollected his fairy wings. Although he had not possessed any in the production, his ass's ears were made of ostrich feathers. Here he evoked for the audience the internalized sensation of what it is like to fly in a dream. During one interval of *A Midsummer Night's Dream* I overheard a child being asked by his younger brother why Bottom is the only human in the play to see the fairies. The reply came directly: 'Because Bottom has an ass's head, and animals can see fairies.'

Bottom's speech continues. His senses are still in that state of half-waking, half-sleeping and there is a hint he has experienced something profound and godly (4.1.204–7) with reference to St Paul's letters to the Church in Corinth from the New Testament (I Corinthians 2:9–10; II Corinthians 12:1–6). Finally, Bottom concludes with the decision to turn his dream into art, a ballad, which he will ask somebody else to write for him. His incommunicable interior life will be adapted as 'Bottom's Dream' by Peter Quince and consumed as part of the royal wedding festivities. He returns to his fellow actors 'to discourse wonders' (4.2.25), but does not get round to it. The communication he had originally intended is superseded by the news that their play of *Pyramus and Thisbe* has been selected. All of their dreams have come true.

Dreams cannot be expressed through words. They need the dimensions of a performance to communicate the sense of the truth that underlies them. A friend of mine once told me that she refused to attend any of the lectures on literary theory as an undergraduate because, she said, 'At the first one, the lecturer said "Wittgenstein said 'There is no truth in literature'", and everyone wrote it down.' You hold in your hands a collection of essays which dare to convey truth, through knowledge and, perhaps most importantly, experience. *Shakespeare and I* is a series of dreams, an anthology of attempts to communicate something real in language, a succession of illustrations which show why personal experience in relation to art, in relation to Shakespeare, matters. All the contributors to this volume share a sense of daring, a declaration that what they have seen and felt, combined with what they can rationally know and demonstrate, is important.

A few of the essays have chosen to be honest about sex and sexuality. Ewan Fernie's essay made me reflect on the idea that not being honest about the texts we read is like not being honest about sex. Like sex, texts have the power to get under our skins. Eric S. Mallin's chapter is an occasion for him at once to admire and be afraid of Othello and Desdemona's marriage, against which he obliquely positions his own. David Fuller's exploration of sexuality is nuanced with the development of his appreciation of Shakespearean verse-speaking; his own interior music of desire finds confirmation and affirmation in the sound of Shakespeare.

All of the essays are about personal formation. Peter Holland (who when he was young used to be treated to rum truffles on the way to the Aldwych Theatre) reflects on how going to the theatre was something (and still is) to be prized, and that from this grew a gradual (now professional) awareness of performance and the energies of its history. Holland's essay reminds me that we can often be best (and most) critical of the things and people we love best of all.

Richard Wilson describes the burning of Virginia Woolf's straw hat in the garden of Monk's House a year after Leonard Woolf had died, and the broken memorial tablet marking the place where her ashes are buried under the tree. For Wilson Shakespeare gives shape (via F. R. Leavis) to a subtle and richly textured formational web. Philip Davis heroically finds personal formation in the text, too, in *Coriolanus*, and in works that speak to the depth of our experience more than we can do on our own. He traces this effect on the textual surface as he reads, as words and experience happen before him.

Simon Palfrey contributes a rites of passage narrative about the trauma of birth and the fears and frustrated joys of growing up. It is difficult to be truly honest about one's parents and one's upbringing – the doubts about love, fragile happiness, waiting for the opportunity to make someone you love a cup of coffee – and it is striking that moments from *King Lear, Coriolanus, The Tempest, The Winter's Tale* and *Pericles* run through Palfrey's account. Shakespeare's words become for Palfrey a way of identifying deeply submerged ghosts and memories, something angry and yet, in their way, as prophetic as Louis Macneice's 'Prayer before Birth'.

Thomas Docherty recalls how, at the age of eleven, class distinctions and sheer boredom prevented him from properly responding to *A Midsummer Night's Dream*. But the annotations in his edition excited his imagination. Through them language became a living thing, something which could be powerfully wielded, and yet remain itself. Julia Reinhard Lupton experiences a similar sense of knowing among material objects and considers, through her persona of Mrs Polonius, a relationship between Shakespeare's stage-craft and her own constructed sense of domesticity. Lupton dreams aloud her sense of being formed by Shakespeare's stage-craft and material world.

Graham Holderness powerfully retrieves and refreshes a narrative of resurrection in his response to *King Lear*, mapping his own rediscovery of Christianity onto his reading of the text, and experiencing a tremendous sense of liberation. Reading becomes something blood-felt and heart-felt. And through this he establishes a theoretical and experiential space in which to understand the nature of his own poetic endeavour. Reading, voicing, and creating here take on something akin to a spiritual exercise.

Philippa Berry laments the English language's lack of power fully to describe the kind of knowledge that is learnt through experience and turns instead to the broader-minded Greek lexicon. Like the other essays in the collection, Berry's seems to come from deep within her. Her Shakespearean formation, like Holderness's, is spiritually focused and rooted in Shakespeare's great gift for depicting particularity.

That Shakespeare is a supremely accommodating and generously hospitable writer is borne out by all the essays. Sarah Klenbort and Philippa Kelly also bring to Shakespeare deeply felt personal issues. Klenbort offers a political and privately inflected kaleidoscope about maternity, masculinity and their attendant anxieties. Kelly bears bravely the effects of raw grief. Shakespeare allows both writers to name and place their doubts and fears. He confirms for Klenbort what she has long felt: that our Early Modern predecessors can illuminate our contemporary experiences of gender. For Kelly Shakespeare becomes the means through which to hope, a perspective on grief that begins to transcend its pain.

Shakespeare and I comes at the end of 'the end of theory' in literary studies (*The Return of Theory in Early Modern English Studies* edited by Paul Cefalu and Bryan Reynolds waits for me, just to my left, as I write this Afterword). New Historicism and Cultural Materialism have pulled academic focus since the mid-1990s, while the dominance of other theoretical models (more prevalent in the 1970s and 1980s) has seemed to decline. A relaxing of theoretical astringency for more than a decade has created the space for the freshly voiced *Shakespeare and I.* This is not to say that the essays here are untheoretical, but that they draw freely on a range of other discourses (including life-writing, pedagogical analyses, and performance criticism). They share the view that human feeling cannot be measured, defined, or argued against. Feelings are messy and often unforgettable, irrational, and will always escape any theoretical paradigm. 'Feelings', though (unless they be historicized Early Modern ones) are unprofessional and do not speak the right kind of language for academic conferences and publication. Yet in daring to share their feelings, desires, confessions, epiphanies, frustrations, regrets, honesty, and fears, the contributors to *Shakespeare and I* are doing precisely what Edgar at the end of *The Tragedy of King Lear* implores us all to do: 'Speak what we feel, not what we ought to say' (5.3.299).

To be truly honest about our feelings is to drop our defences. Writing which is honest, open and in our most fully possessed human language finds its place in the long tradition of confessional literature, memoirs, and essays, the kind of writing which was being re-invented in the Early Modern Period. A much earlier example would be St Augustine's *Confessions* or, even earlier, the book of Ecclesiastes in the Hebrew Bible. In Shakespeare's time confessional writing is perhaps best exemplified by Michel de Montaigne (1533–1592) who, in the address to the reader of his essays, writes:

I desire therein to be delineated in mine own genuine, simple, and ordinary fashion, without contention, art or study; for it is myself I portray. My imperfections shall therein be read to the life, and my natural form discerned, so far forth as public reverence hath permitted me. For if my fortune had been to have lived among those nations, which yet are said to live under the sweet liberty of Natures first and uncorrupted laws, I assure thee, I would most willingly have portrayed my self fully and naked. (Montaigne, 1935, vol. 1, p. 15)

Another great essayist of the period was John Donne (1572–1631) who describes Heaven as a literary space into which the life of each individual is translated differently, 'that Library where every book shall lie open to one another' (Donne, 'Meditation 17', in Rhodes, 1987, p. 125). Later came Sir Thomas Browne (1605–1682) who, like Montaigne and Donne, wrote, as it were, with a mind so copious, generous and open that he felt his way around a subject intuitively, excluding nothing, including everything: 'all places, all airs, make unto me one country; I am England everywhere, and under any meridian' (*Religio Medici*, Browne, 1928, vol. 1, p. 70). Browne's writing is shot through with compelling (some-times absurd) speculation, for example: 'Pythagoras might have had calmer sleeps, if he had totally abstained from beans.' (*On Dreams*, Browne, 1928, vol. 3, p. 232). In his essay for *Shakespeare and I*, David Fuller recalls his former tutor, William Empson, in terms which evoke the Renaissance ideal of learning as something which engages the whole person and in which a love of poetry was an inextricable part of a wide range of interests across what we now call disciplines. All of the essays here gathered share that same spirit of large-mindedness.

I should like briefly to add two more touchstones to this anthology, two writers in whose personal and literary formations Shakespeare played an important part. The first is John Keats (1795–1821). When Keats was a schoolboy, Charles Cowden Clarke tells us, his eyes filled with tears when reading Innogen's lines about the departing Posthumus:

> I would have broke mine eye-strings, cracked them, but
> To look upon him till the diminution
> Of space had pointed him sharp as my needle;
> Nay, followed him till he had melted from
> The smallness of a gnat to air, and then
> Have turned my eye and wept. (*Cymbeline* 1.3.17–22)

For Keats, Shakespeare provided not only inspiration – 'I am very near Agreeing with Hazlitt that Shakespeare is enough for us' (Keats, 'To B. R. Haydon, 10, 11 May 1817'; quoted in Gittings, 1970, p. 14) – but also a language with which to communicate with friends. A long list of Shakespearean allusions resonate throughout Keats' letters. One of the most memorable is in the letter to his brother and sister-in-law at the beginning of 1819. In this Keats suggests that the three of them may be brought closer together in spirit and mood, though separated by distance, if they agree to read a passage of Shakespeare every Sunday at ten o' clock: 'we shall be as near each other as blind bodies can be in the same room'. (quoted in Gittings, 1970, p. 176) Shakespeare here becomes the quasi-spiritual meeting place for different integrities, and makes them interdependent.

The second is Virginia Woolf (1882–1941). For some part of her youth, Woolf was indifferent about Shakespeare. Her father, Sir Leslie Stephen, published some essays on Shakespeare's life; she used to read Shakespeare aloud to her mother. He was very much a part of her family background. However, she recalls finding his plays 'antipathetic. How did they begin? With some dull speech; about a hundred miles from anything that interested me'. (Fox, 1990, p. 54)

It was her brother, Thoby Stephen, the Jacob of Woolf's novel *Jacob's Room*, that encouraged her to turn again to the dramatist. Woolf recalled later how her brother

> had consumed Shakespeare, somehow or other, by himself. He had possessed himself of it, in his large clumsy way, and our first arguments – about books, that is – were heated; because out he would come with his sweeping assertion that everything was in Shakespeare: somehow I felt he has it all in his grasp. (Fox, 1990, p. 7)

The lines of Posthumus from Act Five Scene Six of *Cymbeline* 'Hang there like fruit, my soul,/Till the tree die' (5.6.263–4) were actually the turning point for Woolf's own re-appraisal of Shakespeare. In a letter of 5 November 1901, she recalls reading *Cymbeline* afresh:

> just to see if there mightn't be more in the great William than I supposed. And I was quite upset! Really and truly I am now let in to [the] company of worshippers – though I still feel a little oppressed by his – greatness I suppose. (Fox, 1990, p. 94)

Whereas Keats regarded Shakespeare as the greatest poet, Woolf did not hold back in criticizing Shakespeare's portraits of human nature. While expressing her reservations about the main characters in *Cymbeline*, Woolf also provides the beginnings of her own ideological readings. She asks:

> Why aren't they more human? Imogen and Posthumous and Cymbeline – I find them beyond me – Is this my feminine weakness in the upper region? But really they might have been cut out with a pair of scissors – as far as mere humanity goes. . . . Of course, they talk divinely. (Fox, 1990, p. 94)

In being formed by Shakespeare Woolf creates space for political self-irony with the reference to her own femininity. Her renewal of interest in Shakespeare, through her brother Thoby, marks the start of a lifelong fascination of her own which was to excite and inspire both her works of fiction and her cultural criticism. Shakespeare is to be enjoyed, but can also become the forum for radical, cultural debate.

As well as *Cymbeline*, Keats and Woolf also have Shakespeare's Birthplace in common as a formational milestone. Keats's signature is included in the earliest surviving visitors' book. He made the visit on 2 October 1817 while staying in Oxford with his friend Benjamin Bailey. Keats gives his address as 'everywhere'. When he visited Shakespeare's grave in Holy Trinity Church on the following day Keats evoked a pre-Reformation age by writing that same address in Latin: 'ubique'. Woolf, too, visited the Birthplace on 9 May 1934. Her diary entry is impressionistic, 'road running' she calls it, and spiritually infused. She feels Shakespeare is 'serenely absent-present, both at once; radiating round one; yes; in the flowers, in the old hall, in the garden; but never to be pinned down. . . . His genius flowed out of him, and is still there, in Stratford'. (Woolf, 1997, pp. 112–13)

In visiting Shakespeare's Birthplace both writers join the footfall of many millions for whom the site is an important kind of pilgrimage. The footfall through Shakespeare's Birthplace continues and people from all over the world make their mark in the visitors' book. In the garden, the attentive passer-by will see an effigy of the Indian poet and philosopher Rabindranath Tagore (1861–1941); nearby, in the Shakespeare Centre, is a plaque to one of Tagore's friends and students, the Pakistani poet and philosopher Sir Muhammed Iqbal (1877–1938). Standing inside The Shakespeare Centre and looking out across the garden, it is possible to see Tagore's bust from Iqbal's plaque. Only the width of Shakespeare's garden separates two friends, poets and scholars whose nations are politically opposed; only Shakespeare can hold in tension so profound a political divide by being a large enough cultural meeting place.

We are formed by our dreams, our interiority, our 'undefendedness', the dreams we dare to share. A subtitle for *Shakespeare and I* might be *How Shakespeare Formed Me*. The contributors ask 'Where have I come from? What part did Shakespeare play in that, and why? How might this help me relate to where other people are coming from?' This book requires its readers to be good listeners. Some readers might find it hedonistic. Perhaps it is. But this kind of hedonism is tempered with discernment, with the self listening carefully to itself, and creative expression. It requires no more justification than this: 'speak what we feel, not what we ought to say' (*The Tragedy of King Lear*, 5.3.299). Our revels now have started.

Bibliography

Books cited

Abrams, M. H. et al. (eds) (1993), *The Norton Anthology of English Literature.* Vol. 2, 6th edn. New York and London: W. W. Norton.

Adorno, Theodor (2003), *The Jargon of Authenticity.* Knut Tarnowski and Frederic Will (trans.). London: Routledge.

Allen, Michael J. B. (1989), *Icastes: Marsilio Ficino's Interpretation of Plato's 'Sophist'.* Berkeley: University of California Press.

Amad, Yaser (2009), *The General.* M.A. Thesis, University of Texas at Austin.

Anderson, Linda (2001), *Autobiography.* London: Routledge.

Anderson, Perry (1992), *English Questions.* London: Verso.

Andersson, Daniel (2010), 'Humanism and natural philosophy in Renaissance Cambridge', in Mordechai Feingold (ed.), *History of Universities*, vol. 24. Oxford: Oxford University Press, pp. 69–116.

Arendt, Hannah (1958), *The Human Condition.* Chicago: University of Chicago Press.

— (1993), *Between Past and Future: Eight Exercises in Political Thought.* Harmondsworth: Penguin.

Aristotle (1956), *Metaphysics.* John Warrington (ed. and trans.). London: Dent.

Armstrong, Isobel (2000), *The Radical Aesthetic.* Oxford: Blackwell.

Augustine (1907), *The Confessions of St Augustine* (English). E. B. Pusey (trans.). London: Dent.

— (1908), *The Confessions of Augustine* (Latin). John Gibb and William Montgomery (eds). Cambridge: Cambridge University Press.

Bacon, Francis (1605; 1962), *The Advancement of Learning*. G. W. Kitchin (ed.). London: Everyman's Library, Dent.

Barker, Francis (1984), *The Tremulous Private Body: Essays on Subjection*. London and New York: Methuen.

Barthes, Roland (1977a), *Roland Barthes by Roland Barthes*. Richard Howard (trans.). London: Macmillan.

— (1977b), *Sade, Fourier, Loyola*. Richard Miller (trans.). Jonathan Cape: London.

— (1978), *Image/Music/Text*. Stephen Heath (trans.). New York: Hill and Wang.

Barton, John (1986), *Playing Shakespeare*. London: Methuen.

Bell, Michael (1988), *F.R. Leavis*. London: Routledge.

Belsey, Catherine (1985), *The Subject of Tragedy: Identity and Difference in Renaissance Drama*. London: Methuen.

Bennington, Geoffrey and Derrida, Jacques (1991), *Jacques Derrida*. Paris: Seuil.

Berry, Philippa (1993), 'Authorship overshadowed: death, darkness and the feminisation of authority in late Renaissance writing', in M. Biriotti and N. Miller (eds), *What Is an Author?* Manchester: Manchester University Press, pp. 155–72.

— (1999), *Shakespeare's Feminine Endings: Disfiguring Death in the Tragedies*. London: Routledge.

Berry, Ralph (1989), *On Directing Shakespeare*. London: Hamish Hamilton.

Billington, Michael (2007), *State of the Nation: British Theatre Since 1945*. London: Faber and Faber.

Blanchot, Maurice (2000), *L'Instance de ma Mort / The Instant of My Death*. Elizabeth Rottenberg (trans.). Stanford, California: Stanford University Press.

Bloom, Harold (2005), *Shakespeare's Othello*. New York: Penguin.

Blume, Harvey (2001), 'Stephen Greenblatt: the wicked son' (interview), *Bookwire*. Available online at: <http://www.bookwire.com/bookwire/bbr/reviews/june2001/GREENBLATTInterview.htm> [accessed December 2007].

Boito, Arrigo (n.d.), Verdi, Giuseppe (music), *Otello: A Lyrical Drama in Four Acts (libretto)*. New York: Edwin F. Kalmus.

Booth, Stephen (1995), '*Twelfth Night* and *Othello*, those extraordinary twins', in Peggy O'Brien, Jeanne Addison Roberts, Michael Tolaydo, Nancy Goodwin (eds), *Shakespeare Set Free: Teaching* Twelfth Night *and* Othello. New York and London: Washington Square Press.

Boyse, Kyla R. N. (2007), 'Television'. *University of Michigan Health System.* Available online at: <http://www.med.umich.edu/1libr/yourchild/tv.htm>

Bradley, A. C. (1904; 2nd edn., 1905), *Shakespearean Tragedy*. London: Macmillan.

Bradshaw, Graham (1993), *Misrepresentations: Shakespeare and the Materialists*. Ithaca, New York and London: Cornell University Press.

Bradshaw, Graham and Bishop, Tom and Holbrook, Peter (eds) (2006), *The Shakespeare International Yearbook: Special Section: Shakespeare and Montaigne Revisited*. Aldershot: Ashgate.

Bremmer, Jan N. (1987), *The Early Greek Concept of the Soul*. Princeton: Princeton University Press.

Briggs, Julia (2005), *Virginia Woolf: An Inner Life*. London: Allen Lane.

Browne, Thomas (1928), *The Works of Sir Thomas Browne*. Geoffrey Keynes (ed.), 4 vols. London: Faber and Faber.

— (1964), *Religio Medici and Other Works*. L.C. Martin (ed.). Oxford: Clarendon Press.

Burke, Sean (1992), *The Death and Return of the Author*. Edinburgh: Edinburgh University Press.

Burkert, Walter (1987), *Ancient Mystery Cults*. Cambridge, MA: Harvard University Press.

Calderwood, James (1989), *The Properties of Othello*. Amherst, MA: University of Massachusetts Press.

Cavell, Stanley (1987; repr. 2003), *Disowning Knowledge in Six Plays of Shakespeare*. Cambridge: Cambridge University Press.

Celenza, Christopher S. (1999), 'Pythagoras in the Renaissance: the case of Marsilio Ficino'. *Renaissance Quarterly*, 52, 667–711.

Challen, John (1973), *Drama Casebook: A Chronicle of an Experience*. London: Methuen.

Clinton, Kevin (2003), 'Stages of initiation in the Eleusinian and Samothracian mysteries', in Michael B. Cosmopoulos (ed.), *Greek Mysteries: The Archaeology and Ritual of Ancient Greek Secret Cults.* London: Routledge, pp. 50–78.

Cooper, J. and Hutchinson, D. (eds) (1997), *Plato's Complete Works.* Indianapolis and Cambridge: Hackett Publishing.

Coote, Stephen (1992), *Coriolanus.* London: Penguin.

Crosse, Gordon (1953), *Shakespearian Playgoing, 1890–1952.* London: Mowbray.

— (1986), *Shakespeare and the Stage. Series 3: Prompt books and related materials from the Shakespeare Library, Birmingham.* 10 microfilm reels. Woodbridge, CT: Research Publications.

Cynewulf (1977), 'Elene', in P. O. E. Gradon (ed.), *Cynewulf's 'Elene'.* Exeter: Exeter University Press.

Daileader, Celia (1998), *Eroticism on the Early Modern Stage.* Cambridge: Cambridge University Press.

Dapoxetine Priligy. Available online at: <http://www.dapoxetine-online. biz/notorganic.php> [accessed 28 September 2010].

Davidhazi, Peter (1998), *The Romantic Cult of Shakespeare: Literary Reception in Anthropological Perspective.* New York: Palgrave Macmillan.

Davie, Donald (1976), *Articulate Energy.* London: Routledge and Kegan Paul.

Davies, J. V. (ed.) (1973), *Lawrence on Hardy and Painting.* London: Heinemann.

Dawson, Giles E. (1964), 'London's bull-baiting and bear-baiting arena in 1562'. *Shakespeare Quarterly*, 15(1), 97–101.

de Man, Paul (1979), 'Autobiography as de-facement'. *Modern Language Notes*, 94, 919–30.

de Vries, Hent (1998), '"Lapsus Absolu": Notes on Maurice Blanchot's *The Instant of My Death'. Yale French Studies*, 93, 30–59.

de Waal, Edmund (2010), *The Hare with Amber Eyes.* London: Chatto and Windus.

Derrida, Jacques (1988), *The Ear of the Other: Otobiography, Transference, Translation: Texts and Discussions with Jacques Derrida.* Christie McDonald (ed.), Peggy Kamuf and Avital Ronell (trans.). Lincoln, Nebraska: University of Nebraska Press.

— (1989), *Memoires for Paul de Man*. Cecile Lindsay, Jonathan Culler, Eduardo Cadava and Peggy Kamuf (trans.). New York: Columbia University Press.

— (2000), *Demeure: fiction and testimony*. Elizabeth Rottenberg (trans.). Stanford, California: Stanford University Press.

Dobbie, Elliott van Kirk (1937), *The Manuscripts of Caedmon's Hymn and Bede's Death Song: With a Critical Text of the Epistola Cuthberti de Obitu Bedae*. New York: Columbia University Press.

Dollimore, Jonathan (1991), *Sexual Dissidence: Augustine to Wilde, Freud to Foucault*. Oxford: Clarendon Press.

Dorland's Illustrated Medical Dictionary (2003), 30th edn. Philadelphia: Saunders.

Dostoevsky, Fyodor (2004), 'The Dream of a Ridiculous Man'. In *Great Short Works of Fyodor Dostoevsky*. New York: Perrenial.

— (2006), *Demons: A Novel in Three Parts*. Richard Pevear and Larissa Volokhonsky (trans.). Vintage Books: London.

Dromgoole, Dominic (2006), *Will & Me: How Shakespeare Took Over My Life*. London: Allen Lane.

Duncan-Jones, Katherine (2001), *Ungentle Shakespeare: Scenes from his Life*. London: Arden Shakespeare.

Easterling, Keller (1999), *Organization Space: Landscapes, Highways, and Houses in America*. Cambridge, MA: MIT Press.

Eliot, T. S. (1963a), *Collected Poems 1909–1962*. London: Faber and Faber.

— (1963b), *Selected Prose*. John Hayward (ed.). Harmondsworth: Penguin.

— (1969), *The Complete Poems and Plays*. London and Boston: Faber and Faber.

— (2002), *Collected Poems of T.S. Eliot*. London: Faber and Faber.

Elsner, J. and Rutherford, I. (eds) (2008), *Seeing the Gods: Patterns of Pilgrimage in Antiquity*. Oxford: Oxford University Press.

Falconer, Rachel (2005), *Hell in Contemporary Literature: Western Descent Narratives Since 1945*. Edinburgh: Edinburgh University Press.

Faludi, Susan (1999), *Stiffed: The Betrayal of the American Male*. New York: William Morrow.

Faye, Emmanuel (2009), *Heidegger: The Introduction of Nazism into Philosophy*. Michael Smith (trans.). New Haven: Yale University Press.

Fernie, Ewan (2005), 'Shakespeare and the prospect of presentism'. *Shakespeare Survey*, 58, 169–84.

Ficino, Marsilio (1576), *Opera Omnia*. 2 vols. Basel.

—, Jayne, Sears (trans.) (1985), *Commentary on Plato's Symposium*. Dallas: Spring Publications.

Fiedler, Leslie (1972), 'The Moor as stranger: or, "Almost damned in a fair wife"'. In *The Stranger in Shakespeare*. New York: Stein and Day.

Fox, A. (1990), *Virginia Woolf and the Literature of the English Renaissance*. Oxford: Clarendon Press.

Freccero, John (1986), *The Poetics of Conversion*. Rachel Jacoff (ed.). Cambridge, MA: Harvard University Press.

Frye, Northrop (1957), *Anatomy of Criticism*. Princeton, NJ: Princeton University Press.

Fuller, David (1988), *Blake's Heroic Argument*. London: Croom Helm.

— (2010), *The Life in The Sonnets*. London: Continuum.

Genster, Julia (1994), 'Lieutenancy, standing in, and *Othello*', in Anthony Gerard Barthelemy (ed.), *Critical Essays on Shakespeare's* Othello. New York: G. K. Hall, pp. 216–37.

Gittings, Robert (ed.) (1970), *Letters of John Keats*. Oxford: Oxford University Press.

Grady, Hugh (1991), *The Modernist Shakespeare: Critical Texts in a Material World*. Oxford: Oxford University Press.

— (2000), 'Shakespeare's links to Machiavelli and Montaigne: constructing intellectual modernity in early modern Europe'. *Comparative Literature*, 52, 119–42.

— (2002), *Shakespeare, Machiavelli and Montaigne: Power and Subjectivity from Richard II to Hamlet*. Oxford: Oxford University Press.

— (2005), 'Shakespeare studies, 2005: a situated overview'. *Shakespeare*, 1, 102–20.

Grady, Hugh and Hawkes, Terence (eds) (2007), *Presentist Shakespeares*. Accents on Shakespeare. Oxford: Routledge.

Graf, Fritz (2008), *Ritual Texts for the Afterlife: Orpheus and the Bacchic Gold Tablets*. London: Routledge.

Graham, Claire (1994), *Ceremonial and Commemorative Chairs of Great Britain*. London: Victoria and Albert Museum.

Greenblatt, Stephen (1980), *Renaissance Self-Fashioning: From More to Shakespeare*. Chicago: University of Chicago Press.

— (1991), *Marvellous Possessions: The Wonder of the New World*. Chicago and Oxford: University of Chicago Press.

— (2001), *Hamlet in Purgatory*. Princeton, NJ and Oxford: Princeton University Press.

— (2004), *Will in the World: How Shakespeare Became Shakespeare*. New York: W. W. Norton.

— (2005), *Renaissance Self-Fashioning: From More to Shakespeare*, 2nd edn. Chicago: University of Chicago Press.

— (2011), *Shakespeare's Montaigne*. London: Notting Hill Editions.

Greenblatt, Stephen and Gallagher, Catherine (2000), *Practicing New Historicism*. Chicago and London: University of Chicago Press.

Gross, Kenneth (1989), 'Slander and skepticism in *Othello*'. *ELH*, 56 (Winter), 819–52.

Hagstrum, Jean H. (1992), *Esteem Enlivened By Desire: The Couple From Homer to Shakespeare*. Chicago: University of Chicago Press.

Hallstead, N. N. (1968), 'Idolatrous love: A new reading of *Othello*'. *Shakespeare Quarterly*, 19 (Spring), 107–24.

Harris, Alexandra (2010), *Romantic Moderns: English Writers, Artists and the Imagination from Virginia Woolf to John Piper*. London: Thames & Hudson.

Hassel, Jr., R. Chris, (2005), *Shakespeare's Religious Language: A Dictionary*. New York and London: Continuum.

Heidegger, Martin (1984), *Early Greek Thinking*. David Farrell Krell and Frank A Capuzzi (trans.). San Francisco: Harper and Row.

Holderness, Graham (1999), 'Anglo-Saxon verse'. *European English Messenger*, 8(2), 34–7.

— (2000), *Shakespeare: The Histories*. Basingstoke: Macmillan.

— (2002a), *Craeft: poems from the Anglo-Saxon*. Nottingham: Shoestring Press.

— (2002b), *The Prince of Denmark*. Hatfield: University of Hertfordshire Press.

Holland, Peter (2007), 'It's all about me. Deal with it'. *Shakespeare Bulletin*, 25(3), 27–39.

Hotson, J. Leslie (1925), 'Bear gardens and bear-baiting during the Commonwealth'. *PMLA,* 40(2), 276–88.

Howard, Jean E. (2003), 'The new historicism in Renaissance studies', in Russ McDonald (ed.), *Shakespeare: An Anthology of Criticism and Theory, 1945–2000.* Oxford: Blackwell, pp. 458–80.

Irigaray, Luce (1985), *This Sex Which Is Not One.* Catherine Porter and Carolyn Burke (trans.). Ithaca: Cornell University Press.

Johnson, Samuel (1765), *The Plays of William Shakespeare in Eight Volumes.* London: J. and R. Tonson.

Judt, Tony (2010), *The Memory Chalet.* London: William Heinemann.

Kastan, David Scott (1999), *Shakespeare After Theory.* London and New York: Routledge.

Kermode, Frank (2005), 'Our muddy vesture'. *London Review of Books,* 6 January, p. 17.

Kierkegaard, Søren (1955), *Fear and Trembling and the Sickness unto Death.* Walter Lowrie (trans.). New York: Doubleday.

Kingsley, Peter (2001), *In the Dark Places of Wisdom.* London: Duckworth.

Knight, G. Wilson (1930), *The Wheel of Fire: Interpretation of Shakespeare's Tragedy.* London: Routledge & Kegan Paul.

— (1965), *The Crown of Life: Essays in Interpretation of Shakespeare's Final Plays.* London: Methuen.

— (1967), *Shakespeare and Religion.* London: Routledge & Kegan Paul.

Krapp, George Philip (1932), *The Vercelli Book.* New York: Columbia University Press.

Lamb, Jonathan (2010), 'Parentheses and privacy in Philip Sidney's *Arcadia'. Studies in Philology,* 107(3), 310–35.

Lasch, C. (1978), *The Culture of Narcissism: American Life in an Age of Diminishing Expectations.* New York: W. W. Norton.

Latour, Bruno (2005), *Reassembling the Social: Actor-Network Theory.* Oxford: Oxford University Press.

Lawrence, D. H. (1932), *Collected Poems of D.H. Lawrence.* London: William Heinemann.

— (1934), *Twilight in Italy.* London: Heinemann.

Leavis, F. R. (1932), *New Bearings in English Poetry.* London: Chatto & Windus.

— (1933), 'Joyce and the revolution of the word'. *Scrutiny*, 2(2), 193–201.

— (1943), *Education and the University*. Cambridge: Cambridge University Press.

— (1968), 'The function of the university'. *The Times*, 22 January.

— (1969), *English Literature in Our Time and the University*. London: Chatto & Windus.

— (1970), '"Literarism" versus "Scientism"'. *Times Literary Supplement*, 23 April.

— (1974), 'Reply to Lord Annan'. *The Human World*, 4, 98.

Leavis, F. R. and Thompson, Denis (1932), *Culture and Environment*. London: Chatto & Windus.

Lee, John (2000), *Shakespeare's Hamlet and the Controversies of Self*. Oxford and New York: Oxford University Press.

Lejeune, Philippe (1982), 'The autobiographical contract', in Tzetvan Todorov (ed.), *French Literary Theory Today*. Cambridge: Cambridge University Press, pp. 192–222.

Lerner, Lawrence (1980), *The Man I Killed: Poems*. London: Secker & Warburg.

Levey, Santina M. and Thornton, Peter (2001), *Of Household Stuff: The 1601 Inventories of Bess of Hardwick*. UK: The National Trust.

Light, Alison (2007), *Mrs Woolf and the Servants: The Hidden Heart of Domestic Service*. London: Penguin.

Lohse, Bernhard (1999), *Martin Luther's Theology: Its Historical and Systematic Development*. Roy A. Harrisville (trans.). Edinburgh: T. and T. Clark.

Lopate, Phillip (2008), 'Duration', in Ellen Sussman (ed.), *Dirty Words: A Literary Encyclopedia of Sex*. New York: Bloomsbury.

Lupton, Ellen and Julia Lupton (2006), *D.I.Y Kids*. New York: Princeton Architectural Press.

— (2009), *Design Your Life: The Pleasures and Perils of Everyday Things*. New York: St. Martin's Press.

Lupton, Julia (2011), *Thinking with Shakespeare: Essays on Politics and Life*. Chicago: University of Chicago Press.

— (forthcoming), 'Making room, affording hospitality: environments of entertainment in *Romeo and Juliet*'. In Lloyd Kermode (ed.), *Journal of*

Medieval and Renaissance Studies. (Special issue on Space in Renaissance Drama).

Luther, Martin, Dillenberger, John (ed.) (1961), *Selections from his Writings*. Garden City, New York: Anchor.

MacKillop, Ian (1995), *F. R. Leavis: A Life in Criticism*. London: Allen Lane.

Macrobius, Davies, P. V. (trans.) (1969), *The Saturnalia*. New York: Columbia University Press.

Madelaine, Richard (ed.) (1998), William Shakespeare, *Antony and Cleopatra*. Cambridge: Cambridge University Press.

Malone Society (1961), *Collections, Volume VI: Dramatic Records in the Declared Accounts of the Treasurer of the Chamber*. Oxford: Oxford University Press.

Mann, Thomas (1985), *The Magic Mountain*. Harmondsworth: Penguin.

Marcus, Laura (1994), *Auto/biographical Discourses: Theory, Criticism, Practice*. Manchester: Manchester University Press.

Markham, Gervase (1615), *The English Huswife, Containing the Inward and Outward Vertues which Ought to Be in a Complete Woman*. London: Roger Jackson.

McAfee, Helen (1916), *Pepys on the Restoration Stage*. New Haven: Yale University Press.

Merleau-Ponty, Maurice (1968), *The Visible and the Invisible*. Claude Lefort (trans.). Evanston, Illinois: Northwestern University Press.

Milner, Marion (1937; repr. 1986), *An Experiment in Leisure*. London: Virago.

Minority, True (2006), 'Newport News'. *Urban Dictionary*. Available online at: <www.urbandictionary.com/define.php?term=Newport+News>.

Montaigne, Michel de (1910; repr. 1935), *The Essays of Montaigne*. John Florio (trans.), 3 vols. London: J. M. Dent.

— (1980), *Essays*. John Florio (trans.), 3 vols. London: Everyman's Library, Dent.

— (2003), *The Complete Essays*. M. A. Screech (trans.). London: Penguin.

Montiglio, Silvia (2000), *Silence in the Land of Logos*. Princeton: Princeton University Press.

Nagy, Gregory (1991), *Greek Mythology and Poetics*. Ithaca: Cornell University Press.

Nairn, Ian and Pevsner, Nikolaus (1965; repr. 2003), *The Buildings of England: Sussex*. Harmondsworth: Penguin (repr. New Haven: Yale University Press).

Neill, Michael (1994), '"Unproper beds": race, adultery, and the Hideous in *Othello*'. Repr. in Anthony Gerard Barthelemy (ed.), *Critical Essays on Shakespeare's* Othello. New York: G.K. Hall, pp. 187–215.

Newton, John (1965), '*Scrutiny*'s failure with Shakespeare'. *Cambridge Quarterly*, 1 (2), 144–77.

Nietzsche, Friedrich (1887; 1913), *The Genealogy of Morals*. Horace B. Samuel (trans.). New York: Boni and Liveright.

— (1967), *On the Genealogy of Morals*. Walter Kauffmann (ed.), Walter Kauffmann and R. J. Hollingdale (trans.). New York: Random House.

— (1998), *Philosophy in the Tragic Age of the Greeks*. Marianne Cowan (trans.). Regnery Publishing: Washington, D. C.

Oliver, Simon (2005), *Philosophy, God and Motion*. London: Routledge.

Pascal, Blaise (1995), *Pensées*. A. J. Krailsheimer (trans.). Harmondsworth: Penguin.

Pepys, Samuel (1970–83), *The Diary*. Robert Latham and William Matthews (eds), 11 vols. London: G. Bell and Sons Ltd.

Phillips, Adam (2005), *Going Sane: Maps of Happiness*. London: Fourth Estate, Harper-Collins.

Pickstock, Catherine (2010), 'Stones ring: the mystery of the senses'. *The Reader*, 40, 54–5.

Poisson, Jayme (2011), 'Storm in a teacup'. *Sydney Morning Herald*, 9 July, A1: Print.

Poole, Adrian (1988), *Coriolanus*. London: Harvester.

Prior, Moody E. (1951), 'The Elizabethan audience and the plays of Shakespeare'. *Modern Philology*, 49 (2), 101–23.

Racine, Jean (1962), *Tragédies choisies*. Collection Internationale. New York: Doubleday.

Reisz, Matthew (2010), 'Style points'. *Times Higher Education*, 15 July. Available online at: <http://www.timeshighereducation.co.uk/story.asp?sectioncode=26&storycode=412480> [accessed 12 June 2011].

Rhodes, Neil (ed.) (1987), *Donne: Selected Prose*. Harmondsworth: Penguin.

Richards, I. A. (1924), *Principles of Literary Criticism*. London: Routledge and Kegan Paul.

Rickman, Alan (2007), '2007 prize giving speech'. Available online at: <http://www.latymer-upper.org/txt/speeches-1.html>

Rilke, Rainer Maria (1992), 'Archaic torso of Apollo', in Stephen Cohn (trans.), *Neue Gedichte/New Poems*. Manchester: Carcanet.

Rowe, M. (2010), 'Iago's Elenchus: Shakespeare, *Othello* and the Platonic Inheritance,' in Gary Hagberg and Walter Jost (eds), *The Blackwell Companion to the Philosophy of Literature*. Oxford: Blackwell, pp. 174–92.

Sambursky, S. (1987), *The Physical World of Late Antiquity*. Princeton: Princeton University Press.

Sanders, W. (1987), *The Winter's Tale: New Critical Introductions to Shakespeare*. Brighton: Harvester Press.

Sanders, W. and Jacobson, H. (1978), *Shakespeare's Magnanimity*. London: Chatto.

Sandwell, Barry (1996), *Presocratic Reflexivity: The Construction of Philosophical Discourse c. 600–450 BC*. London: Routledge.

Secomb, Linnell (2002), 'Autothanatography'. *Mortality*, 7(1), 35–46.

Sessions, Ina Beth (1947), 'The dramatic monologue'. *PMLA*, 62, 503–16.

Shapiro, James (2005), *1599: A Year in the Life of William Shakespeare*. London: Faber and Faber.

Sheehan, Thomas (ed.) (1981), *Heidegger: The Man and the Thinker*. Chicago: Precedent.

Shellard, Dominic (1999), *British Theatre Since the War*. New Haven: Yale University Press.

Sidney, Philip (2004), *The Defence of Poetry and Selected Renaissance Literary Criticism*. Gavin Alexander (ed.). London: Penguin.

Siorvanes, Lucas (1996), *Proclus: Neoplatonic Philosophy and Science*. Edinburgh: Edinburgh University Press.

Smith, John (1657), *The Mysterie of Rhetorique Unvail'd*. London.

Stallworthy, Jon (ed.) (1984), *The Oxford Book of War Poetry*. Oxford: Oxford University Press.

Stevens, Wallace (1957), *Opus Posthumous*. Samuel French Morse (ed.). New York: Knopf.

Stevenson, Robert Louis (1999), *The Strange Case of Dr Jekyll and Mr Hyde*. M. A. Danahay (ed.). Broadview.

Storer, Richard (2009), *F. R. Leavis*. London: Routledge.

Tambling, Jeremy (1990), *Confession: Sexuality, Sin and the Subject*. Manchester: Manchester University Press.

Trewin, J. C. (1987), *Five & Eighty Hamlets*. London: Hutchinson.

Tribble, Evelyn (2005), 'Distributing cognition in the globe'. *Shakespeare Quarterly*, 56(2), 135–55.

Tudeau-Clayton, Margaret (1998), *Jonson, Shakespeare and Early Modern Virgil*. Cambridge: Cambridge University Press.

Van Domelen, John E. (1987), *Tarzan of Athens: A Biographical Study of G. Wilson Knight*. Bristol: Redcliffe.

'Vick, Michael [Biography]' (2007), *Biography.com*. Available online at: <http://www.biography.com/search/article.do?id=241100&page=1>

Voss, Angela (2002), '*Orpheus Redivus*: The musical magic of Marsilio Ficino,' in Michael J. B. Allen, Valerie Rees and Michael Davies (eds), *The Platonism of Marsilio Ficino*. Leiden: Brill, pp. 227–42.

Walker, D. P. (1958; 1995), *Spiritual and Demonic Magic: From Ficino to Campanella*. Philadelphia: Pennsylvania State University Press.

Weber, Alan S. (1996), 'New physics for the nonce: a stoic and hermetic reading of Shakespeare's *Antony and Cleopatra*', in George Walton Williams and Barbara J. Baines (eds), *Renaissance Papers*. Raleigh: Southeastern Renaissance Conference, pp. 93–107.

Weintraub, Karl (1978), *The Value of the Individual: Self and Circumstance in Autobiography*. Chicago: University of Chicago Press.

Wells, Stanley (2003), *Shakespeare for All Time*. Oxford: Oxford University Press.

White, Jack (2003), (Interview), *The Believer*. Available online at: <http://www.believermag.com/issues/200305/?read=interview_white> [accessed 25 July 2010].

Williams, Raymond (1984), 'Seeing a man running'. *The Leavises: Recollections and Impressions*. Cambridge: Cambridge University Press.

Wilson Nightingale, Andrea (2004), *Spectacles of Truth in Classical Greek Philosophy*. Cambridge: Cambridge University Press.

Witmore, Michael (2008), *Shakespearean Metaphysics*. London: Continuum.

Woolf, Virginia (1953), *Between the Acts*. Harmondsworth: Penguin.

— (1997), *Travels with Virginia Woolf*. Jan Morris (ed.). London: Pimlico.

Woolley, Hannah (1673a), *The Gentlewoman's Companion*. London: A. Maxwell.

— (1673b), *The Gentlewoman's Guide to the Female Sex . . . Whereunto Is Added a Guide for Cook-Maids, Dairy-maids, Chamber-maids, and all others to go to Service*. London: A. Maxwell.

Wordsworth, William (1997), *Selected Poetry*. Stephen Gill and Duncan Wu (eds). Oxford: Oxford University Press.

Wright, M. R. (1995), *Cosmology in Antiquity*. London: Routledge.

Audio and Video Recordings

Olivier, Laurence (dir), William Shakespeare, *Richard III*. London Film Productions, 1955.

Racine, Jean, *Phèdre*, selected scenes, with Marie Bell as Phèdre. Everest Records, FRL 1505 (USA). [The complete recording from which this is taken (2LPs, n.d.[1950s?]) is in the Bibliothèque nationale de France, enregistrements sonores, FRBNF 38288507. Marie Bell can also be seen as Phèdre in a production directed by Pierre Jourdan recorded in 1968 (currently available on DVD in the United States).]

Sackler, Howard (dir), William Shakespeare, *Antony and Cleopatra*, with Pamela Brown as Cleopatra. Issued 1963 on LP, SRS/M235; subsequently on cassette, HCA 137.

Wagner, Richard, *Die Walküre*, Act I, cond. Bruno Walter, with Lotte Lehmann as Sieglinde. Recorded 1935, issued 1936, HMV DB 2636-43; re-issued on LP, 1962, COLH 133.

Wagner, Richard, *Tristan und Isolde*, cond. Wilhelm Furtwängler, with Kirsten Flagstad as Isolde. Recorded 1952, issued 1953, HMV ALP 1030–5.

Zeffirelli, Franco (dir), William Shakespeare, *Romeo and Juliet*. Paramount, 1968.

Index

Adorno, Theodor 119, 120
affordances 144–60 *passim*
Althusser, Louis 5, 18n. 3
anamnesis 87, 88, 96, 101, 104, 105
Arendt, Hannah 142, 148, 155, 158
Aristotle 179, 182, 198n. 6,
    199–200n. 18, 204
Augustine, Saint 164–5, 264
autobiography 163–77

Bacon, Francis 204, 213
Barker, Francis 5
Barthes, Roland 38–9n. 1, 166,
    197–8n. 5
Bell, Marie 67, 68, 70, 72
Belsey, Catherine 5, 18n. 2
biography 19, 38–9n. 1, 119
Blanchot, Maurice 167–8, 173
Brook, Peter 215–16, 218–19
Brown, Pamela 68, 72
Browne, Thomas 83, 265

Cavell, Stanley 44, 233, 256
chairs 144–51, 154, 157, 158, 159,
    160n. 2, 160n. 4
Chapman, George 188, 198n. 10,
    199n. 14
cognition 150–1, 160n. 5, 178–9,
    181, 185
conversion 40, 45, 147, 163–5,
    168–72, 176, 185
criticism 1–14, 21–3, 38, 69, 74–7,
    115–24, 205, 253, 256, 264,
    267
    see also subjectivity of criticism

Crosse, Gordon 104–5
cultural materialism 2, 5–7, 18n. 3,
    263
Cynewulf 168–73

Dante 175, 183, 195–6
Davies, John 16, 107–10, 112,
    114–16, 119, 121–2, 123
de Man, Paul 166
demons 21, 23–5, 28–30, 37, 181,
    193
Derrida, Jacques 137, 167–8, 172–4
design 147–8, 157
(sexual) desire 24–38, 40, 43–6, 50–1,
    53, 56, 61–3, 68, 70–5, 180–1,
    182–3, 193–4, 228, 261, 264
    see also eros
Dollimore, Jonathan 22, 26, 165
dreams 30, 78, 84–5, 102–3, 227–8,
    236, 239, 258–61, 268
Dromgoole, Dominic 104
Dryden, John 99–100, 103, 206

education 62, 74, 77, 93, 107–8,
    111–12, 115, 117, 121, 122,
    124, 126–35, 140, 175, 183,
    231, 237, 239, 242, 251–53
Eliot, Thomas Stearns 67, 69, 110,
    114, 122–3, 175, 177, 222
Empson, William 74, 265
eros 180–1, 183, 190, 192, 194, 197

Ficino, Marsilio 181, 188, 193,
    197n. 4, 198n. 10, 198n. 11,
    198–9n. 12, 199n. 13

Flagstad, Kirsten 67, 68
football 77, 133, 136–9, 225–6, 236
Foucault, Michel 5, 18n. 3
Frye, Northrop 76

Greenblatt, Stephen 7, 8, 9, 18n. 1,
	18n. 6, 18n. 7

Hegel, Georg Friedrich 63
Heidegger, Martin 118–20, 124, 179
hospitality 149, 155–60
housekeeping 149, 155–60

Keats, John 265–6
Kelly, John 71–82
Kierkegaard, Søren 23–4, 233

Lawrence, David Herbert 107, 109,
	120–1, 122
Leavis, Frank Raymond 16, 115–25,
	262
Leavis, Queenie Dorothy 116, 120
Lehmann, Lotte 67, 68
Lejeune, Philippe 165–6
Lerner, Lawrence 109
literature 1–18, 19–23, 37, 38n. 1,
	74–7, 126–7
Luther, Martin 22–3, 34–6, 57n. 8

Macrobius 196
Mann, Thomas 19–20
Markham, Gervase 152, 159
marriage 37, 40–60, 66, 70, 100,
	104, 156, 159, 259, 261
materialism/materiality 158–9, 179,
	183, 192, 233
memory 30, 67, 79, 86, 87–105,
	109–13, 117, 122–5, 127,
	158, 171, 177, 183, 195,
	201–2, 205, 213, 223–4, 228,
	229, 230, 231, 237–57, 259

Milner, Marion 202–3, 206
Montaigne, Michel de 10–12, 13, 14,
	18n. 7, 114, 206, 264, 265
mourning 15, 78–86, 124, 173–4,
	176–7, 246–7, 256
music 62–3, 66–9, 74, 76, 92,
	186–7, 188–9, 262

Nietzsche, Friedrich 8–9, 39n. 1, 214

Olivier, Laurence 72, 88, 90, 91, 93,
	122, 201

parents/parenthood 37, 80, 82,
	87–93, 111, 127, 130, 139,
	152–3, 201–2, 209–12, 216,
	217–18, 221–3, 225–8, 231,
	235, 240, 246
Pascal, Blaise 11, 211
Pepys, Samuel 96–105
performance 64, 67, 68, 73, 74,
	87–106, 109, 124, 152, 211,
	261
Plato 178–82, 186–9, 193–4,
	197n. 1, 197n. 4, 198n. 10,
	199–200n. 18
presentism 7–9, 18n. 4, 18n. 5

queer *see* sexuality (homosexuality)

Racine, Jean 15, 63, 70–1
	Phèdre 67, 70–1, 72, 73, 74
rape 27–8, 32, 36–7, 223, 224,
	255
religion,
	Buddhism 76
	Christianity 25, 31, 40, 168,
		170–1, 174–5, 176, 181
	Judaism 18n. 6, 147
	and theology 22–3
	see also spirituality

ressentiment 29, 117, 159

Rilke, Rainer Maria 21, 96, 158

sex, sexuality 25–6, 29–30, 46,
    48–52, 53, 57n. 6, 58n. 10,
    58n. 12, 227, 230, 231
  homosexuality 62–3, 73–4, 75,
    227, 230
  masturbation 244–6
Shakespeare, William (works)
  1 Henry IV 98, 99, 144, 192, 194,
    198–9n. 12
  2 Henry IV 19
  All's Well that Ends Well 43, 147,
    160n. 7
  Antony and Cleopatra 15, 26, 61,
    64–70, 71, 72, 73, 74, 105–
    6n. 1, 190, 201, 211, 217
  As You Like It 72, 109, 116
  Comedy of Errors, The 136
  Coriolanus 17, 107, 201–2,
    203–18, 221, 225, 226–8,
    231, 247, 262
  Cymbeline 109, 247, 265, 266–7
  Hamlet 79, 81, 82–3, 92, 93, 96,
    102–3, 105, 121, 122, 148,
    171, 208, 209, 212
  Henry V 93, 116
  Henry VIII 180
  Julius Caesar 201, 212
  King John 15, 80
  King Lear 16, 84–6, 88, 95, 96,
    109, 113, 125, 136, 161–3,
    174–6, 221, 243, 244, 247,
    262, 263, 264, 268
  Love's Labour's Lost 111
  Macbeth 20, 23, 56n. 2, 81, 90,
    103, 149, 216
  Measure for Measure 15, 20,
    24–38, 106
  Merchant of Venice, The 16, 183–90

Merry Wives of Windsor, The 180
Midsummer Night's Dream, A 16,
    102, 114, 116, 126–35,
    139, 141, 142, 154–5, 191,
    198–9n. 12, 212, 258–61, 262
Much Ado About Nothing 91
Othello 15, 40–60, 72, 83–4,
    90, 122, 147, 159, 160n. 6,
    160n. 9, 246, 261
Pericles 255–6, 262
Rape of Lucrece, The 199n. 14
Richard III 23, 24, 72, 74, 88,
    90, 95
Romeo and Juliet 73–4, 147,
    151–2, 153–7, 158, 159
Sonnets 73, 188
  Sonnet 111, 218
Taming of the Shrew, The 149
Tempest, The 17, 103, 109, 140–1,
    151, 217, 247, 250, 256, 262
Timon of Athens 122
Titus Andronicus 17, 221–2,
    222–3, 224–5, 228, 231
Troilus and Cressida 109, 113, 122
Twelfth Night 220n. 6
Winter's Tale, The 16, 109–11,
    114, 116, 123, 147, 157–8,
    218, 247, 251, 253–5, 262
Sidney, Philip 182
spirituality 24–5, 29–38, 82, 174–6,
    179–83, 188–96, 263,
    265–6, 268
Stevens, Wallace 66, 75, 153
Stevenson, Robert Louis 20–2, 23
stools 144–51, 153, 156, 157, 158,
    159, 160n. 4
subjectivity of criticism 1–18,
    21–2, 39n. 2, 75–7, 104,
    171–2, 175–6, 179, 182,
    192, 222, 248, 252–3,
    256, 264

theory 10, 21, 22, 24, 114, 120, 172,
179–80, 186, 187, 261, 263–4
trauma 63, 119, 233–4, 246, 249,
262

Verdi, Giuseppe 48, 49, 92
Vick, Michael 225–6
violence 20, 25, 36, 46, 54, 61,
64, 65, 72, 114, 142, 206,
213, 221–32, 241, 243,
248–50
Virgil 148, 155, 185–6, 196,
200n. 1
Von Ephrussi, Elisabeth 93–6,
103, 105

Wagner, Richard 62, 63, 66, 67,
95, 96
Whiting, Leonard 73–4
Wilde, Oscar 4, 72
Williams, Raymond 116
Wilson Knight, George 16, 110–11,
112, 117, 120, 123, 124
Wolfenden, Lord (report, 1957) 61
Woolf, Virginia 113–15, 116, 262,
266–8
Woolley, Hannah 148–9, 152
Wordsworth, William 172, 191,
199n. 16

Zeffirelli, Franco 73–4

SHAKESPEARE

Series Editors: Ewan Fernie, The Shakespeare Institute, University of Birmingham, UK and Simon Palfrey, University of Oxford, UK

Philippa Kelly

THE KING AND I

Shakespeare

'An innovative new series . . . Series editors Simon Palfrey and Ewan Fernie have rejected the notion of business as usual in order to pursue a distinctive strategy that aims to put "cutting-edge scholarship" in front of a broad audience. With its insistent appeal to the contemporary, this is fresh Shakespeare for readers turned off by the prospect of dry-as-dust scholarship'
- Shakespeare Quarterly

Shakespeare Now! is a series of short books that engage imaginatively and often provocatively with the possibilities of Shakespeare's plays. It goes back to the source - the most living language imaginable - and recaptures the excitement, audacity and surprise of Shakespeare. It will return you to the plays with opened eyes.

Λ continuum

For further details visit
www.continuumbooks.com